Globalization and Rural Development

About the Authors

G. Palanithurai (1953)

Prof. Ganapathi Palanithurai, Chairperson, Rajiv Gandhi Chair, Chairperson, The Hunger Project of Tamil Nadu Council, Gandhigram Rural University is an academic activist working with the people in rural areas for building the capacity of the leaders and people to reinvent and strength grassroots democracy and to achieve sustainable Rural Development. His policy advocacy role at the governmental level is increasingly felt at present in all the three levels, namely sub-regional, regional and national as he does more field work than theorization. He has been associating himself with Central Planning Commission, State Planning Commission of Tamil Nadu, and State Finance Commission of Tamil Nadu and he carried out several research studies in decentralization for both governments. His activities are supported by Population Foundation of India, the Ford Foundation, UNICEF, Rajiv Gandhi Foundation, Ministry of Rural Development, Ministry of Panchayati Raj, UNDP, SDC, World Bank, Action Aid, Department of Rural Development, Government of Tamil Nadu and DANIDA (Danish-Indo Development Agency) in specific areas of activities in connection with empowerment of people. He is in the network of the Non Governmental Organisations for Panchayat activities. He involves himself in capacity building exercise for local body leaders. He has evolved training module and manual for local body leaders. He has to his credit fifty two books, one hundred and seven articles in reputed referred research journals, twelve working papers, eighty two monographs, and thirteen review articles on three major areas, namely, Legislative Behaviour, Ethnicity and Panchayati Raj System. He has prepared twenty five commissioned reports for government and multilateral agencies. He is currently the editor of the journal *Grassroots Governance* and member of the editorial committee of different journals. He is editing a bimonthly newsletter entitled *Global and Local* for the Ford Foundation Project. He is associating himself with both print and electronic media to cover the issues of Local Governance. He was a recipient of Fellowship from Sastri Indo-Canadian Institute, New Delhi and World Academy of Art and Science, USA. He has visited the US and Canada, on academic assignments. He was a visiting fellow in the MiGill University, Canada in 1989. He held the position of Dean, Member Syndicate, and Member Finance Committee of Gandhigram Rural University. Currently he is Dean Students Welfare, Gandhigram Rural University. He is a life member of Indian Institute of Public Administration, Indian Association of Public Administration, Indian Association of Political Science and Indian Association of Canadian Studies. He was a member of the Expert Committee constituted by the Government of Tamil Nadu, to monitor the training programme for local body leaders. He is a member of the advisory committee of the Ministry of Panchayati Raj, Government of India. He is a member of Board of Studies of seven universities. He is a member in the High Level Committee constituted for devolution of powers to Local Bodies in Tamil Nadu.

R. Ramesh

Dr. R. Ramesh (1968) obtained his Ph.D. in Rural Development from the Gandhigram Rural University. He has worked for a variety of projects with varied scope and scale, for almost 20 years now. He served as a Training Expert for a DANIDA assisted project on water and sanitation for five years. He also served as a Project Officer for the Terre des Hommes—a Netherlands based INGO—with its India Country Office in Hosur (near Bangalore) that is working for the cause of children in difficult situations. He has a real flair for empirical research and field-based reporting. A proposal he wrote on 'Establishing Community-managed Domestic Water Supply System' won for Gandhigram Trust the World Bank's India country Level Development Marketplace Award—2004. He has co-authored with Prof. G. Palanithurai a book titled : *Globalization Issues at the Grassroots* (also from Concept Publishing Company Pvt. Ltd.). His other (co-authored) books include : *Analysing Community Problems—Tentacles of PRA Methodology* and *Standpoints on Globalization*. He has published around 20 articles, five of them in international journals. He is currently working as Assistant Professor of Rural Development at Bahir Dar University in Ethiopia.

GLOBALIZATION AND RURAL DEVELOPMENT

G. PALANITHURAI
R. RAMESH

CONCEPT PUBLISHING COMPANY PVT. LTD.
NEW DELHI-110059

ISBN-13: 978-81-8069-750-0

First Published 2011

Published and Printed by

Since 1974

Concept Publishing Company Pvt. Ltd.
Regd. Office:
A/15-16, Commercial Block, Mohan Garden
New Delhi-110059 (India)
Phones : 25351460, 25351794, *Fax* : 091-11-25357109
Email : publishing@conceptpub.com,
Website: www.conceptpub.com

Editorial Office:
H-13, Bali Nagar, New Delhi-110 015, India.

Cataloging in Publication Data--Courtesy: D.K. Agencies (P) Ltd. <docinfo@dkagencies.com>

Palanithurai, G. (Ganapathy)
Globalization and rural development / G. Palanithurai, R. Ramesh.
p. cm.
Includes bibliographical references and index.
ISBN 9788180697500

1. Rural development--Government policy--India--Tamil Nadu. 2. Globalization--Economic aspects--India--Tamil Nadu. I. Ramesh, R., 1968- joint author. II. Title.

DDC 307.72095482 22

FOREWORD

The concepts of globalization and decentralization came into prominence in India almost simultaneously during the early Nineties. Though *Prima facie* they appear antithetical to each other, in reality one complements the other. Interestingly several commonalities and linkages are noticeable between these two ideas particularly in the Indian context. Both have significant implications for rural development. Both were largely conceived and introduced by the Government of India and the States had no option but to support and implement. While globalization came into meet our own economic necessities coupled with an international compulsion to fall in line with the rest of the world, decentralization was comparatively home grown. Admittedly, the constitutional amendments on decentralization were introduced to fulfil an electoral commitment made by the ruling party with a genuine intent to provide effective self governments at the local level. These local governments do have a primary duty to protect and safeguard the interests of their citizens even against the ill effects, if any, of the globalization process.

Implementation of both these initiatives over the last fifteen years either whole-heartedly or half-heartedly has given rise to several important questions. Are these concepts really independent to each other ? Are they beneficial to the people, particularly the rural poor ? Can they significantly contribute to rural development in India ? What has been the impact of these processes in the delivery of services, poverty reduction and provision of basic minimum services to the needy ? What lessons have we learnt in the process over these years ?

Answers to these questions are absolutely necessary, as both globalization and decentralization have come to stay and appear irreversible. The study undertaken by Gandhigram Rural University is a sincere attempt in this direction. Their attempt has been to find answers not on the basis of desk research or discussions and perceptions but on hard data collected through empirical studies conducted in State of Tamilnadu over a period of time. Their study has focused on key sectors that are extremely relevant to the rural poor such as primary education, drinking water, public health and employment keeping an eye on gender and inclusion. They have attempted a SWOT analysis of globalization in the context of decentralization and arrived at different options available to India.

The concluding chapter offers valuable suggestions to handle globalization at the grassroots levels in such a way that natural resources are effectively managed in the interest of the community and opportunities become available to the poor for better livelihood and self improvement through the process of globalization. This makes a refreshing break from the usual conclusions such studies make, namely advising the State to provide more and more social safety nets to mitigate the possible adverse impact of globalization. Their emphasis instead has been on self reliance. These suggestions though made in the Indian context have great relevance to other developing countries as well. I am sure this book will not only be a valuable addition to the development literature but will also serve as a practical guide to the practitioners and the stakeholders all over the developing world.

S.S. Meenakshisundaram

PREFACE

We are well past debating : if globalization is good or bad; and if globalization should be supported or opposed. By now, almost everyone has learnt sufficiently well that this flood gate cannot be shuttering down raising hands against it. All that one needs to think seriously about is how to manage the challenges, and remain afloat. How to make use of the opportunities so that the poor are not hurt ? How to strengthen the grassroots level institutions, so that they are not offended by the new-wave market forces or deep-seated bureaucratic-rigidity ? In other words, how to manage globalization in such a way that the poor also benefit, and get out of the poverty trap? One can observe that globalization has definitely escalated the levels of aspirations of the people, including that of the poor. If the poor are able to reap the benefits is a different question. It is time to observe if the long cherished desire of 'making everyone benefited in the long-run' is likely to turn into reality, or is it only an illusionary idea floated around by some easy-chair economic theorists.

When liberalization policies are introduced, one of the significant concerns of a country like India—where poverty and prosperity co-exist—is the concentration of schemes and programmes that would prepare the poor to take hold of opportunities that globalization bring about. How to make sufficient domestic preparations so that the society is competent enough to face and manage with newer ways of doing things? This domestic preparation includes education including primary, higher and technical education; training and capacity building of the local institutions; capability enhancement of the mediocre; public health care system; position of the state policy in allocation of resources especially land, water, power, etc. In a nutshell, the need for protecting the pedestrians in a world that is at break-neck speed cannot be ignored.

The government through several centrally sponsored schemes has made concerted attempts to deliver basic services, build infrastructure including rural infrastructure, generate private and local employment opportunities, and ensure that societal capacity is enhanced to make use of the opportunities that sprout. These include—besides the special policy and legislative instruments for the establishment of Special Economic Zones, and flagship programmes like Education for All, Health for All, expanding the scope of Public Distribution System, National Rural Employment Guarantee Scheme. The government spends more than 95,000 crore annually on these programmes. The functioning of these programmes, and the way they have helped the poor benefit from such programmes require empirical evidence.

The Rajiv Gandhi Chair for Panchayati Raj Studies, Gandhigram Rural University, Tamil Nadu with a grant made available by the Ford Foundation, New Delhi conducted a series of empirical verifications to record the impact of Liberalization, Privatization and Globalization policies on the rural sectors, and on the rural poor between January 2008 and October 2009. Each chapter in this book is a field-based study conducted in various districts of Tamil Nadu. Village Panchayats and NGOs were also active participants in this research endeavour. The research pursued viewed things from the standpoint of the poor, the women, and the elected local bodies (viz. the Panchayats). The main frame of reference was if the reform measures introduced as part of LPG policies benefits or hurts the poor; if it adjusts with or challenges local institutions; and what does it boil down to ultimately. The outcome of each of this study was presented to a team of academics, researchers, and administrators in government service in Chennai during November 2009 for validation. It is their prodding that motivated us to get this printed, for wider audience. Academics, researchers, activists, and Panchayat functionaries would find this book useful to get into grips with operation of LPGs at the grassroots level.

I must thank all the Panchayat Presidents and NGOs in Tamil Nadu, who with a lot of enthusiasm shared their views, knowledge and information with us on various reform initiatives in actualization in their respective areas of work. The research team, S.P. Ramesh, Ms. K. Chandra, P. Selvamani, and G. Venkatesan, involved in holding a series of interviews across districts in Tamil Nadu and documenting them deserve appreciation. Our thanks are also due to Dr. Bishnu N. Mohapatra, Programme Officer, The Ford Foundation, New Delhi, for his encouragement, and to the Ford Foundation for supporting this series of field-based studies.

January 2010 **G. Palanithurai**

CONTENTS

List of Boxes

ABBREVIATIONS AND ACRONYMS

ABL	:	Activity Based Learning
Act	:	Tamil Nadu Panchayats Act 1995
AEO	:	Assistant Education Officer
ANM	:	Auxiliary Nurse Midwife
ASHA	:	Accredited Social Health Activist
ASI	:	Archaeological Survey of India
AYUSH	:	Allopathic, Yoga, Unani, Siddha, and Homoeopathy
BDO	:	Block Development Officer
BRC	:	Block Resource Centre
CBO	:	Community Based Organisations
CEO	:	Chief Education Officer
CHC	:	Community Health Centre
CM	:	Community Management
CPR	:	Common Property Resource
CRC	:	Cluster Resource Centre
CSR	:	Corporate Social Responsibility
DC Land	:	Depressed Class Land
DD	:	Demand Draft
DD	:	Deputy Director
DDA	:	Demand Driven Approach
DDHS	:	Deputy Director of Health Services
DEEO	:	District Elementary Education Officer
DoLR	:	Department of Land Resources
DPWS	:	District Patient Welfare Society
DRDA	:	District Rural Development Agency
DRO	:	District Revenue Officer
DVD	:	Digital Video Disc player
EB	:	Electricity Bill
EDI	:	Education Development Index

EFA	:	Education For All
FDI	:	Foreign Direct Investment
FGD	:	Focus Group Discussion
FII	:	Foreign Institutional Investment
GER	:	Gross Enrolment Ratio
GO	:	Government Order
GoI	:	Government of India
GoTN	:	Government of Tamil Nadu
GRU	:	Gandhigram Rural University
HDI	:	Human Development Index
HH	:	Household
HM	:	Head Master
HP	:	Hand Pump
HSC	:	Health Sub Centre (Health)
HSC	:	House Service Connection (Water Supply)
IAY	:	Indira Awaas Yojana (House Scheme of the government for the poor)
IEC	:	Information, Education and Communication
ILO	:	International Labour Organisation
IMF	:	International Monetary Fund
IPHS	:	Indian Public Health Standards
LHV	:	Lady Health Visitor
LPCD	:	Litre Per Capita Daily
LPG	:	Liberalization, Privatization and Globalization
LPM	:	Litre Per Minute
MDG	:	Millennium Development Goals
MNC	:	Multi National Corporations
MO	:	Medical Officer
MoRD	:	Ministry of Rural Development
MoU	:	Memorandum of Understanding
NCERT	:	National Council for Educational Research and Training
NER	:	Net Enrolment Ratio
NFHS	:	National Family Health Survey
NGO	:	Non Governmental Organisation
NREGA	:	National Rural Employment Guarantee Act
NREGS	:	National Rural Employment Guarantee Scheme
NRHM	:	National Rural Health Mission
NSS	:	National Sample Survey
O & M	:	Operation and Maintenance
OHT	:	Over Head Projector
ONGC	:	Oil and Natural Gas Commission

OPD	:	Outdoor Patient Department
PAA	:	Project Affected Area
PAP	:	Project Affected People
PAV	:	Project Affected Villages
PDS	:	Public Distribution System
PF	:	Public Fountain
PHC	:	Primary Health Centre
PORD	:	Post Office Recurring Deposit
PPR	:	Private Property Resource
PQLI	:	Physical Quality of Life Index
PRI	:	Panchayati Raj Institution
PWD	:	Public Works Department
PWS	:	Patient Welfare Society
R & R Policy	:	Resettlement and Rehabilitation Policy
RGNDWM	:	Rajiv Gandhi National Drinking Water Mission
RTI	:	Right to Information
RWSS	:	Rural Water Supply Service
SCR	:	Student Classroom Ratio
SCSP	:	Scheduled Caste Sub Plan
SEZ	:	Special Economic Zone
SHG	:	Self-Help Group
SIPCOI	:	State Industries Promotion Corporation of India
SSA	:	Sarva Shiksha Abhiyan
STSP	:	Scheduled Tribe Sub Plan
TACID	:	Tamil Nadu Corporation for Industrial Infrastructure
TB	:	Tuberculosis
TIDCO	:	Tamil Nadu Industrial Development Corporation
TIIC	:	Tamil Nadu Industrial Investment Corporation
TNHSP	:	Tamil Nadu Health Systems Project
TSC	:	Total Sanitation Campaign
TWAD Board	:	Tamil Nadu Water and Drainage Board
UP	:	Upper Primary
UPS	:	Union Primary School
VEC	:	Village Education Committee
VHN	:	Village Health Nurse
VHSC	:	Village Health and Sanitation Committee
VP	:	Village Panchayat
VRS	:	Voluntary Retirement Scheme
VWSC	:	Village Water and Sanitation Committee
WHO	:	World Health Organisation

CHAPTER ONE

Rural Development in Globalizing India

DEMANDS OF THE TIME

At a time when countries of the world are fast adopting to market oriented neo-liberal economic policies, the demands of the time are multi-faceted. If we can take them as urgent, important, and long-term : the urgent among them is poverty reduction; important among them is economic growth; and the long-term among them is sustainability of this model of development. A country needs international trade relations and economic growth; businesses need profits; and the poor need their basic necessities such as employment and fair wages, food security, health care, education for children, safe drinking water supply, and dignity in the way we steer development; the civil society institutions look for integrity in democratic practice. The views differ depending upon vantage-points. The aspirations are varied. But still ultimately what is desirable is dignity in development; a world free of poverty and hunger; equity in distribution of economic growth; a society that is equitable and just with peace.

Economists, especially the neo-liberals, argue in favour of economic benefits to the country; industrialists ponder over business prospects and profitability across countries and continents; environmentalists argue in terms of sustainability of resource use; development professionals raise questions of poverty reduction and equity. We seem to live in a time that is most interesting in human history. The basic argument in favour of globalization policies is that they lay strong grounds for capital formation, exchange of technology, knowledge generation and information dissemination, and above all communication connectivity. The flow of capital through Foreign Direct Investment (FDI) and Foreign Institutional Investment (FII), coupled with private participation in economic development and employment generation have resulted for the Indian economy to be agile, and spoken about in the world forums.

GLOBAL INTERDEPENDENCE

The countries of the world are interdependent than ever before in human history. Global challenges, global oil price hike, global inflationary tendencies, global terrorism, global financial meltdown—there is nothing local these days. There is nothing independent these days. Countries of the world are interdependent. The new slogan is: Be Indian and Buy Global. Buy global—but we are not responsible because it is not within our control, nor within the control of anybody in the 'global assembly'. It is global because we are all connected but nobody is in-charge. The best example is the global financial meltdown that started on Wall Street that became the topic of discussion on all streets. The effect has been global but the wrath sure enough goes down to the local as well. From where does this growth model emerge is significant.

SYSTEM OF NATURAL LIBERTY

The current model of development, we pursue is what made Adam Smith (1723-1790) who after his death came to be recognised as father of modern economics or path finder of scientific economics, called 'System of Natural Liberty'. He believed that each individual should be allowed to pursue and advance his own interests. This system, he argued, would result in the greatest wealth for both the individual and the society. Indeed, the effort of the individual to serve himself would bring the greatest possible benefits for society as a whole and for other individuals (Daniel R. Fusfeld, 1970).

In Adam Smith's opinion, government interrupted economic progress. In the system of natural liberty, there were only three proper functions of government: (a) establishing and preserving justice; (b) defending the nation; and (c) creating and preserving certain public institutions, which no individual or group is interested in creating and preserving, e.g. roads, communications, and education (Adam Smith, 1776). Today, our contemporary economists and policy makers have gone a step further expanding the natural liberty by providing even roads, communications, and education for individual contractors and private companies to maintain and earn profits from. The role of the government has been contracted to be even smaller than what Smith envisioned. However, Smith was aware of the tendency of businessmen to serve their own interests at the expense of the public (Adam Smith, 1776).

COMPARATIVE ADVANTAGE

Similar ideas can be found in the propositions developed and promoted by David Ricardo (1772-1823), a classical economist again. Ricardo said that policies which limited trade in order to protect domestic producers would injure the nation that established them. Free trade was the road to economic health internationally as well as domestically. Ricardo was able to prove that it would benefit the economy. He showed that as long as it costs less to produce cloth in England than it does to produce wheat, compared with costs in other countries, it will benefit Englishmen to shift their resources to cloth manufacturers, export the product, and import wheat from other countries.

For example, suppose an Englishman must work one day to produce a yard of cloth and two days to produce a bushel of wheat. Then wheat requires twice as much as effort as cloth. Suppose also that a Frenchman works one day to produce each product. In this case, Englishmen should produce cloth (one day's labour), export it to France, trade it one-for-one for wheat, and import the French wheat. In this way, Englishmen would get, for one day's labour, the wheat it would otherwise require them two day's to produce. The Frenchmen would also benefit. They could produce wheat, ship it to England and trade one bushel for two yards of cloth, and ship the cloth to France. They would also receive products worth two days' effort for one day's actual work. Both countries would benefit from this division of labour and free exchange (Daniel R. Fusfeld, 1970).

Analogy can be traced in the works of contemporary economists such as Jagdish Bhagwati (2004). Going back to classical liberalism, John Stuart Mill (1806-1873) developed concepts and theories that opposed to government ownership of natural resources because he wished to preserve the institutions of private property, but favoured a large tax on profits derived from their exploitation because those resources rightly belonged to all (Daniel R. Fusfeld, 1970). A free-market economy will use all its resources, is the basic argument.

TRAGEDY OF THE COMMONS

One seminal work that seriously questioned this model of development or this idea of resource use is 'The Tragedy of the Commons' published in 1968 by a biologist called Garret Hardin. He proposed a hypothesis that seeks to explain why Common Property Resources (CPR), or better put, open access resources, are over-exploited, degraded and depleted (Hardin, 1968). The logic of the tragedy is purely economic and can be stated as: unregulated access to a CPR creates a decision-making environment in which incremental private benefits to an individual from the increased use of the resource markedly exceed the incremental private costs associated with the increased use.

The readers can find that these concepts revolve around in our arguments and interpretations in the current work of empirical evidences collected on the workings of Liberalization, Privatization and Globalization (LPG) policies on the ground in the form of cases in various districts of Tamil Nadu. The basic tenor is finding out if the free-market oriented reformist policies facilitate development in favour of the poors, and their basic necessities such as food security, basic education, health care, drinking water service delivery, employment generation, information access etc. or not; and recording the voices of the poors in this respect. In trying to conceptualise the field-based participatory learning with the poor rural communities, the arguments by various political economists and the advocates of decentralised development have been constantly referred to.

Reference to decentralization is very essential in the context of India, after the 73rd Constitutional Amendment made the local self-governments, the legitimate body to plan and implement rural development programmes drawing support from state machinery, and taking cue from various policies pertaining to development such as education policy, health policy, policy and Government Orders on rural drinking water supply, employment generation policy etc.

UNDERSTANDING DEVELOPMENT

Development is used differently in diverse contexts. Generally speaking development implies a change that is desirable. Society is dynamic, and so, what is desirable at a particular time, place and in a particular culture may not always be desirable at other places or at other times at the same place and in the same cultural milieu. Therefore, it is impossible to think of a universally acceptable definition of development. But a development index generally includes aspects such as: (i) increase in real income per capita (economic growth); (ii) improvement in distribution of income (equity); (iii) political and economic freedom; and (iv) equitable access to resources, education, health care, employment opportunities and justice (Katar Singh, 2009).

SUSTAINABLE DEVELOPMENT

The idea of sustainable development has been defined in many ways, but the most familiar definition remains that given in the Brundtland Commission report, *Our Common Future* (1987): 'development which meets the needs of the present without compromising the ability of future generations to meet their own needs'. Sustainable development strategies aims at ensuring a better quality of life for everyone, now and for the generations to come. This means meeting four objectives at the same time, at home and around the world: They are: (i) social progress that recognises the needs of everyone; (ii) effective protection of the environment; (iii) prudent use of natural resources; and (iv) maintenance of high and stable levels of economic growth and employment.

Another definition, from the Real World Member Forum for the Future, sees sustainable development in this way: 'sustainable development is a dynamic process which enables all people to realise their potential and improve their quality of life in ways that simultaneously protect and enhance the Earth's life-support systems'. The starting point for definitions of sustainable development is the diagnosis of unsustainable trends in the economy, and in our exploitation of natural resources. The core concept behind this are that (a) the main goal of economic development should be to create conditions for people to enjoy a better quality of life, not simply the pursuit of quantitative growth in the economy; (b) the pursuit of development must include policies to eliminate poverty importantly; (c) all parts of the society must be involved in decision-making about the measures that will bring about the transition to sustainable economic and social systems over the coming decade (Ian Christie & Diane Warburton, 2001).

These definitions underscore the need for society to ensure inter-generational equity in the sense that present level of consumption and well-being. Constancy of natural capital stock—including natural resource and the environment—is a necessary condition for sustainable development (Katar Singh & Anil Shishodia, 2007). More and faster production, and more and faster consumption would definitely lead to economic growth. At the same time in the process it naturally leads to faster environmental degradation and much faster depletion of resources required depriving the future generation of a kind of life that the current generation is living. That which would be much depleted is the open access resources or the commons.

Another adversity in a country like India where one-fifth of the world's poors live is, those who are not able to catch up (make use of the opportunity) because of lack of education, or due to inaccessibility to financial, information and knowledge resources might be left behind in lurch. This will create two camps, where one section of the people make use and reap the benefits, whereas another group would get further marginalised and impoverished. This disparity in distribution of benefits of economic growth shall naturally result in wider inequity in society than it existed before. So, ensuring social development, especially better quality education for the poor children, safe drinking water, better health care, local employment opportunities, access to information resources for the poor, access to institutional sources of finance as part of economic growth are imperative, and a practical necessity, if at all equity should be ensured. Studies conducted by the International Labour Organisation (ILO) at macro level especially on social development and on fairness globalization have come out with results that indicate deteriorating conditions of labour and especially women as a result of profit-orientation (ILO, 2004).

DEVELOPMENT AT THE GRASSROOTS

Another debate going on analogous to the debate on globalization and identifying ways to managing globalization is 'what constitutes development' (Stan Burkey, 1993). Is it economic growth rate *per se* as being repeatedly reported by the Government of India; Is it enabling the ultra-poor earn more than $ 1 a day, as being advocated by the World Bank; Is it a combination of education, health and employment (Human Development) related indicators as is being advocated by the UN? As a counter weight to the national economic statistics approach to measuring poverty, the Physical Quality of Life Index (PQLI) has been developed. Various ways of putting together the index have been proposed as well (David Macarov, 2003). Viewed closely these—enhancing basic educational facilities or enabling the ultra-poor getting out of the poverty trap—are issues to be addressed at the grassroots level, which require disaggregating the problem rather than in aggregating. That is localising rather than globalizing. Localisation (or disaggregating) means working with local self-governments, and aggregating means promoting globalization ideas. In India both globalization and localization exercise commenced almost simultaneously. A little background about it would be pertinent here.

DECENTRALIZATION : SOME BACKGROUND

Two concepts have occupied development literature more than anything else in the past couple of decades. One is 'globalization' and the other is 'decentralization'. Some describe these concepts as one being complementary to the other while others describe them as being antithetical to each other. At face value, they represent two extreme poles. Neither of them is new. But both of them have taken a new incarnation in the past decade. In the context of India, both of them, obviously, have historical routes, and they have legitimate sanctions too.

Globalization, in its primary sense means expansion of economic transactions and the organisation of economic activities across the political boundaries of nation-states. So, it is not only a matter pertaining to market economy, but also to political democracy (Deepak Nayyar, 2002). Decentralization is the process of dispersing or delegating decision-making authority relatively away from a central authority closer to the point of service or action. One of the main features of decentralization is a bottom-to-top flow of decision effecting ideas (Wikipedia, 2001). That is a devolving political, administrative, and fiscal powers and responsibilities from a higher level Central Government to the smallest institution at the grassroots level (Palanithurai, G., 2001). Globalization advocates doing away the borders and boundaries in order to ensure efficiency; decentralization advocates breaking up in order to bring things up in an effectively manageable unit.

DECENTRALIZATION AND GLOBALIZATION

There are several commonalities between globalization and decentralization. One commonality is that both the ideas emerged in India during the period 1990-95. Globalization was really started out of compulsions of economic situations in India during the late 1980s. Soon after we started liberalisation, privatisation and globalization exercises, it was incidental that we started decentralization exercises also simultaneously. But, we were not aware at that time that these two concepts [globalization and decentralization] have relevance. These are two independent events, but took place more or less at the same time. Neither globalization nor decentralization is concept of Indian origin as indicated in the works of economic theorists of the past two centuries.

The World Bank and IMF propagated the idea of free-market economy as a way to get on faster growth path. Similarly, from organisations like the World Bank again, there was an international pressure to take up decentralization. It was taken not merely out of compulsion, but out of necessity due to the conditions that prevailed here. During early 1990s, India was selling off most of its gold reserve. Now, we have grown to the stage of buying gold in order to enhance gold reserve level. Whereas the condition in 1990 was that we had to mortgage our gold stock in order to get foreign exchange and for importing the items we need.

To put it very appropriately one can say that globalization was an Indian local compulsion. It was a little before that time, late Shri Rajiv Gandhiji discussed with District Collectors, and several officials at various levels and came out with the idea that Panchayati Raj is the answer. He tried to pass an amendment in the Constitution to bring Panchayati Raj System. It did not pass parliamentary support. So, on one side the economic compulsion made us introduce globalization; and on another side the political compulsion made us introduce decentralization. Though these are international concepts, they came in India out of local compulsions. It was demand of the time.

As a theory these two are not based on any erroneous concepts. The concept of globalization is 'you produce only those things that you can produce at cheap production cost, so that you can make it available for the consumers at lowest possible price. You can sell it universally, and economise. Instead if everybody started producing irrespective of access to raw materials or skill and technology requirements, then it will become costly, which the consumer has to bear unnecessarily. Wherever there is a place where you can produce something cheap, why not you take it and give it to other person instead of asking him to produce at a higher cost. Everybody should get access to goods and services at lowest possible price, is the idea of globalization.' After all, the world is bigger than any country. So, instead of producing and consuming within a country, why not go for global production and distribution.

In principle globalization is a good concept. The same holds good for decentralization also. The basic tenet of decentralization is: why all powers should be centered at Central level in Delhi. Why can't we have some powers in Delhi, some in Chennai, some at the districts, and some at the village level. So, if it is drinking water, let the decisions pertaining to that take place at local level; if it is something relating to defence let that decision be taken at Central Government level. It would be something like an activity mapping at various levels—each with certain responsibilities and powers.

Another significant commonality with globalization and decentralization is that we implemented neither globalization nor decentralization the way it was intended to become operational. How we carry out these two exercises made the difference. In States like Kerala decentralization is reported to be functioning better than many other States. In Tamil Nadu, it gives a mixed picture in some places it is active, and in many places they are not active.

Especially at District level, Panchayats in Tamil Nadu are very weak. In Kerala, the village Panchayats and district Panchayats are said to be strong, whereas the Block Panchayat is said to be almost defunct with very little powers or activities.

The last similarity we need to know is that we cannot shy away from any of these two concepts—globalization and decentralization. Both the processes are irreversible. Both mean development. Decentralization is about local level planning and rural development administration, and globalization is about social development through economic growth. All over the world now, globalization has become an accepted principle. There is no point if we start talking now, that we should give up or try for a reverse gear. The same thing holds good for decentralization as well. For the next 25 to 30 years we are not definitely going to find an alternative to decentralization or Panchayati Raj System.

How we respond to these changes, and how to make ourselves happy given the situation we live in, that is the major question we need to find answer for. Globalization is not an end in itself. Similarly decentralization is also not an end in itself. It is a route; it is a process. The whole purpose of globalization or decentralization is to enable people lead a happy life. In Bhutan they have Happiness Index in place of the Human Development Index (HDI) we are talking about in India. After all, ultimately what everyone is searching for in life? Peace and happiness. So, whatever policy you make, you keep the poorest man in view: If this policy will be of some use to bring about happiness in the 'poorest man's life'. This is what we need to bear in mind, instead of raising ideology-based questions about any policy change—including that of globalization policies.

Given the trend, globalization and decentralization will make significant changes in India. They could be such as: (i) Our public health care system is still poor; (ii) Primary Education, we have not been as successful as we intend to become. If we can provide good quality education to all our children, they can withstand all that one argues as challenges in the globalized era. We need to have good health care system including safe water and proper sanitation system. We need to have access to good quality education for all our children. The third important thing is (iii) livelihood options. This is about employment, income, and food security of the families. One can empirically analyse if improvement is being made in these fronts, before arriving at any conclusion on the contribution of reform measures/privatization, liberalization and globalization in India.

DEVELOPMENT CHALLENGES

In order to do away the ideological positioning for or against globalization policies, it is good to have an understanding that trading and exchange of expertise, and technology have been taking place even in Ninth and Tenth Century. There are certain social aspects and certain commercial aspects that are vulnerable to extinction. Occupations that are vulnerable to competition will be thrown away, and it is there throughout history, and not after globalization. Perhaps, globalization has intensified it. Globalization is like evolution. Like with evolution there would be extinction, and there would be rebirth. How are we going to manage globalization is the basic question?

How globalization can influence the state as an institution is a vital question. When we mention state—we need to bear in mind it has three elements, viz. the Central Government (Union Government), the provincial government (State Government), and the local government (Panchayats). Discussing about these institutions is important because all these institutions are being touched by globalization. Even before globalization got on the fast-lane, there were threats. But they were all localised. But, now many of the threats are global in nature. It transcends across national borders very easily. Today's problems like global warming, deforestation, nuclear threat can wipe out humanity which has never happened in the past at a global scale. It has happened in some province or in some part of a province, but not at a global scale. This is the first and foremost difference between the current phase of globalization and the one we had in the past. The second difference is nowhere in the past communication has been so instantly possible as today. Both good news and bad news can travel at lightning speed. There was interesting report about mobile phones in India that 85 per cent of the mobile phones have a recharge value of less than Rs. 10. Technology can be used for good, and for bad. Technology is value-neutral. It is what we make of it counts.

Globalization demands change. Change to an unprecedented level. It demands change in the way one thinks, does business, and requires reforming the way one has led his/her life so long. Opportunities come with challenges as well. The advocates of globalization argue that when change requires you to face life with new opportunities and challenges, if you look at only the challenges and forget to take notice of the opportunities, you cannot attain development. However, studies prove the disparities in income and opportunity structures, as fallout of liberalization and privatization policies. The gaps in good *versus* poor jobs are easily seen in the expanding Indian economy.

The task lies in developing the economic base of the local communities. The task lies in building the local capacities to take cognizance of the kind of development taking place, and seize technological and informational opportunities to convert them as income possibilities. The task lies in making use of the liberalised trend in banking and micro financing institutions for enhancing the access one has had to financial sources for multiplication of prospects in small business ventures. How to make rural development as a 'community-determined process' is the challenge. How to stimulate local economic activity and employment is a task. It is also the duty of the intellectuals, researchers, academics and policy makers to come with ideas on how to make globalization work for the poor. So, the responsibility of the educated should be to think how best I can make use of globalization to benefit my village, and my family. This can create be a movement and creating ripples.

Globalization is never one way. People refer to Mahatma Gandhi and *swadeshi* to oppose globalization. Gandhiji said: '*Let the wind come from east, west, and north, but I shall refuse to be blown out of my roots*'. That was resolute thinking. That was progressive thinking. People should not misquote great leaders of this nation. Facing globalization and making wise use of globalization is in the hands of everyone of us. Our traditionalist and conservative thinking should not stand in the way blocking progress the humanity makes. That part of it which makes people feel inferior or make them blank, passive, meek and submissive is what is dangerous about it.

In the name of rural development we are doing several good things in a sporadic way. But, they do not take place in a massive scale. The principal goal of local economic development is to stimulate local employment opportunities in sectors that improve the community using existing human, natural, and institutional resources (Edward J. Blakely & Ted K. Bradshaw, 2003). For example, the idea of Rural Business Hub was launched with a view to provide markets and publicity for produces/products from rural areas. It should also serve to 'value-add' these products. Khadi should not always remain that pale white. Khadi should be produced in colour prints also so as to suit the contemporary demands of the consumers. We should know how to put consumers mind in product development. It looks logical when the neo-liberals argue that only when there is competition, people would get good quality product at cheaper prices. This is the crux of free-market economy. Instead of thinking *coca cola* is hitting local soft drinks such as *Nanari Sarpath,* or bottled beverages one should find ways to enhance one's business strategy through changes in quality, price, publicity and promotion measures to take the local soft drinks or *Cola* to the level of *Coca Cola*.

That which should get down on business mode should be presented in business mode only. Business cannot be run like a charity house, although business has its social responsibility dimension. Unfortunately in India, even NGOs today are also getting into business mode. The influence of business has craftily entered the NGO sector as well. NGOs call their Annual Plan and Operational Plans as 'Business Plans'. They are adopting several business models in the guise of attaining sustainability of their 'businesses'. When they go to lend a poor SHG woman, they explain various 'loan and insurance products' they have. NGOs appoint 'Business Development Managers'. SHG loans have become 'products' now. Similar is the case with several of the advertisements in the media including in the Television channels, and their influence on local cultures and the way people think. This leads us to an important question frequently raised in the context of globalization that is the psychic war between local cultures, organisational cultures and market forces.

THE PSYCHIC WAR : CULTURE AND MARKETS

Globalization can be viewed as a psychic war. It is a war on your psyche. Once you threaten a society, which is really vulnerable in certain respects, that you do not have strength; that you do not have capacity to grow; that you do not have the capability to take hold of your own problems, it silently attacks on your psyche. This is creating a passivity or inferiority complex, and you carry on your business with the psyche operating in your favour. It is not the product. It is a whole psyche saying that Indian products do not match the world market, so you better change. So, the products are not the real issue. That psyche war or submissiveness to the ideas that whatever that comes from outside India is good and whatever is produced here is inferior, that is the major issue. How to face this cultural war is the real problem.

To cite an example, in India, we all face poverty-driven diseases such as malnutrition, anaemia, miscarriages and other tropical diseases such as malaria etc. Suddenly we got down to addressing life-style diseases—the diseases that come because of our life-style—HIV-AIDS, cardiac problems, diabetics, obesity etc. How did we get this change in perception? This is because people in developed countries think that these are the major health problems. Suddenly you drive all your resources into this. All your major tropical diseases such as TB, malaria, filaria are not looked at because the 'they say' that the life-style diseases are the major problems we are going to suffer from. In India we had, more or less, won the war on leprosy, we were working on curing TB. Nobody talks about population control now. China and India are not looked at as countries with creativity, ethical and ethnic beauty. They are seen as big marketplaces. You do not talk about population now. It does not any more pose a threat. Suddenly how these values change? People from outside India imposing values on us. This is a danger of multiple channels of information-reach and influencing without letting you realise that the way you need to think is being inculcated and formatted. You know that inner tranquillity is questioned. This becomes a country whose psyche and culture questioned.

Another important dimension to this problem is that it is the duty of the Panchayats to protect rural livelihoods including the services of the rural artisans. As far as rural artisans are concerned, we have lost the war. Artisans are no more the service sector for us. Artisans are basically cultural sector for us. But, in the name of economic efficiency we allow all their livelihood resources being robbed. They are very fast being ripped off their raw material bases. You no more wear cotton, our weavers are gone. You no more use pottery products, how can potters survive. Now you think you do not need them. Construction works are going on all over in all the States. There is a lot of possibility for pottery products being used in construction such as flooring, tiles, flower vases, etc. if we really want to support pottery. Pottery articles are organic and non-toxic, unlike Teflon coated materials. We can have our gas stove, but we can use pottery materials in the kitchen. It can be a movement. On the one side we are breaking the tradition and we are making no efforts to revive the tradition.

Box 1.1: Cultural Revival in Actuality

It happened in a village near Wardha in Gujarat state. The *Diwali* was over. But, the potters were left with a lot of mud-lamps unsold with them. Nobody buys them after *Diwali.* The Panchayat headman, came to know about it. What he did was he mooted an idea: 'See, we have all celebrated *Diwali* happily with our family at our homes. Why don't we all celebrate *Diwali* one-day at the local temple? Each family bring 20 or 30 mud-lamps to the temple. We shall light them at the temple, and celebrate a community-*Diwali* this year. It was such a vibrating festival with over 2000 mud-lamps shining at one place. So, culturally what has he done? He revived it in a different manner, and made it a community thing. In another sense, protecting the potters is a responsibility of the community, they depend on. He was right in that respect also.

Source: Dr. Vibha Gupta, *Global and Local*, September-October 2006.

There is no such cultural revival (see Box 1.1) taking place in India. Works on cultural revivals, which sustains traditional livelihoods, and which keeps the community together are very much needed at a time, when globalization is eroding the tradition and culture. Storing water in plastic pots is unhealthy, and it could earn toxicity as hours go by. Plastic pots are easy to carry and so they can be used for fetching water. But, when it comes to storing it is always good to store in mud pots. Now, we need to re-educate the people, showing the science behind certain cultural practices such as wearing *khadi;* why plastic *bindi* should not be used; why use flowers on head; why store water in earthen pots and so on. We need to understand the logic of all that had been coming with culture. We must find ways to scientifically put it across to people. Thus, we can save some of the traditional industries and artisans.

In order to protect the interest of the jute farmers and jute workers of Bangaladesh, that country came up with a policy: 'We have plenty of jute, no more plastics. Jute must be used as the primary material in any kind of packing'. That was the policy. Just one single policy all those involved in that sector have been protected, and they are selling at massive quantity. Such policy measures are necessary. Whatever policy that is pursued one must see if that helps the common ordinary man in the villages. Protecting the interest of the industrialists they can do it themselves. They do not need a state policy for survival. It is the poor who needs state policy for their survival and sustenance.

THE SWINGING STATE

In whose interest should a state act is a vital question. Act in the interest of the market or act in the interest of the poor, who are vulnerable to the vagaries of market conditions and the changing state policies to be able to accommodate global economic trends. As we have become part of the global economy now, keeping track of global economic trends, while at the same time taking domestic level action for economic growth are important objectives too. They cannot be brushed aside completely tilting towards ideologies that base local community-centredness. Economic growth and social development are twin important objectives. One cannot be achieved without the other. Economic growth demands private investments too. This is a kind of balancing act that the state and policy makers have to do often times. They need to protect the interest of the poor, while at the same without losing private investment that would generate additional employment, contribute to global trade, and economic growth.

HUMANISING THE STATE

One thing about globalization is one cannot clearly think about it, and say categorically this is what it is, and this is how it will behave. This is so, especially because the principles that operate are essentially based on market forces. Consequently, it happens people are either for or against it. You either support it or oppose it. Some trends are clear that indicate or provide evidence to come to a conclusion where it works how. One such evidence in several places where globalization has brought about in several countries, is nation-state becomes weak? It is possible one may argue that India is an exception to this. Secondly, the power of labour shall become weak. The organised labour power would become weak. The unorganised state or informal economy grows; inequality becomes wider. It means rich people become richer, but the poor may not become poorer, instead the rich becoming richer might widen the gap between the rich and the poor. Collective action becomes difficult, as it triggers the individuals to run faster in the competitive world.

The importance is to the investor and knowledge-based worker. Traditional economic activities tend to get whipped out especially agro-based industries—for example, Kerala Coir has picked up, but handloom has fallen into a deep pit. Some consider that if globalization has to operate, the state needs to be kept weak, therefore, powers should be decentralized at various levels.

As far as decentralization is concerned there are two types of decentralization. One is rolling back the state. That is there is no need for a government. The other is humanising the state. Instead of rolling back, how to humanise the state is a vital question. This is not rolling back the state. This is about humanising the state. It is government failure in many of the places that gives way for the market to emerge to fill that gap. The state is powerful but it is no good to interact with the state. It is often rule-based and not human-faced.

In globalization there are several good ideas, and potentials. For good governance one common definition given world-wide is: 'equity'. If we gave a thought about equity the poor may not have become poorer by income criterion. They become vulnerable as a result of the unprecedented changes taking place. It means they are exposed to unprecedented shocks, stress and risk. They become defenceless because of lack of means to cope without damaging loss (Robert Chambers, 2003). They become less powerful, because they were not prepared to face such damage, shock or stress. Consequently, they get excluded in the kind of development taking place. They are not able to make sense of the goings-on to fit them in, and get along. They get excluded. This process causes exclusion in gaining technological or economic benefits, not necessarily impoverishment. We should understand this distinction.

When we find the formal economy does not support the poor. We get down to informal economy such as SHGs. The government may slowly support it for political reasons. But, all said and done it is an informal economy. In Tamil Nadu as well as in Kerala, almost everyone has a mobile phone. The Kerala Government has removed 'mobile phone' as a proxy indicator of a person or family being below poverty line. Having been put out by the mainstream development of the economy, the poor get sidelined on the track of informal economy such as SHGs, government's rural employment programme etc. to earn a living and for survival. They get shelter into such social safety nets.

One argument we can positively present is that the social capital built up such as Panchayats, and SHGs are results of decentralization. The ethnic food, ethnic dress, traditional medicines or Indian System of medicine have all started finding important place because of the fear that globalization might wash away these. Panchayats are provided with computers to be able to retrieve any information the district administration is required to supply to the State government, any moment.

The thinking of formal linking of rural producers with urban markets, value-addition, quality consciousness and Rural Business Hub etc. are aspects we have started seriously thinking about as a result of globalization or these are cultures that globalization has brought about. These are aspects pertaining to local economic development and individual entrepreneurship. Earlier the thinking was the state should do everything for the village. Now, after decentralization we have started thinking about local development, we claim Gram Sabha can decide what is important to a given Panchayat. For local economic development, how international contacts through NGOs can help is a positive thinking. We can also think of Panchayat level Investors Meet. Like the State government is facilitating the industrialists to commence business, the Panchayats can also invite investors to set up industries in their Panchayat area. But, the aspects pertaining to employment for local people, and environmental sustainability, and corrosion of local cultural sectors such as rural artisans should not become poorer, as a result.

INFORMED CITIZEN FOR MARKET AND DEMOCRACY

After the 73rd Constitutional Amendment Act and introduction of Panchayati Raj Act in every State, one cannot think of rural development without having

Panchayats in mind. In a democracy the right thing may not get done; but popular thing will get done. Panchayat is strength of number and numbers really matter.

One of the imperatives for rural poverty reduction or rural development to take place in every Village Panchayat office must have information on aspects like: land classification within the Panchayat; what are their common assets; what crops are cultivated; where, how and at what price they are marketed; animal population; fodder sources; employment pattern; irrigation sources; irrigation infrastructure that require protection and maintenance; river sand; stone; and woods etc. They must go into planning how to make the best use of their resources without allowing others from exploiting them for making private profits. The Panchayats should take care of their own demands. Poverty reduction cannot wait for the sake of beach beautification. Whose priority matters or whose reality counts most is the real question. You cannot leave your weavers sleep hungry; you cannot let your potters gasping for breath; you cannot leave your agricultural wage earners get employed in road expansion projects in other States. Unless there is a social bearing in the whole thing poverty reduction or rural development cannot become a reality. In all these processes there has to be an underlying empowerment of our being—of our being an Indian, of belonging to this culture, this soil, this society, and this environment. The best way to manage globalization can be with a strong self-sustaining footing of this country.

Secondly, demanding financial or fiscal transparency putting to use Right to Information Act (RTI) is something every Panchayat President should get to know. The revenue raising capacities are with State governments or Central government. In India revenue raising capabilities are not coterminous with expenditure responsibilities. Fiscal Decentralization is necessary to correct this mismatch between expenditure and revenue responsibilities at various levels of government and match them through inter-governmental fiscal transfers. After 73rd Amendment Act, fiscal decentralization takes place from States to Panchayats. Various departments are implementing programmes in the villages. They include: rural development, social welfare, agriculture, horticulture, forestry, irrigation, women and child development and so on and so forth. They receive fund allocation every year. Not all these funds are expended through Panchayats. But, all these funds are expended within the villages of some Panchayats only.

One practical question in this regard is : How much of money reported to be spending in villages are routed through Panchayats—sector-wise, and scheme-wise? This is a vital question for local self-governments. Are the Panchayat functionaries aware of the amount of money that is going to be spent in his/her Panchayat area in a given year—by various departments? If they were not aware of it how would they be able to make action plans for rural development, agricultural development or poverty reduction with Gram Sabha? How would they be able to demand the type of schemes they are in need of in their respective Panchayat area? The question is simple: How much money have they [the government] allocated for our village for carrying out various sectors of work?

There are 99 centrally-sponsored schemes, totally planned to spend Rs. 95,000 crore. NREGS itself is Rs. 37,000 crore; and SSA (Education for All) is Rs. 13,000 crore. Just eight important schemes equal to Rs. 85,000 crore. The rest 91 schemes get in total, the rest Rs. 10,000 crore (GoI). Each Panchayat should track how much money is coming into (your) Panchayat area under these eight schemes? Roughly Rs. 2 crore to Rs. 4 crore are reportedly spent in each Panchayat depending upon the size of the Panchayat. This is an important area for Panchayat leaders to act upon. If real participatory rural development should take place, the information empowerment at the grassroots level is significant. One legally or constitutionally recognized body that has all the rights to demand for information from various departments is Panchayat Office.

There are several possibilities at the Panchayat level. For example, 'activity mapping' is important for State and Centrally sponsored schemes at Panchayat level. We need to create separate windows for Panchayats. Reform of fund flow mechanisms from State treasuries through bank transfers can be done, so that the money flow is clearly seen. All Panchayats should be ensured of minimum level of infrastructure and staff. The State government can use the agency function of Panchayats through well designed contracts; and the State can build up the taxation power of Panchayats, concentrate on property taxes and user charges. If all these can fall in place gradually, at least the information transparency can be attempted immediately. Panchayats in Tamil Nadu are weak more because of lack of transparency in financial allocations, than because of poor financial devolution.

The first thing that can reveal grassroots level democracy or transparency in financial devolution is all the Panchayat Presidents should write to each department asking through an RTI petition: 'How much money are you going to spend in my Panchayat during the current year—please provide work-wise details?' This one question can take rural development and poverty reduction efforts in Tamil Nadu villages to next level of development. If people started asking for information, then officials get alert, and keep away from doing any malpractices, especially when they know you are aware and that you are watching. You should know that within 30 days you need to be given an answer for the RTI application. The moment this RTI application is filed, it starts ticking. How do we manage this reality as best as we can is what it matters. The law is in favour of Panchayats, and decentralized administration. It is how Panchayats make use of it that matters. It is upto Panchayats to make use to whatever advantage they can put that too.

REFERENCES

Adam Smith (1776). *The Wealth of Nations*, Bantan Classics (2003), New Delhi.

Brue, McConnel, (2007). *Essentials of Economics*, Tata McGraw Hill Publishing Company, New Delhi.

Daniel R. Fusfeld (1970). *The Age of the Economist: Ideas That Shape The Way We Live*, The Ladder Edition, Pyramid Publications, New York.

David Macarov (2003). *What the Market Does to the People: Privatisation, Globalization and Poverty*, Clarity Press Inc. Atlanta and ZED Books, London.

Deepak Nayar (ed.) (2002). *Governing Globalization: Issues and Institutions*, Oxford University Press, New Delhi.

Edward J. Blakely & Ted K. Bradshaw (2003). *Planning Local Economic Development : Theory and Practice*, Vistaar Publications, New Delhi.

Hardin (1968). *The Tragedy of the Commons.*

Ian Christie and Diane Warburton (2001). *From Here to Sustainability : Politics in the Real World*, produced by the Real World Coalition, Earthscan Publications Ltd., London.

ILO (2004). *Fair Globalization Creating Opportunities for All*, available at www.ilo.org/wcsdg.

Jagdish Bhagwati (2004). *In Defence of Globalization*, Oxford University Press, New Delhi.

Katar Singh (2009). *Rural Development: Principles, Policies and Management*, (3rd Edition) Sage Publications, New Delhi.

Katar Singh and Anil Shishodia (2007). *Environmental Economics : Theory and Applications*, Sage Publications, New Delhi.

Meenakshisundaram, S.S. (1994). *Decentralization in Developing Countries*, Concept Publishing Company, New Delhi.

Palanithurai, G. (2001). *Towards Decentralization of Power*, Rajiv Gandhi Chair for Panchayati Raj Studies, Gandhigram Rural University, Gandhigram.

Robert Chambers (2003). *Whose Reality Counts : Putting the First Last*, ITDG Publishing, London.

Sakiko Fukuda-Parr and A.K. Shiva Kumar (2005). *Readings in Human Development*, Oxford University Press, New Delhi.

Sikdar, *Contemporary Issues in Globalization*, Oxford University Press, New Delhi.

Stan Burkey (1993). *People First : A Guide to Self-reliant, Participatory Rural Development*, ZED Books, London & New York.

Thomas R. Dye (2004). *Understanding Public Policy*, Pearson Education Inc., Delhi.

Vaish, M.C. & Sudama Singh (2006). *International Economics*, Oxford and IBH Publishing Company, New Delhi.

Vibha Gupta (2006). *Global and Local : Views and Counter Views*, Rajiv Gandhi Chair for Panchayati Raj Studies, Gandhigram.

WEDC (1987). *Our Common Future*, Oxford University Press, London.

Wikipedia—*The Free Encylopaedia Online, 2002.*

Yujiro Hayami and Yoshihisa Godo (2006). *Development Economics: From Poverty to the Wealth of Nations*, Oxford University Press, New Delhi.

CHAPTER TWO

PRIMARY EDUCATION FOR ALL

REFORMS IN BASIC SERVICES IN TAMIL NADU

The Government of India on a sharing basis with the Government of Tamil Nadu has initiated several reform measures in the delivery of basic services. The vital of them include : (i) Primary Education, (ii) Primary Health Services, and (iii) Drinking Water Supply. Reforms in basic services are being implemented since 2000-01. The package of reforms in primary education sector is addressed as *Sarva Shiksha Abhiyan* (popularly known as SSA) meaning Education for All; the package on reforms in primary health care is addressed as National Rural Health Mission (NRHM); and the package on reforms in rural drinking water supply is addressed as *Swajaldhara* Rural Drinking Water Project. Reform initiatives involving the basic services require review and analysis because the impact of policy changes in the basic services are mainly supposed to offset the costly privatised service; and enabling the reach of quality services to the common man. If they fail to deliver what these reform measures are supposed to deliver, it tends to affect the poor rural residents more than anybody else.

The critical links among policy objectives, policy actions, and their impacts on key stakeholder groups, with a focus on gainers and losers should be made public and be brought to the notice of the policy makers. While all of these services are largely available with the private sector also, the influence of market principles, often, keeps the poor away from availing these services. Unless the government made way and facilitated reach of these facilities to the poor through the service delivery network of the state, the course of development (a) tend to leave the poor deprived of these services, and (b) the private sector tend to sweep up the market and ignore the poor.

OBJECTIVES OF THIS STUDY

- Study the changes—both positive and negative—that have come about after introduction of reform measures in the delivery of basic services viz. primary education, drinking water service delivery and primary health care and in Tamil Nadu.

- Find out the relative nature, type, and pace of changes that are taking place at the delivery basic services after reform measure of the government *vis-à-vis* the changes that are coming about with the privately-managed services.
- Record the aggregated views of different stakeholders involved in pushing the reform agenda forward especially at implementation level and the effect on them on the rural poor.

METHODOLOGY OF THE STUDY

Methods and Tools Used: The study has used mixed methodology meaning both qualitative and quantitative methods. Two short questionnaires were used for collecting primary data. One questionnaire was used for collecting school level information;. and the other for collecting household information, especially of household expenditure on education. The questionnaires are given in the annexure. Besides this, the study mainly involved Direct Observation and On-the-Spot Analysis of situations and responses of the stakeholder groups.

Data Sources: The study has made use of both primary as well as secondary data. Secondary data were collected from DISE, and from the website of the Government of Tamil Nadu. In order to collect primary data chain of interview was held with Headmaster and school teachers, BRC and CRC Team members of SSA, parents of children from both government-run schools and privately-managed schools, and with Village Panchayat functionaries who are said to be the members of Village Education Committee. Experts in Primary Education have been interviewed to make sure that the study covers all aspects, a study of this kind should cover. The study covered 17 villages in Tamil Nadu and interviewed 120 parents of children studying either in government schools or at private matriculation schools.

SCOPE OF THIS STUDY

The study covers primary education reforms in Tamil Nadu. The channels of reform flow have been tracked from the schemes introduced for promoting enrolment, access, transition tracking, quality of education, infrastructure development in schools, availability of teaching-learning materials, outcomes levels in terms of enhancement in retention levels, completion rate etc.

The study is confined to primary education only, and is limited to government-run primary schools and privately-managed schools in Tamil Nadu State. One of the good things that have happened as an outcome of Education Sector Reform is data pertaining to school education has been to a large extent streamlined. What seems to be missing is the qualitative information or the narrative account behind the numbers being compiled, which can actually speak louder than dead numbers. This study has precisely aimed at capturing the qualitative changes through chain of interviews, Direct Observations and on-the-spot analysis.

Policy reform involving changes in primary education sector has been studied taking into account the following viewpoints:

- Providing Access to School
- School Infrastructure
- Quality of Education
- Privatisation/Public-private Partnership in primary education
- Social Inclusion and Gender
- Decentralization
- Highlight of findings

EDUCATION SECTOR REFORM

There are newspaper reports stating that government primary schools in some villages are being closed for want of children, and due to teachers not having been appointed for long. There are private individuals and charitable institutions commencing chain of schools—like chain of hotels and resorts—that run successfully as business models.

> "*Seven Union Primary Schools have been closed in Gujiliamparai Block of Dindigul due to want of children*".
>
> —*Dina Malar*, 14th April 2008

> "*Eurokids—a chain of privately-managed schools calls for franchises to open and run play school in various districts of Tamil Nadu*".
>
> —*The Hindu*, 7th May, 2006

> *"Members of the district wing of the Tamil Nadu Primary School Teachers Association staged a dharna in front of the office of the District Elementary Education Officer in Pudukottai, demanding a revision of the teacher-pupil ratio from the existing 1:40 to 1:20 for ensuring quality education particularly to the rural students"*.
>
> —*The Hindu*, Wednesday, June 20, 2007

The 86th Constitutional Amendment of 2002 led to inclusion of a New Article 21-A in Part III of the Constitution that made Free and Compulsory Education to all children of 6-14 years of age a Fundamental Right. Pending enactment of a suitable follow-up legislation envisaged in Article 21-A, the 86th Constitutional Amendment has not yet been enforced. However, it is imperative to give good quality elementary education to all children in the age group of 6-14 years. Policies and programmes in this direction are also necessary for honouring the country's commitment to the 'Millennium Development Goals' and 'Education for All'.

(I) SARVA SHIKSHA ABHIYAN (SSA)

SSA meaning Education for all is a pre-condition to be able to face the rapid changes that are taking place in the socio-economic and technological milieu of the country. If the poor and marginalized segments of the society should also be benefited by globalisation 'free and compulsory education should be made a fundamental right of every child'. This would ultimately result in an inclusive society ensuring equitable distribution of the impact of reform measures. Hence, the Constitutional 86th amendment made free and compulsory education a fundamental right for all children in the age group of 6-14 years (S. Chandrasekhar, Abhiroop Mukhopadhyay, 2006).

The Sarva Shiksha Abhiyan (SSA) is being implemented in partnership with States to address the needs of children in the age group of 6-14 years. The achievements reported by the Government of India under SSA up to September 30, 2007, include construction of 1,70,320 school buildings, construction of 7,13,179 additional classrooms, 1,72,381 drinking water facilities, construction of 2,18,075 toilets, supply of free textbooks to 6.64 crore children and appointment of 8.10 lakh teachers besides opening of 1,86,985 (till 31.3.2007) new schools. About 35 lakh teachers receive in-service training each year. Central allocation for SSA in 2007-08 was Rs. 10,671. With significant success in enrolling children in schools, the SSA's thrust areas are now on reduction of dropouts and improving quality of student learning.

Sarva Shiksha Abhiyan (SSA) forms the cornerstone of government interventions in basic education for all children. SSA, launched in November 2000 was to support and build on primary education in the country. The programme aims at ensuring five years of primary education for all children in the age group of 6-14 years by 2007, and eight years of schooling by 2010. The precise goals of SSA are: (i) all children in schools, education centre, alternate school, back to school camp by 2007; (ii) bridge all gender and social category gaps at the primary stage by 2007 and at elementary education level by 2010; (iii) universal retention by 2010; and (iv) focus on elementary education of satisfactory quality with emphasis on education for life (Gursharan Singh Kainth, 2006). The Government of Tamil Nadu ventures to achieve all these by taking following measures :

- Providing free education, free uniform, free meals, free books and stationery, free bus pass etc.
- Providing access to school to a population of 1000, or within 1 km.
- School infrastructure be improved appropriately.
- Improving the quality of education through innovative ABL methodology.
- Special scheme for social inclusion and education of girl children.
- Village level Education Committee as a way of decentralisation in ensuring transparency, accountability and good governance at the local level.

There are also administrative structure such as Block Resource Team, Cluster Resource Team and constant training of teachers in new ABL methodology etc.

(II) PROVIDING ACCESS TO SCHOOL EDUCATION

The government of Tamil Nadu—with a view to providing universal access to school education, and to realize the goal of education for all—put in practice an important access related criterion, viz. providing access to schools for a population of 1000 or within 1 km. The State Report Cards on education put across that Tamil Nadu has 24,201 government primary schools in 21,950 villages. It means one habitation has more than one school. This does not include 9,715 private primary schools, which together make 33,916 schools in 21,950 villages (DISE, 2005-06). Besides this, there are new government primary schools coming up year after year, and there are also private schools opened alongside. One can take it that Tamil Nadu has achieved access criterion more than what is required. There are also cases where in our attempt to open a new school in one village, we have inadvertently caused closure of another school in the neighbourhood village.

At primary schools in Tamil Nadu there are 38,82,092 children on roll (19,90,557 boys + 18,91,535 girls) and 1,15,568 teachers employed (2005-06). The education mill is on the grind always. Although one cannot claim all school-going age children are in school, one can say that the trend is comfortable except for the hazard of child labour in some pockets of Tamil Nadu. The number of out-of-school children in the State is reported to be

1,12,000 where the ratio of boys and girls are almost equal in number. The official reports present that only 30,728 of them are child labourers. The fact could be over 70,000 of them should be child labourers, and only the rest did not pursue school education due to various reasons. One of the reasons reported is lack of access to school. But, given the coverage, the number of schools *vis-à-vis* villages in Tamil Nadu lack of access cannot be a reason for not going to school. Perhaps, migration of parents in search of employment, uninterested children of unaware parents, disability of children could be taken as reasons. The districts with high incidence of child labourers reported are: Krishnagiri, Salem, Namakkal, Dharmapuri, Coimbatore and Madurai. Despite the existence of anti-child labour legislations, and SSA effort of 100 per cent enrolment, child labour/out-of-school children are present. That a significant number are out of school need not be taken that all of them are child labourers. Children of unaware parents, who are uninterested in studies tend to loiter in the village not going to school.

There are governmental and NGO action taking place to educate the labouring children also through evening coaching centres (*Nila Palli*) for gradual elimination of child labour in the State. The average drop-out rate at primary level has also come down significantly from 3.17 per cent to 1.54 per cent in 2005-06 (DISE, 2005-06). All the districts in Tamil Nadu report a transition rate of almost 97 per cent from Primary to Upper primary level.

All specially trained teachers—with Diploma in Teacher Education and with even higher qualifications—are with the government schools or with Union Primary Schools. Elementary Education in the State has been on focus for quite a few years now with centrally assisted schemes like Sarva Siksha Abhiyan (SSA). But the strength of children in primary schools is declining year after year. So much so, for want of children, many of the schools especially in rural areas of Tamil Nadu are two classroom schools with two teachers to handle all the five primary classes. The children strength in all the five classes put together are so meagre that the school is eligible to get only two teachers as per government norms. Thus, Union Primary Schools are thinning down, in pupil strength as well as in number of teachers with each school. One of the obvious and immediately understandable reasons is declining birth rate in the state in the last decade. Are there other reasons beyond this that cause thinning down of enrolment in Union Primary Schools in the State such as the privatisation of education, for example? This required deeper probe through chain of interviews across districts with various types of stakeholders essentially parents, teachers, school principals, Education Officers, promoters of SSA etc.

Privately-managed and government-aided schools have also joined the government/Union primary schools in providing universal education for all. However, the strength in Union Primary Schools in rural areas is losing ground very fast. In fact, some of the schools such as the ones existed in places like Parapatty, and Chenkulathupatty in Dindigul district have shuttered down for want of children. It seems a list of schools closed down in the last five years can be generated given the number we get in each district. The privately managed schools are thriving and making headway increasing the number of enrolment each year setting wider net through providing school bus service etc. The community in general has become sceptical about the quality of education and the childcare provided by the government-run union primary schools. However, poor it might be in terms of infrastructure, private schools tend to thrive. It must be a blend of myth-and-reality that all the private schools offer quality education. But they have gained the parents' validation and support, notwithstanding high tuition fees, and other paraphernalia.

Despite schemes like SSA, free education, free meal, free uniforms etc. the Union Primary School is looked down upon by parents. The enrolment in government schools has come down from 63.6 per cent (2004-05) to 59.8 per cent in 2005-06. Therefore, although declining birth rate could be an important reason, there is no denying the fact that the general community trust on the quality of education and childcare provided at Union Primary Schools is also a significant reason for declining enrolment rate at the government schools in the State. However, there is widespread awareness on the importance of education even amongst the poorest of families.

Public inaction is one of the important reasons for dull Union Primary Schools in the State. The public are fast washing their hands off Union Primary School, mainly because they have an easy alternative available (privately run schools with van facilities for picking up and dropping back children) that suite different types of income categories. There is no community based action, or action from Panchayats to set right school system at the village level. They are still in the hands of AEO or Education Department of the State government although they are said to be Panchayat Union Primary Schools. The Panchayats play very little role in managing or setting right the problems of enrolment, retention or in improving the school infrastructure, or quality of education. The administrative structure of Union Primary Schools, and place of local Panchayats is such that the Panchayat functionaries feel they have no role to play in matters relating to basic education.

There is every reason to believe that if Panchayats could take action to set right things at government run primary schools, a considerable number of schools can be improved. Overcoming the discouragement effect of parents is very much required (Dreze & Sen, 2005)

Another standpoint one can take to view this problem is that no matter who does it : be it government schools or the private matriculation school— the ultimate goal is : 'Education for all'. There is nothing to comment that government is weaning away from providing a basic need of the citizenry. What requires to be controlled is the high tuition and other fees charged by private matriculation schools. This stems from the fact that in the sphere of education private participation or public-private participation has been in existence even during the first plan period when mixed economic system started taking roots. However, critiques awake only when it comes to quality of education offered, and cost of education, affordability of private education for children from poverty stricken families.

Talking in terms of market, primary education today is no small market. All said and done, given the number of villages in Tamil Nadu, there are about 40 lakh children at primary level alone and hardly one-third of them are in private schools. The rest go to government primary schools only. The State Government of Tamil Nadu has really achieved remarkably in providing access even in remote and hilly areas. Tamil Nadu has already reported that it has achieved cent-per-cent access at Primary level in the year 2002-03. However, it has been reported in school mapping 2005-06 that 364 habitations are still eligible for getting EGS, and 126 of them are eligible for Primary School. It is true that the quantum of out-of-school children has come down very significantly, whereas schools are closing down one after another for want of children. Access does not seem to be the problem. Therefore, this blind 'eligibility to get sanction' need not be taken as criterion, especially when it comes to opening new Primary Schools. What is required is facility and infrastructure upgradation in the existing schools, and to change the poverty of image that government schools are mired in over the years. Not another new school.

(III) SCHOOL INFRASTRUCTURE

If one made a list of what are the physical infrastructures required at primary school level, the list could go something like this. A building with proper ventilation and lighting, a roof made of material that is poor conductor of heat, partition facility between classes, adequate furniture and required electrical fittings, drinking water facility, sanitation facility separately for boys, girls, and teachers, and a compound wall to ensure that common people do not misuse the school infrastructure for illegitimate purposes. SSA may or may not have helped in terms of enhancing the quality of education or in reducing the dropout rate or improving the completion rate at schools, but, one thing that teachers at primary schools are thankful to SSA is for it has made them sit on chairs that clearly has four legs, which otherwise used to be two-legged chairs or three-legged ones.

As part of reform measures infrastructure development in primary schools is a significant step taken by the Government of Tamil Nadu with a view to enliven primary education in the State. The Centre has also come with SSA to improve quality of government-run schools. The Reform package in school education has come essentially as SSA Scheme that aims not only at enrolling every one of the school going-age children at school but also providing quality learning environment and quality infrastructure at government-run primary schools. That the government primary schools lack infrastructure facilities is a well-known fact. But, when it comes to building up infrastructure, do we have a sense of priority, and how good we are, in maintaining those assets are the crux of the matter. The teachers are, to some extent, contented at the moment because what they did not get after years and years of request have been provided to them under SSA—their chairs changed, and the school has got a new cupboard to keep the registers, and wooden racks and plastic trays to keep the ABL cards on.

When one makes a personal observation of the kind of infrastructure development taking place in government-run schools, one could not help thinking that there is some fundamental problem in prioritization, management and maintenance of infrastructure. Before getting down to such an analysis we need to study the reports of existing infrastructure as given by the State. The State Elementary Education Report Card 2005-06 states that average student-classroom ratio (SCR) is 26. Averages do not make sense in matters pertaining to student-classroom ratio in a State like Tamil Nadu where there are more than 33,916 schools. Another thing reported is 96 per cent of the schools have drinking water facility. Our personal observation and chain of interviews with school teachers and school children reveal that perhaps, in 96 per cent of the schools 'drinking water arrangement is made' because there is anyway noon meal requires to be cooked. Water from the main village collected in a stainless steel container and kept for children to take. It is not a facility in use. It is only an arrangement, which is *ad hoc*. That the report, 57 per cent of schools have common toilets can be challenged if one paid visits to these schools. There is also report, that 45 per cent of the primary schools have toilets separately for girls. The few toilets—although in dilapidated condition—in use are for the teachers only. In most of the-primary school buildings there is no electric power connection given. Where it has been given, electric wires have been nailed on the wall; neither the head master nor the teachers know if they are usable. A countable few schools have electricity connection in use. One interesting thing to note here with regard to water and sanitation facility is that figures given in the State Report Cards are averages combining primary schools run by private management also. Perhaps, the private schools make up for the huge tilt that otherwise might let the Union Primary Schools lose ground completely.

The fact one gets during field visits is that it is cent-per-cent true that almost all the primary schools have been provided with water connection, water tanks and toilets more than one, and more than once. If one made a rough calculation of the amount of money invested for establishing water and sanitation facilities in these government-run schools, one would get anywhere between Rs. 1 lakh to Rs. 5 lakh. Most of them remain disused. Renovation of the existing toilets and water lines that remained disused could have served the purpose. It could also have saved the place that another set of toilets and water supply facilities that occupied.

Another dimension to this issue is that when one facility (be it water or toilet) ran into disuse, another new unit has been sanctioned, which again remain non-functional—for reasons such as there is no water line for use, the pan is no good and so flushing is not possible or there is no fencing and so villagers have made it disgusting to enter and so on and so forth. Anyway, the investment made on water and sanitation infrastructure has gone into the gutters. Even after implementing a host of water supply and sanitation programmes, one lesson that our policy makers or planners do not seem to get into their heads, somehow, is that a set of facilities given to rural schools without proper fencing would definitely be misused by the local miscreants. There is hardly any government run primary school that has fencing. In fact, some goats become solitary learners in rural school classrooms on Sundays. It is astounding to find that there are schools with asbestos sheet roofs, which WHO strongly advises not to use. The children have to put up with the heat being conducted by the asbestos sheets, which are potential spoilers of a learning environment.

It should be recorded that reform efforts through SSA has helped build school infrastructure which did not get attention for several years in a row, not adequately though. However, infrastructure provided with no arrangements for maintenance or adequate funds to take up repair works etc. results in recurrent capital investment ultimately rendering the facility unusable at any point of time. Although everything costs money at private matriculation schools, infrastructure does matter in creating a quality learning environment. In the absence of even the basic facilities such as a good black board to write on, drinking water facility, urinal facility, and a fence to create an impression among the community that this an institution, what use would EDUSAT be of.

(IV) QUALITY OF EDUCATION

Reforms in Education initiated in 2000-01 in India aims at rapidly expanding the supply of education, achieving equity in the provision of education, and significantly improving the quality of education. The Education For All mission in Tamil Nadu has several interesting components such as providing access, infrastructure development, teacher development, Activity Based Learning (ABL), creating a learning environment, measuring learning outcome levels and so on. Talking in practical terms, all these if implemented sincerely should be able to produce far-reaching results. Besides this, two other things required are : (i) liberal social sector budget provisions to make it operational; and (ii) a determination on the part of the teachers in government run schools to change their outlook and enhance their commitment levels. All of them in government-run schools are professionally qualified unlike the teachers in the privately-managed (especially rural) schools where most of the teachers are unemployed graduates with no professional qualification in teaching methodologies or college dropouts.

The major chunk of budget allocation for primary education used to go in the form of teachers salary—almost 96 per cent. But, SSA has improved the situation making provision for building maintenance, and for construction of new buildings etc. But, given the number of schools to share this provision, effectively a school gets hardly Rs. 7,000 per year. The provision of Rs. 500 per teacher to make learning materials of their choice and creativity has not reached most of the teachers in Tamil Nadu. However, some of them interested in ABL spend their personal money and prepare learning materials to satisfy the visitors/BRC, though not with the purpose of making learning effective. All said and done, it glaringly reveals during our field visit to every school, that what stands on the top of the mind to all the teachers including the so called resource teachers and the Block Resource Teachers is the ABL method, the cards, the tray and the rack. ABL is expected to serve as the single common denominator to ensure 'quality education'. All the Block Resource Teams, like in any other project, have developed a handful of show-case schools where they can take the visitors to. They are not many of them in each district. There are 385 Block Resource Centres and 4,088 Cluster Resource Centres in the State that are involved in providing on-the-job-training of teachers in Union Primary Schools.

ABL is a method of learning. This method has a set of learning tools, and special kits which facilitate faster learning in an interesting way. It could be definitely a shade better than the methods we have had hitherto. We need to also comprehend and figure out the purpose this is supposed to serve. Change in the learning method is one, and change in the learning environment and teacher-outlook is another. The need to change the poor image the general community holds about government-run school is the most important aspect of it all. The myth created by privately-managed schools that they offer quality education stands stronger than the reality ABL is bringing about in the children with government-run schools. For effective learning to take place, the entire environment should be conducive including the parents' image of the school and the teachers' conviction in the method. The relationship building, or image repairing works have to be taken up too.

Our interaction with the parents and the general community clearly put across that wherever the school headmasters have been active the schools have good image among the general community. Wherever teachers come to school on time, the image has been good. Wherever the teachers share the performance of children with the parents the school image has been good. Wherever the government paid teachers' school-going age child goes to a private school, the image has been poor. Where the teacher is a known money lender or owner of a grocery shop, he is primarily viewed so and secondarily as a teacher; wherever the school has taken initiative to rope in the Village Panchayat functionaries or the PTA, and improve school infrastructure, the image of the school has been good. All these reveal that it is not only method of teaching within the classrooms. It is much beyond it. It requires change in the outlook of the teachers and the commitment levels to enhance the quality of education, and thus the image of public service.

Fantasising is not development. Or the development need not result in fantasy creation. In a place where there is no clean water to drink, what value would a laptop computer or SSA studio get? In a classroom where there is no electric power connection, what purpose would an educational VCD with nursery rhymes in English serve? Development should be gradual and progressive. If some of the privately-managed schools go in for these they have fulfilled their other basic requirements, and facilities. There can be no quick or short-cut ways to make development gain ground or to make education take place at primary level. The privately managed schools have gone to the extent, one parent who pays Rs. 16,600 for admission in lower primary class in a town-based private nursery school, says: "You pay more and you get more, and I am sure I would get what I pay for. Tell me how many of them getting admission in IITs and IIMs are from Government Higher Secondary schools". The range of knowledge and skills a child gets exposed to in a privately-managed school are really fantastic. For private schools it is a matter of survival that they have to show teaching outcome and quality. In rural private schools, if not many, the children's grasp of vocabulary, mathematics, and expression are definitely a shade better than the dumb one that comes from a government primary school.

Regarding the ABL in action at Union Primary Schools, the teachers' view is that where the number of children to be handled is more, it is difficult for the teachers to ensure that learning takes place. Many teachers are of the opinion that ABL would be ideal for a group of 20 or less. One of the observations they shared with this research team is that under ABL those who are generally bright get going level after level, and those who are generally weak in studies keep watching them with no idea of what is this all about. If the number to be handled is less it is possible for the teacher to take the weak also along. When it is more, the attention that the studious get is more than those who are weak and wanting.

Besides poverty, one of the factors that still facilitate admission in government primary schools is the *Balwadis* (Child Care Centres). Incidentally, in a good number of villages, the *Balwadis* are situated next to the Primary Schools. The workers at the *Balwadi* and the teachers in the primary schools become friendly, and so getting the children enrolled at Primary class take place even without the parents knowing about it. The *Balwadi* teacher sends children who have reached five years old to go and sit at the primary school. Thus, *Balwadis* serve as a source of feeder to the Primary school. The middle class send their children to private Nursery Schools or to the Play Schools in the town. In that respect, *Balwadis* are, again for the poor only. This can be extrapolated that children who attend *Balwadis* are most likely to get admitted in government Primary schools, and the children who are sent to Nursery Schools are most likely to get admitted in privately managed primary schools. But the pace at which privately-managed school get going, unless the *Balwadi* as feeders continue to function, it would be difficult for government primary schools to pull on. One of the dangers noticed during field visit is that where the number of children keeps going down year after year, the teacher instead of putting in extra efforts to enhance performance, and enrolment tends to apply for transfer to some other school.

This discussion brings forth another vital question, what is so special about education in privately managed schools that the parents do not mind burning a hole in their pockets to be able to get their children admitted in such schools. The response from majority of the parents is attention paid to 'English language teaching' which has emerged as a global language; better childcare and habits of cleanliness; and right to fight with the management if the parents are not satisfied with any of the aspects of schooling—be it teaching or childcare. The privately managed schools has to respond appropriately in time, otherwise, the matter would start spreading in grapevine communication and create a bad image for the school, resulting in poor admissions in the subsequent years. With due respects to one or two exceptions, the teachers in government schools: 'don't care' especially when it comes to child care. The quick response they have in defence is : 'even their parents don't care'.

What quality education comprises of or what should quality education ultimately result in, is a matter of contention. But the fact remains that the general dissatisfaction with the state of education in government-run schools has made way for proliferation of privately-managed schools. The situation is, given a choice—but for the money factor—even the poorest of parents prefer to send their children to private matriculation schools only.

Reporting that the quality of education, infrastructure and parents opinion about government schools are poor, we are not making a case here for public provision of every aspect of education, or denying that private provision has a role. Rather, we are arguing for seeing the promotion of education as irreducibly social concern, even when basic education is effectively provided through private channels. In every modern economy, health and education is divided to a varying extent between public provision and private supply. However, this does not detract from the overarching importance of public discussion and social planning in these sectors.

Box 2.1: Mangudi Government Middle School

The general trend with regard to school education in Tamil Nadu is that Union Primary Schools or government schools in general are struggling to keep afloat. In fact, there are Union Primary Schools being closed for want of children in some of the villages. As opening of private matriculation schools has been liberalised, the attraction the children (or rather the parents!) get from private schools is multiple, which offer a big challenge to the very existence of Union Primary Schools. The disaster is that private matriculation schools with even abysmally poor levels of infrastructure and teacher competence pose threat to the existence of Union Primary Schools.

(*Contd.*)

BOX 2.1 : (*Contd.*)

Mangudi Government Middle School in Aranthangi Block (Pudukottai)—a tiny village about 7 km from Aranthangi town has proved to be otherwise. It receives applications from children wanting to withdraw from private matriculation school willing to join this government school in Mangudi. That sounds interesting. The drive of the parents is that their wards should get good quality education that would help him go on his own in the future. If they can get it in a government school, that would be excellent for a poor parent who does not have to burn a hole in his pocket for the sake of paying the school fees, and charges on extra curricular activities like computer classes, cycle-riding and so on. The parents who admitted their children once in private matriculation schools are withdrawing them from there and seek admission in Mangudi Government School.

Mangudi Government Middle School has 238 children (115 girls and 123 boys). They come from about 9-10 villages in the neighbourhood, viz. Mangudi, Idaiyuriyendal, Ettiyathali, Maruthangudi, Nattumangalam, Manjalkarai, Poovathakudi, Konnaikkadu, and Thenundavayal. Reportedly, about 60 per cent of the children belong to MBC category; 35 per cent BC; and 5 per cent belong to SC category. The parents are landless wage earners or are involved in small-hold farming.

At least 19 children have come back to join this school from private matriculation schools at the beginning of the current academic session. The reason stated is the quality of education and child care offered in Mangudi Government School is better than that offered in any of the private matriculation schools in the vicinity. First of all, the school looks clean and green with plants and trees all around. Lessons especially at Upper Primary level are taken up with Power Point Slides with an LCD Projector. The colour televisions in all the classrooms are connected to view one lesson, just in case the same thing is to be shown to all the children. The school computer lab has ten computers, which children feel free to use. Be it operation of the audio system, video lessons, or computers connected to LCD, we notice it is the children, who handle everything. That in itself could be stated as a skill that children pick up, and learn at this school. The school receives at least three sets of newspapers, and a few magazines—all with donations from local donors. Many of the facilities have been obtained approaching government schemes, NGOs and individual donors.

The able-leadership of the Head Master and the commitment of every one of the teachers are the factors behind this success. The Head Master Mr. Jothimani (42) recipient of several awards says: "It is the team work of the teachers here and the support that started flowing once individuals and organizations understood that we stand for a commitment. For children to learn, they should feel the freedom to make mistakes in answering a question or operating a gadget like audio-system. Intimidation and the fear of penalty in private schools stand in the way of learning and experimenting. We allow them try their hands without fear. If we allow the fear-factor to operate so that children can be prevented from plucking a flower or leaf—that is being a watchman. Maintaining school environment clean and green should go into his blood as his value system, to call myself a teacher, otherwise I would only be a watchman."

It is interesting to learn that this gentleman (Head Master) who also hails from a village called Aliyanilai (near Aranthangi) has two PG degrees, one M.Phil, and an M.Ed behind his name, and is pursuing Ph.D. degree in Bharathidasan University on 'the use of media in Tamil language teaching'. His proficiency in the use of computers could be noticed when Class 7 and 8 students performed a demonstration in the use of computer lessons to this research team under his supervision. Use of educational technologies to put across lessons is done even at primary level. A child in Class 7 is able to operate computer, type in Tamil, browse the net to learn English grammar lessons. This school serves as a motivation for many schools in the surrounding area to build schools with quality education and child care.

There are private matriculation schools that are market-driven, and commercially oriented. There are government schools that are oriented towards providing education as a basic service to the poor. When a government school starts delivering quality education and offering admirable child care, parents tend to seek admission in government schools only.

(v) Cost of Primary Education and Affordability

The analysis of cost of education brings up several issues that look irresolvable unless through brave policy action at the government level. There is problem—with government-run primary school—of giving everything free; and with privately-managed schools there is problem of charging for everything including the handholding a child gets to go to the urinal. Our survey of thirteen private schools located both in rural areas as well as in mediocre towns like an average district headquarters reveal that for one child a parent has to spend anywhere between Rs. 2,000 to Rs. 7,000 per year in a typical rural private schools. It ranges between Rs. 15,000 to Rs. 40,000 per year to children who travel from rural areas to urban schools in any of the commutable medium level town in Tamil Nadu. The message that privately-managed schools communicate is very clear and quite understandable that they are meant only for the children from well-to-do families. Educational expenses of households have become an important in household expenditure. It takes away almost 10-20 per cent of the household income for a single child family. It works out double of it in a family where there is more than one child.

In rural villages, minus a countable few children from well-to-do families who go to private matriculation schools in the locality or town, all the local children go to union primary school only. There are attractions offered by privately-managed schools by sending school van, making children wear shoes and necktie etc. which is trying the ability of the moderate-poor to stretch. But, one very significant factor that forces the parents to keep their children in government-run schools is 'poverty'. Those who are a little well-to-do or they think they have the 'manageability' they decide to send their wards to private matriculation schools despite high costs. Those who are really dependent on daily wages, and the Public Distribution System (PDS) for rice and essential commodities, have no option but the local Union Primary School. There is not one single individual interviewed by this research team who opined that they send their children to government-run school 'in appreciation of the quality of education imparted'. 'Poverty' is the main factor, invariably, uttered by almost all the parents.

The reasons uttered by the parents who send their children to private-matriculation schools paying through the nose (in the same order as it was reported to this research team by most of the parents) are: (i) English language education, (ii) Foundation years need to be made strong with good teaching, (iii) Safety and better childcare, and (iv) Possibility to get exposed to a variety of extra curricular activities. But what makes them think that the child should learn all these in the formative years? A further probe reveals that (a) they are preparing their children for the future to get admission in reputed institutions of higher learning, (b) increasing the prospects of employability, (c) making sure that the child gets prepared to deliver to the demands of the market. Thus, quality education has become a commodity available in the market with private matriculation schools. Those who have affordability can buy and benefit. For those that are poor, the government schools offer education minus quality.

Minus, of course, the daily wage earners who depend truly on Public Distribution System (PDS) as the main source of food and grocery items to the family; even the moderate poor send their children to at least the local private school rather than to government schools. The general perception of the community is private schools in the city or in far away places are highly quality oriented. It could be partly true because of the competition existing among private matriculation schools in the city—that they have to maintain quality. But, it becomes a myth when people think more the distance, greater the quality. It has almost become a matter of prestige in the society that if a family admits a child in a private residential school, the family scores a better social standing. Rather than the educational status of the parents, it is the economic status of the family that determines if a child would get admitted in government school or private school. It follows that better economic status of the family provides an impetus to the family to look for better quality education from any source that is available—and their least faith is government schools. Another parallel could be corroboration of the fact that government schools are for the economically poor.

(vi) SOCIAL INCLUSION AND GENDER PARITY

One of the achievements of SSA could be that it has brought about a new perspective on special focus groups, viz. girls, children with special needs and SC/ST children. Tamil Nadu has already ensured cent-per-cent access to all habitations as per norms. The arrangement is such that if not a school, at least an EGS centre would be run in such remote places where there are not enough children to construct a new school. That is with a view to providing additional access to enrol and retain girls and SC/ST children in some select pockets, the government has opened EGS centres.

The gap in NER between All and SC is only marginal with 0.75 per cent, and the gap in the case of ST with 1.80 per cent. The gender-wise variation is marginal too, for example, among SCs NER of boys is 97.79 per cent and girls is 97.85. The attendance rate in Primary level is 96 per cent in general, and it is 93 per cent and 90 per cent among SCs and STs respectively, which is acceptable in rural schools. As far as transition from Primary to UP is concerned it is as high as 99.40 per cent in districts like Kanyakumari. Unfortunately, it is 97 per cent among the SCs and 91.60 per cent among the STs. These have shown improvement, but it still requires concerted action.

It is obvious the marginalised cannot mobilize capital nor take hold of technology. But, it is possible for them to get education and become knowledgeable. Hence, education could be a great equalizer. Unequal distribution of knowledge can be stated as one of the prime sources of inequality in society. Equalising society by diffusing knowledge to all is possible. Hence, Education for all is serving as a good tool. The noon-meal is also serving as a driving force for many poor SC and ST children to attend schools. The State Government of Tamil Nadu described EFA as a path-breaking effort of the government in providing education, for the provision it makes to reach the inaccessible, the disabled, the girl children and the STs and so on. The programme has also reached a Net Enrolment Rate of 98.48 per cent, the remaining being in special schools, and in residential camps. Of significance is the fact that there are more women than men teachers at Primary level. Women teachers make up nearly three-fourths of the total number of teachers constituting 73.95 per cent.

The children from the marginalised sections of the society cannot imagine about studying in private matriculation schools given the cost of education in private schools *vis-à-vis* the free meal and uniform given at government schools. The difference people make out is very straight and quite explicable: *government schools are for the marginalised and the private schools are for the rich.* There are also MNCs opening limited liability educational companies commencing from play school to an array of computer courses, including summer special courses for children. Social inclusion has no meaning for private market promoters.

Although girls from marginalised sections have come to join in schools in large numbers, it is also noticeable in rural areas, that a well-to-do peasant family admits both son and daughter in privately-managed primary school. But, when it comes to further education at upper primary level, to be able to manage the household expenditure the girl is admitted in a government school nearby, whereas the boy travels by school bus to the same private school. This kind of gender disparity is also seen in the study villages. The quality difference in government-run schools *vis-à-vis* the privately-managed schools is bound to bring about disparity in educational achievements shown by male and female children from within poorer segments. This would naturally reflect in the future of these children.

It has become something like, for those who seek 'quality education', it is private matriculation schools; and for those who seek 'education', it is government schools. Talking specifically about rural Tamil Nadu, one can point-blank say that government schools are for marginalised and for the girls in poor and middle income families; and private schools are for the middle class and above. Chain of interview with various categories of population put across that the cost and quality factors with government and privately-run schools have brought about this disparity. Those from government schools are repeatedly impressed of their inherent inferiority that such children remain subordinate to those from matriculation schools.

A common response of parents to the poor functioning or non-functioning of a government run village schools is to send their sons to study in other villages, or in private schools. But, the same response is less common in the case of girls, because parents are often reluctant to allow their daughters to wander outside the village or to pay the fees that would be necessary to secure admission in a private school. The breakdown of government school typically affects female children much more severely than male children.

This is not to say that low levels of female education in Tamil Nadu are exclusively due to the poor functioning of the schooling system. The problem of low parental motivation for female education needs attention on its own, in addition to the issue of poor functioning of the schooling system.

History of school education has it that in order to do away the class and caste divisions in schools, uniforms were thought of and introduced. The government of Tamil Nadu reports: Free uniforms worth Rs. 91.22 crore distributed to 59 lakh students studying from 1st to 8th standard in the State. One statement uniformly we get—in almost all the schools visited, and from the parents of union primary schools—is that free uniforms issued are totally unusable. Children use them hardly one month because of their interest in wearing a new cloth. It is unusable because it is under-sized for everyone of the child. Shirts are above belly-button level, and the skirts are well above the knee level that girl children feel uneasy to go out with them.

There is a sound reason in giving free education, and even in providing noon-meal as many of the poor parents consider it a source of keeping children hunger-free when they are away in the field earning the day's wage. But, one widespread opinion of teachers as well as the parents of poorer children is that free uniform scheme could have been made more useful, provided a little attention is paid in stitching them properly. Provision of free noon-meal, and free uniforms have really improved the school enrolment ratio, from the statements made by parents that they do not have to worry about them. There are cases that the free-cycle scheme for children reaching the higher secondary level education has motivated completion of secondary education. Improving the school infrastructure and quality of education offered in government-run schools has to be concentrated to make poorer children achieve.

It should be recorded here that for many a poor wage-earner household where both husband and wife eke out a living doing errand works in the vicinity, school is the place where their children get free noon meal, safety and shade. Quality of education is not what they look for, unless specifically probed about it during a survey such as the current one. For them going to school means: the child walks to or hops into a free-bus with no compulsion about uniforms, gets free meal, chant some alphabets in chorus, and stays safe until the parents return home in the evening. Learning is secondary. Their idea of school is: a free childcare centre run by the government—even if the teacher did not turn up a day, the attendant woman would take care of the noon meal of the child. They are contended.

(VII) DECENTRALIZATION

That teachers at elementary education level and Union Primary Schools should be under the direct control of local administration, meaning with the elected Village Panchayats is a matter of debate for quite some years. There are arguments in favour of it that local schools should form part of local administration activity. Anything to do with school development should be decided locally, and implemented with the concurrence of the community. It should be decentralized and should not remain with the State government. Moreover, the teachers would tend to be more accountable to local leaders than to officials on supervisory function who would be able to visit them hardly once in a month or so. Anything to do with elementary education teachers—from salary disbursal to leave application—should go through the local administration is the argument.

From the point of view of educationists, decentralization in education means that the local teachers should be allowed to frame their own curriculum based on a common set of guidelines or syllabus prescribed. There should not be centralized curriculum making by the NCERT or any high level centrally appointed body for that matter. Their argument is, advocating a uniform pattern of curriculum all over the State would be meaningless and irrelevant in many a district. There are activists with very strong conviction in decentralization to the extent that they advocate even regional dialects of Tamil should be approved at elementary school level. This idea did not make much headway. However, involvement of Village Panchayats in school developmental activities got constitutional sanction and official recognition.

The 73rd Constitutional Amendment made provision for creation of a body called Village Education Committee (VEC), which would be an auxiliary body of the Village Panchayat. This committee headed by one of the Village Panchayat functionaries would chair the developmental activities pertaining to local school. The State Government of Tamil Nadu reports that there are 43,113 Village Education Committees in the State. There is provision within the framework of SSA that VEC should be formed wherever they have not been formed, and they should meet once in a month or bi-monthly as required, and discuss issues relating to the school. This would devolve power at local level. The basic premise is that instead of the State doing it, giving it to the local people would strengthen grassroots level democracy, and train people in practicing democracy at village level. The SSA has a blanket sanction of Rs. 7,000 towards maintenance of rural school buildings, for which the VEC has to decide what works to take up. This is only Rs. 2,000 for government-aided schools. Of course, private schools do not come into this. Similarly, when there are some new school buildings to be constructed or water and sanitation facility to be arranged VEC has to discuss and decide the nature of the plan and approve it.

Field observations of the functionality of VEC reveal that where there are new works to be taken up, and funds are made available by the government, the leaders are dynamic and are watchful. Their involvement is substantial and noticeable. Where only the usual maintenance grant of Rs. 7,000 is provided, the VEC members sign blindfolded and ask the school headmaster to take care of it. Another interesting dimension to this is where the headmasters or one of the teachers is really dynamic and show interest in working closely with the Panchayat functionaries, the VECs are active. Unless the initiative is taken from the school side, the Village Panchayat functionaries tend to keep away from school affairs, and it looks as if Panchayats have nothing to do with schools. There are a handful of cases in point. M. Kalathur at Kujiliamparai Block of Dindigul district has constructed school building with the active involvement of VEC. Similarly, the initiative of the school headmasters in Thomaiyarpuram and Bhoothamarathupatti in Dindigul again keeps the VEC functional and closely associated with school activities, to the extent of mobilizing local financial support for school infrastructure development. The undercurrent seems to be either there should be funds made available to execute the decisions of the VEC or the school headmasters, besides their regular duty, should do a little more to rope in the Village Panchayat functionaries.

Another body that we need to bear in mind while discussing about VEC is Parent Teacher Associations (PTA). PTA is an expression in existence since long. One or two members of PTA also are made members of VEC as per a Notification given by Government of Tamil Nadu through the Department of Rural Development (Gazette, 2005). But, the question in many places is, PTA is a parallel body when VEC exists. Be it VEC or PTA hardly 10-15 per cent of them are functional. A law can only be a facilitating tool or an instrument that legally approves functioning of a body. It is people at appropriate levels—schools or Panchayats—should take initiative to achieve the mission the body is visualized to achieve.

Box 2.2 : School as a Significant Pillar of Panchayat

Union Primary School, Neduvasal North in Thiruvarankulam Block (Pudukottai) could be stated as a good school in the making. The task the school headmaster has taken up goes beyond the boundaries of the school, extending to overall development of the community, being school as the focal point of assembly and discussion. Thus, the school ropes in the parent community, local Panchayat, local SHGs, and the government officials within that jurisdiction. "*In a Gram Sabha meeting, if I am not able to make suggestions—including sources of funds for enhancing local development activities—I feel culpable that expect the Panchayat functionaries to pay heed to my call with regard to school development*" says Mr. Karupiah, the School Head Master at Neduvasal North.

The Union Primary School at Neduvasal North has 83 children (34 girls and 49 boys). Most of the children belong to potters family—MBC category. The school is located in a hamlet that is hidden behind the Neduvasal main village. Reportedly, the area is very poor by literacy rate and in child health standards. The Head Master has assumed charge by deliberately choosing to work for this school, which was located in another congested place in the same village. The first thing he did was to go round the village late in the evenings, educating parents sitting at the sit-outs of houses, and in common places in a very informal manner. His walk into the village late in the evenings, talking to community members, and passing on information to parents about the progress each child is making in studies, and simultaneously supervising children do home work sent across positive message about him in the locality. That he usually visited the settlements between 7.00 and 8.30 pm made the school children to keep the books open, read or write so as to enter oneself into the good books of the HM. This made the children browse book at home as well. The genuine interest he manifested in discussing about child development issues with parents elevated the image of this School Head Master amidst the local community. They could not absent themselves when he called for PTA meeting or VEC meeting. The Panchayat functionaries cooperated as well.

The old school with sufficient space that was located in a congested corner of the village had to be redone. The HM with the support of the VEC and the SHGs approached the District Collector and got orders to use a common land that was under encroachment. He got the land by eliminating the encroachment, keeping the Panchayat, local SHGs and the District Collector. He has mobilised funds for constructing new buildings. The new school building is located on the village main road now. Besides the furniture etc. supplied by the SSA, he has got computers, computer furniture, LCD projectors, play materials etc. as donation from individual and institutional donors, from NGOs, and under government schemes. He has made it a point to 'avoid taking currency in hand as donation'.

(*Contd.*)

Box 2.2 : (*Contd.*)

He has got DD drawn in favour of the District Collector to be paid as community contribution under *Namakku Name* Scheme. His request to almost every donor has been in terms of materials only such as computers, furniture, LCD projector, waterline connection, fans, play materials, uniforms to children and so on.
He invites the Panchayat President to convene Panchayat meeting at the school premises; he calls the SHG to use a class-room in the school for conducting SHG meetings. He convenes Village Education Committee (VEC) meeting at the school. He has taken PTA and VEC meeting as important places to make decisions relating to school development. Thus, he has made the local people feel free to enter the school, and participate in school activities. The community members could not help attending school meetings because the HM is so close, and he frequently visits them.
As far as education is concerned child get quality education making use of computers, LCD, VCD players etc. He uses computers and LCD for handling classes, he has received play materials donation worth Rs. 2.2 lakh. He has got a few bi-cycles on donation for children to learn to ride cycles. He has extra curricular activities with the support of other teachers where children learn computer operation, cycle-riding, stage acting, and so on. He has promoted the school keeping Panchayat and the local community as the prime partners in school activities. This is really a school with a distinction or a good school in the making. His future plan includes full-fledged rain water harvesting at school, and making the school look like a garden for children to play and stay pleasantly. His emphasis to other teachers in the school is let the children find coming to school enjoyable. Do not force anything down the throat. All that it would take is a little extra of our personal time at school daily. We should be prepared to do it because we are a privileged few who get assured salary every month unlike the parents of the children who come to school here. His question is: "*as teachers we are given pre-service training, and in-service training; we are supplied brilliantly designed books and activity-cards; we are paid well, and the children are given study materials and lunch free... around 220 days in a year and five years in a row, most of the time when the child is awake he spends at school; when the child leaves for Upper-primary classes, if he turns out to be good-for-nothing—as teacher—am I not responsible for what he is. My children in the future should get into the IITs and IIMs. I must lay the foundation for it here and now.*"

(VIII) THE LANGUAGE DEBATE

Tamil has been made compulsory subject in all the schools irrespective of type of management—be it government or private. The increasing importance of the English language is gaining, especially after globalization has caught hold of the private matriculation schools to the extent that many parents send their wards to private schools more with the expectation of the child picking up the English language at an early age. There are Tamil supporters who champion the cause of Tamil arguing that English language should not be introduced at Primary level at all. Given a choice between English and Tamil most parents tend to choose only English taking into consideration the societal changes and job market demands today. This is a matter of serious concern in wake of globalization and market economy. Tamil—supposed to be one of the oldest languages of Dravidian origin—is under severe threat due to the demand for English knowledge in the job market. This is a critical condition created against Tamil by the new economic and social order.

Since the universalization of elementary education has become an important goal, it is also essential to push this vision forward to move towards universalization of secondary education. It has, therefore, been decided to launch a centrally sponsored scheme, viz. Scheme for Universalization of Access to Secondary Education (SUCCESS) and improvement of quality at secondary stage during the Eleventh Five Year Plan. The main objective of the programme is to make secondary education of good quality available, accessible and affordable to all young students in the age group 15-16 years (*Economic Survey 2007-08*).

MAJOR FINDINGS

On an average one habitation in Tamil Nadu has more than one school. This does not include 9,715 private primary schools, which together make 33,916 schools in 21,950 villages (DISE, 2005-06). Besides this, there are new government primary schools coming up year after year, and there are also private schools opened alongside. One can take it that Tamil Nadu has achieved access criterion more than what is required. There are also cases where in our attempt to open a new school in one village, we have inadvertently caused closure of another school in the neighbourhood village.

Talking in terms of market, primary education today is no small market. Given the number of villages in Tamil Nadu, there are about 40 lakh children at primary level alone and hardly one-third of them are in private schools. The rest go to government primary schools only. The State Government of Tamil Nadu has really achieved remarkably in providing access even in remote and hilly areas.

The number of schools and accessibility to schools are not problems any more. It is the quality of education, the quality of infrastructure, and poverty of image that Union Primary Schools hold in the minds of the local community that make the problem.

SSA does not seem to have the support of neither the teachers nor the parents. The reasons are: Majority of the teachers think they cannot handle children at different levels paying individual attention; the parents think that the children do not have any home work to do or anything to write. The only stakeholder category that is happy about ABL is the school children, who enjoy whiling away the time, or playing with cards, with almost no need to write anything.

Reforms while focusing on improving the primary education mostly through government-run schools, and government aided schools. The private matriculation schools are market-driven. Especially the cost of education in private management schools is alarmingly high. It is ingenuity of the state to control the charges being collected in the name of quality education.

It is only partially true that the private schools offer quality education. But notwithstanding high tuition fees, and other paraphernalia, they have gained the parents' validation and support. Despite schemes like SSA, free education, free meal, free uniforms etc. the Union Primary School is looked down upon by parents. The enrolment in government schools has come down from 63.6 per cent (2004-05) to 59.8 per cent in 2005-06. Therefore, although declining birth rate could be an important reason, there is no denying the fact that the general community-trust on the quality of education and childcare provided at Union Primary Schools is also a significant reason for declining enrolment rate at the government schools in the state.

There is hardly any government run primary school that has fencing. There are schools with asbestos sheets used as roofing material. There are no toilets and if at all it existed, it is under the lock and key of the teachers who will use it. It is not meant for children. The government is planning about providing laptops, and EDUSAT, whereas schools do not have electricity connection, nor proper drinking water and sanitation facilities.

Under ABL those who are generally bright get going level after level, and those who are generally weak in studies keep watching them with no idea of what is this all about. If the number to be handled is less it is possible for the teacher to take the weak also along. When it is more, the attention that the studious get is more than those who are weak and wanting.

Besides poverty, one of the factors that still facilitate admission in government primary schools is the *Balwadis* (Child Care Centres). Incidentally, in a good number of villages, the *Balwadis* are situated next to the Primary Schools. The workers at the *Balwadi* and the teachers in the primary schools become friendly, and so getting the children enrolled at Primary class take place even without the parents knowing about it.

One general trend noticed in villages is that the children who attend *Balwadis* are most likely to get admitted in government primary schools, and the children who are sent to private nursery schools are most likely to get admitted in privately managed primary schools. But the pace at which privately-managed school get going, unless the *Balwadi* continue to function as feeder, it would be difficult for government primary schools to pull on.

The general dissatisfaction with the state of education in government-run schools has made way for proliferation of privately-managed schools. The situation is, given a choice—but for the money factor—even the poorest of parents prefer to send their children to private matriculation schools only. Educational expenses of households have become an important household expenditure. It takes away almost 10-20 per cent of the household income for a single child family. It works out double of it in a family where there is more than one child.

The reasons uttered by the parents who send their children to private matriculation schools paying through the nose (in the same order as it was reported to this research team by most of the parents) are: (i) English language education, (ii) Foundation years need to be made strong with good teaching, (iii) Safety and better childcare, and (iv) Possibility to get exposed to a variety of extra curricular activities, in that order.

The long-term vision of parents revealed that (a) they are preparing their children for the future to get admission in reputed institutions of higher learning, (ii) increasing the prospects of employability, (iii) making sure that the child gets prepared to deliver to the demands of the market. Thus, quality education has become a commodity available in the market with private matriculation schools. Those who have affordability can buy and benefit.

It has almost become a matter of prestige in the society that if a family admits a child in a private residential school, the family scores a better social standing. Rather than the educational status of the parents, it is the economic status of the family that determines if a child would get admitted in government school or private school. It follows that better economic status of the family provides an impetus to the family to look for better quality education from any source that is available—and their least faith is government schools.

The study revealed that the gap in NER (net enrolment ratio) between all, and SC is only marginal with 0.75 per cent, and the gap in the case of ST with 1.80 per cent. The gender-wise variation is marginal too, for example among SCs NER of boys is 97.79 per cent and girls is 97.85. The attendance rate in Primary level is 96 per cent in general, and it is 93 per cent and

90 per cent among SCs and STs respectively, which is quite acceptable in rural schools. As far as transition from Primary to UP is concerned it is as high as 99.40 per cent in districts like Kanyakumari. Unfortunately, it is 97 per cent among the SCs and 91.60 per cent among the STs. These have shown improvement, but it still requires concerted action.

Although girls from marginalised sections have come to join in schools in large numbers, it is also noticeable in rural areas, that a well-to-do peasant family admits both son and daughter in privately-managed primary school. But, when it comes to further education at upper primary level, to be able to manage the household expenditure the girl is admitted in a government school nearby, whereas the boy travels by school bus to the same private school. This kind of gender disparity is also seen in the study villages. The quality difference in government-run schools *vis-à-vis* the privately-managed schools is bound to bring about disparity in educational achievements shown by male and female children from within poorer segments.

Provision of free noon-meal, and free uniforms have really improved the school enrolment ratio. There are cases that the free-cycle scheme for those attaining the higher secondary level education has motivated completion of secondary education.

Field observations of the functionality of VEC reveal that where there are new works to be taken up, and funds are made available by the government, the leaders are dynamic and are watchful. Their involvement is substantial and noticeable. Where only the usual maintenance grant of Rs. 7000 is provided, the VEC members sign blindfolded and ask the school head master to take care of it. Another interesting dimension to this is where the head masters or one of the teachers is really dynamic and show interest in working closely with the Panchayat functionaries, the VECs are active. Unless the initiative is taken from the school side, the Village Panchayat functionaries tend to keep away from school affairs, and it looks as if Panchayats have nothing to do with schools.

ACTION POINTS

- The willingness of government appointed teachers to put in efforts to improve the image of union primary schools, and to deliver quality school turn-outs are urgent need to repair the image the general community has about union primary schools.
- The undercurrent under decentralization is that there should be funds made available to execute the decisions of the VEC or the school

headmasters, besides their regular duty, should do a little more to rope in the Village Panchayat functionaries.

- The quantum of out-of-school children has come down very significantly, whereas schools are closing down one after another for want of children. The study has found that physical access to school is a problem. Therefore, this blind 'eligibility to get sanction' need not be taken as a criterion, especially when it comes to opening new Primary Schools. What is required is facility and infrastructure upgradation in the existing schools, and to change the poor image that government schools have earned over the years. Not another new school.
- The need to change the poor image the general community holds about government-run school is the most important aspect to be addressed. The myth created by privately-managed schools that they offer quality education stands stronger than the reality ABL is bringing about in the children with government-run schools. For effective learning to take place, the entire environment should be conducive including the parents' image of the school and the teachers' conviction in the method. The relationship building, or image repairing works have to be taken up too.

CONCLUSION

Quantitatively the school education in Tamil Nadu is doing extremely well. Close to 100 per cent of the children at school going age are in schools. Even the so called child labourers also attend bridge courses and evening classes called *Nilappalli*. The transition tracking from one level to another, monitoring of children who drop out, and pinning down the habitual absentees and taking action about them have been established well. The incentives in terms of free uniforms, free meal, free books and stationery items, free bus pass and so on, for parents to send their children to attend school are plenty. The SSA has also pumped in a lot of funds and ideas for improving the enrolment, and to improve the retention level in schools. There is nothing to question about the competence level of teachers in government schools. However, in terms of image-repairing of government-run schools amidst the parents community, delivering quality education and showing commitment or genuine interest in child care the government-run schools have a lot to learn from the privately run schools. It lays more in the hands of the teachers, and grassroots level institutions such as the Panchayats than that is required in terms of policy facilitation or governmental support.

ANNEXURE

SCHOOL EDUCATION SURVEY

District : Block :
Panchayat : Habitation :
No. of Schools in the village : Government/Aided/Unaided
Total No. of Children in the village :
Name of the School : Government/Aided/Unaided
Person Interviewed :
Access: (Further distance from where children come to this school)

Number of Classes

	Boys			*Girls*			*Total*	*Teachers*			
	Others	*SC*	*ST*	*Others*	*SC*	*ST*		*Male*	*Qualif.*	*Female*	*Qualif.*
1st Std.											
2nd Std.											
3rd Std.											
4th Std.											
5th Std.											
Total											

Non-Teaching Staff

INFRASTRUCTURE

- Number of Classrooms
- Average Student—Classroom ratio
- Classroom facility
- Teaching aids
- Seating/Desk Facility
- Drinking Water Facility
- Girls' Toilet

- Boys' Toilet
- Common Toilet
- Teachers' Toilet
- Water for the toilet
- Compound wall
- Electricity Facility : Plug points/lights/fans
- Playground
- Play materials
- Disabled children
- Any Development Grants
- Medical Camp
- Other Language classes

TEACHERS

- Male-Female teacher ratio
- PTA teachers appointed, if any?
- Pupil-teacher ratio
- Single teacher schools
- Percentage of schools with 3 or less teachers
- Teachers with professional qualification
- (Staff benefits)

OUTCOME

- Gender Parity Rate
- Repetition Rate
- Dropout Rate
- Percentage of Passed out children to total enrolment
- Percentage of appeared children passing with 60 per cent and above marks.

QUALITY OF EDUCATION

- ABL
- Project work
- Assessment method

PARENTS PARTICIPATION

- Parents meeting
- Frequency of meeting
- Participation/Contribution

EXTRA CURRICULAR ACTIVITIES OFFERED

- Cycling
- Music
- Martial arts

Fees (Per term/year)

Fees & Charges	*Class 1*	*Class 2*	*Class 3*	*Class 4*	*Class 5*
Admission Fees					
Tuition Fees					
Books and Note books					
Examination Fees					
Van charges					
Uniform					
Private Coaching					
Others					

HOUSEHOLD EXPENDITURE SURVEY ON EDUCATION

Name of the Child/Children :
Name of the School and Place :
Educational Status of Parents : Father : Mother :
Occupation of the Parents : Father : Mother :

1. Government Service
2. Employment in Private Limited Companies
3. Employed in Private Business
4. Own Business
5. Wage earners

Educational Expenditure on Child (Per Year)

	Class 1	*Class 2*	*Class 3*	*Class 4*	*Class 5*
Admission Fees					
Tuition Fees					
Books and Note books					
Examination Fees					
Van charges					
Uniform					
Private Coaching					
Others					
TC					

REASON FOR CHOOSING PRIVATE SCHOOL?

- Easy Access
- Better Quality of Education
- Sending to Private School is a matter of social status
- Better discipline and child care
- Any other reason (Specify)

REASON FOR CHOOSING GOVERNMENT SCHOOL?

- Easy Access
- Poverty (Free education)
- Free noon meal
- Better Quality of Education
- Better discipline and child care
- Any other reason (Specify)

Monthly Income of the Family

Income Range	
Around Rs. 2000	
Rs. 2000-5000	
Rs. 5000-10,000	
Rs. 10,000-20,000	
Above Rs. 20,000	

Percentage of income spent on education of children

REFERENCES

Chandrasekhar, S.; Abhiroop Mukhopadhyay (2006). Primary Education as a Fundamental Right—Cost Implications, *Economic and Political Weekly*, September 2, 2006.

DISE (2005-06). *Elementary Education Report Card—Tamil Nadu State, 2005-06.*

Francis Abraham, M. (2006). *Contemporary Sociology: An Introduction to Concepts and Theories*, Oxford University Press, New Delhi.

Government of India (2007-08). *Economic Survey 2007-08*, Ministry of Finance, Economic Division, Oxford, University Press.

Government of Tamil Nadu (2005). *Tamil Nadu Government Gazette—Extraordinary,* Notification by Government dt. 19th July, 2005, Rural Development Department, Chennai.

Gursharan Singh Kainth (2006). A Mission Approach to Sarva Shiksha Abhiyan, *Economic and Political Weekly*, July 29, 2006.

Jean Dreze and Amarta Sen (2005). *India: Development and Participation*, Oxford.

Kumar Rana *et al.* (2005). Public-Private in Primary Education: A Case Study in West Bengal, *Economic and Political Weekly*, April 9, 2005.

Manabi Majumdar (2006). Primary Education: Debating Quality and Quantity, *Economic and Political Weekly*, March 4, 2006.

Robert Jenkins and Eimar Barr (2006). *Social Exclusion of Scheduled Caste Children from Primary Education in India,* UNICEF, New Delhi.

Vimala Ramachandran (2003). Backward and Forward Linkages that Strengthen Primary Education, *Economic and Political Weekly*, March 8, 2003.

Vimala Ramachandran (2005). Why School Teachers are Demotivated and Disheartened? *Economic and Political Weekly*, May 21, 2005.

Vimala Ramachandran, Aarti Sahjee (2002). The New Segregation: Reflections on Gender and Equity in Primary Education, *Economic and Political Weekly*, April 27, 2002.

CHAPTER THREE

Reforms in Drinking Water Service Delivery

INTRODUCTION

Water is a state subject in India, and so, the State Government of Tamil Nadu has made huge investments in domestic water supply installations—besides the assistance offered by the Central Government of India. Yet, the problem of unreliable rural water supply remains unsolved. The expected level of service has not reached and the benefits have not materialized as desired. Many supplies have fallen into disrepair after a short period or are not fully utilized, as they are not properly managed. Inadequate, unequal and intermittent supply, and unhygienic pit tap and wastage of water are some of the symptoms. Several studies including that of the World Bank's conducted world-wide proved that the fundamental reason is centralised arrangement of Operation and Maintenance of the Water Supply System resulting in user community developing an attitude of recipient of services.

In order to solve the problem of user community disowning the water supply installations when it comes to setting right repairs or maintenance, the concept of community-managed water service delivery system was introduced in Tamil Nadu, as part of sector reform measures.

The essential objective of the approach is to achieve sustainability by preparing rural communities to manage their water supplies themselves once the implementing agency has withdrawn support. It entails :

- Participatory processes to create a sense of ownership among the users upon the water supply system.
- Tailoring service levels to the demands of the community people.

- Building the capacity of community people to operate, maintain and manage their systems.

The Government of Tamil Nadu has sent across a Government Order requiring the Village Panchayat Presidents to collect user charges for drinking water. It puts the main responsibility of sustainable water supply squarely with user communities. The Panchayat Presidents are of the view that the State government gives even non-essentials such as Television sets free-of-cost keeping the vote bank in mind, whereas it wants the Village Panchayats to make cost-recovery of a basic service such as drinking water that a State is supposed to essentially deliver to the citizenry. The Panchayat Presidents want the State government to understand that Panchayat level functionaries are also politicians at another rung of the same political ladder.

ADEQUACY OF WATER AS A BASIC SERVICE

There are some Tamil press, often, reporting with names of villages, that those villages are undergoing severe water crisis, and that we have passed so many years after independence, but still the community members of those villages are drinking water fetched from 'open ponds—an unprotected source'. The community has developed the practice of using a nut for cleansing water (commonly know as 'The Clearing Nut', and among the biologists it is known as *Strychnos potatorum*). The Nut is used as a cleanser.

Truly, this practice of using water collected from 'pond' is in vogue sporadically in Tamil Nadu villages, especially in Madurai, Ramanathapuram, Dindigul and Sivagangai districts. This research team also visited those villages and witnessed people using 'pond' water for drinking and cooking purposes. A key probe on this matter brought to light an interesting fact. They have enough piped water supply facilities. They have also been provided with hand pumps that serve as standby source in the event of power failure. They use the piped water for all domestic purposes minus cooking and drinking. For cooking and drinking, they bring water from 'pond' cleansed with the Clearing Nut. This is not a matter of dearth of facilities for supplying water, rather a matter of habit that these communities have been nurturing over the years which they are not able to give up, despite the fact that there is piped water supply made available.

Talking about the quantity of supply, there is hardly any village in Tamil Nadu that has inadequate supply of water. The Government of Tamil Nadu reports that there are hardly 0.5 per cent of habitations that are finding it difficult to get potable water. That means to say that there are villages that have quality problems. If one analyzed the 'quality parameters'—the chemical, physical or biological properties of water, in some places it renders water unusable for drinking. Attention needs to be paid to such villages. But, in reality what happens is: based on the quantum of funds allotted to TWAD Board, the Board makes a list of villages using supply-drive approach. There are a fixed number of villages that the Board shall support for additional facility creation. There is also *Swajaldhara* Scheme made available on demand-driven basis, whichever Panchayat demands facilities can make use of. Therefore, the assessment or report on the adequacy of the existing facilities plays a very insignificant role in determining the facility requirement in a given village. Funds made available to TWAD Board (to be expended within the financial year), and the number of schemes under *Swajaldhara* that require to be reported for comfortability of reporting, are the two determining factors.

REFORM INITIATIVES

The Government of Tamil Nadu started experimenting with the concept of community-managed water supply system since 1996. The idea was integrated in the government water supply schemes initially through Water Sector Reform Project assisted by the Rajiv Gandhi National Drinking Water Mission since 1999. It became fully operational as a demand-responsive project all over Tamil Nadu since 2002 with the World Bank assisted *Swajaldhara* Drinking Water Project. This is a demand-responsive project meaning the community should demand augmentation of water service delivery to get the Project assistance Thus, in the State of Tamil Nadu, the concept of community-managed water supply system is being implemented for almost a decade now. It should be noted here that this experiment apart, water supply schemes with the regular supply-driven approach of the government is also being implemented side-by-side. Under the demand responsive scheme the community that demands facility improvement should be prepared to contribute at least ten per cent of the total cost of the scheme. This money should be mobilized from the soon-to-be users house-to-house.

As per the existing arrangements, Village Panchayat is responsible for providing drinking water service delivery in rural areas. There would be a Village Water and Sanitation Committee that would act as an executive body of the Gram Sabha as far as water supply related matters are concerned. This is expected to greatly reduce the financial burden of State government in making capital investments, and in Operation and Maintenance of the technical installations. The users of water service are classified as House Service Connection (HSC) holders, and Public Fountain (PF) users. Generally hand pumps are used as standby source only, when there is power failure that water could not be pumped to the Overhead Tank for distribution. The hand pump users could also be classified under PF users.

Besides other things, two significant points of rural water service delivery as noted in the reform measures are: (i) the Village Panchayats shall make all efforts to make sure that each individual gets 55 litre per capita (lpcd) supply daily; and (ii) the users shall take the responsibility of Operation and Maintenance (O & M) including the cost involved for operation and maintenance. The cost recovery aspect was thought of taking into consideration the ever increasing expenditure that the government had to incur in rectifying the repaired installations, and rejuvenating the infrastructure periodically, which prevented the government from moving to newer villages in remote areas that always fell in 'not covered' category or 'partially covered' category.

The arrangement for cost recovery was enabled through a Government Order that authorized the Village Panchayats to collect Rs. 1000 as deposit from HSC holders and Rs. 360—as minimum annual water supply charges from each household. As the common water collection points (PFs) are meant for the use of the poor, it was left to the discretion of the Panchayats to collect not more than Rs. 120 as annual water service delivery charges. This is one of the reform measures. There is also Public-Private Participation in water service delivery—but mostly in urban areas especially for industrial use.

Reform in rural water service delivery has put the responsibility of drinking water management squarely on Village Panchayats. It is not simply a matter of institutional transfer, rather a matter of preparing the Panchayats to shoulder additional burden.

THE NEO-LIBERAL ECONOMIC TINGE

Often enough, the critiques of neo-liberal economic policies argue that the very concept of decentralization was promoted side-by-side with globalization policies so as to develop a legally recognized local body to make 'the principle of cost recovery' possible at the grassroots level. In the context of drinking water sector reform, an action that furthers this statement is: instead of giving adequate financial resources, the Village Panchayats have been given legal authority to make cost recovery from users of water service delivery. However, decentralization has certain advantages compared to privatization which primarily aims at profit. The expectation of the reform initiatives is that the local body should be able to recoup at least the Operation and Maintenance (O & M) expenses from the water users. The reform prescription is that the State government can pitch in when there is any major replacement to be made or additional facilities to be erected which might involve capital expenditure.

OPERATION AND MAINTENANCE

The problems with regard to establishing village level Operation and Maintenance are manifold—starting from the manipulation that the officials teach the Panchayat functionaries about collecting capital cost contribution to cost recovery for O & M. The first and foremost among them is, there is TWAD's free water scheme that is being implemented in parallel lines with *Swajaldhara*. The TWAD's Scheme does not require people's contribution nor community commitment to O & M, whereas *Swajaldhara* wants the user community to take responsibility in contributing to the capital investment, and also to the O & M expenditure. This creates a discrepancy. The Panchayats show interest in getting free scheme of the TWAD rather than the *Swajaldhara*'s that require a lot of commitment on the part of the community and the Panchayats.

Secondly, the community contribution required for capital cost is usually paid from the common fund of the community, where common fund is not available; the arrangement is made in such a way that the contractor-to-be pays the contribution on behalf of the community. This is a short-cut that has been adopted in many Panchayats, wherever *Swajaldhara* has been implemented.

The rural people who have never paid for water is asked to pay Rs. 360 a year for water service delivery. Although common water collection points are meant for the poor who cannot afford to pay the annual water charges, there is also a G.O. that authorizes collection of Rs. 120 a year from the users of common water collection point. The logic put forth is that any service user—be it HSC holder or PF user or user of a hand pump—should pay towards Maintenance (O & M). Recovery of this O & M expenditure from each household rests with the Village Panchayat President.

Panchayats in Tamil Nadu have a peculiar way of collecting 'house tax'. That is, the Panchayat clerk sitting at Panchayat Office prepares cash-receipts for house-tax. Then he goes door-to-door, hands over the cash-receipt and collects the money. This explains the method of tax collection/cost recovery practised at Panchayat level. The same thing holds good for collection of drinking water charges as well. The Panchayat clerk has to go door-to-door. People have not been cultured to pay user charges/taxes at the Panchayat Office. The collection is also inconsistent in the sense, no Panchayat can ensure cent-per-cent collection in any given year. This is socio-political in the sense, partly the community and mostly the way they have been cultured that should be attributed as reasons.

People have questions such as: *why not the Panchayat pay from Panchayat funds that it receives from the government?* So much so, the Panchayat Presidents also strongly feel that it is unbecoming for an elected representative to go round asking for user charges, especially for drinking water. In order to justify their stand or corroborate their statement, they ask: *When the State government thinks every poor household should own a TV and it supplies it free, is it unfair that the Panchayat President thinks let every household get sufficient quantity of drinking water free?*

The Panchayat functionaries have a series of questions about the State government's idea of using the local bodies for cost recovery from the community. It includes: The State government procures a sack of paddy for around Rs. 430 from farmers. [*Note*: But selling at Rs. 430 does not give fair returns to the farmers]. It processes it into 50 kg of rice. It is sold at Rs. 2 a kg at PDS, which is at a loss of almost Rs. 250 per bag to the State government. The Panchayat Presidents who are asked to make a cost recovery for water services seek an explanation for State incurring such a loss on provisioning rice at Rs. 2.00. If rice is an essential commodity, water is essential as well. It is an essential lifeline of the people.

A good political strategy need not be a good economic policy. An over-smart political strategy often turns out to be a bad economic policy. The influence of politics on economics and the *vice versa* have been a disturbing factor in sustaining economic growth and reforms. When one layer of the State adopts a policy that is fiddly or heavy-handed, it naturally reflects at other layers as well.

The reform initiatives in water supply sector have helped the Panchayats to think about and learn drinking water management at the local level. The Panchayat Presidents tend to think of delivery options such as: (a) providing all the houses with House Service Connections—so that all households pay the activation charges that is the Caution deposit; (b) providing only common water collection points so that although the income to the Panchayat might be reduced so also the expenditure on water wasted; (c) providing a combination of House Service Connections as well as common water collection points, where the rich get yard taps for which they pay, and the poor get water free. There are also regulations brought about in terms of timings of supply.

PHYSICAL INFRASTRUCTURE

Nine (point five) out of ten Village Panchayats that have got *Swajaldhara* scheme implemented in their villages are Panchayats that are potentially award-winning in some sector of development or the other such as total sanitation, SHG activities and so on. One cannot say that the Villages that have demanded implementation of *Swajaldara* scheme were water starving or were badly in need of a water supply scheme. The official statistics of Government of Tamil Nadu provides that hardly 0.5 per cent of the habitations in Tamil Nadu get less than 10 lpcd. Most of the habitations (66%) get full coverage, and around 33 per cent of them get partial coverage. The problem in some of the places where no coverage is reported is also due to problems of hydro-geological conditions, and not due to any administrative or financial reasons. It requires a confession from the officials implementing the scheme if they went out searching for Panchayat Presidents who would come with community contribution to have the scheme implemented, rather than a Panchayat that was undergoing a severe drinking water crisis.

The major factor that seems to determine water lifting technology choice in the study villages, in the order of priority, are: (i) community affordability of contribution towards capital cost; (ii) higher duty pumping device that helps fill the Over Head Tank faster; (iii) easy operation and possibility for local maintenance; (iv) pumping efficiency in terms of reduction of power consumption. It proves that only the financial affordability towards capital cost contribution rather than standard service norms that determines the technology choice. The community has developed a mindset that higher horse-power pumping device is important to pump ground water at a faster rate. They fail to understand that a higher horse power water lifting device would lead to: (a) heavy electricity bill, (b) more wastage of water, and (c) faster depletion of the ground water.

In many of the villages the existing capacity of the OHTs is more than the standard requirement as per population. Where the facilities are less than the requirement, the shortage in piped water supply arrangement is made up by the excess number of hand-pumps. In many of the Panchayats visited, the size of the OHT is larger than the requirement by more than 100 per cent. It must be remembered that more the facilities, more the expenses on maintenance; similarly, the more the facilities, the more the chances of wastage of water. All these would result in higher operational expenses for the Village Panchayat. Either way, it adds to the O & M expenditure of the Village Panchayat. The State may provide the facility. But, when the O & M burden rests with the community, the officials involved in the planning exercise should advise the community on right choice of technology and facilities to reduce the expenses on O & M.

Field visits and calculations of standard water supply norm *vis-à-vis* population strongly suggests that the Panchayats as well as the scheme implementing officials have given overriding priority to matters related to finance. They have not paid adequate attention to technically assess the adequacy or inadequacy of the physical infrastructures that existed, and that which would be additionally required. Making the community contribute financially is taken as an achievement, which hides all other realities such as actual requirement as per technical standards, and responsibilities of Operation and Maintenance etc. This eventually takes shape in the form of O & M burden on the Village Panchayats.

In all the study villages coverage-wise there are no habitations within Village Panchayats or households within habitations which remain uncovered in getting water service. In most of Panchayats studied people have accessibility to House Service Connection, a Public Fountain or a Hand Pump within 200 metres. It is very occasional in a few villages people walk up to 500 metres to collect drinking water. There is no village where people walk more than 500 metres for the purpose of collecting protected water. There is no problem with regard to access criterion.

The users of common water collection points in some of the Panchayats enjoy water service almost to the level of Municipalities, Corporations and Metropolis. The average quantity of water supplied to PF users is 66 lpcd. This is definitely excessive draft of water. The reason was that water was used for purposes other than, for which it was meant. They use drinking water for washing of utensils, cleaning of clothes, watering of plants, kitchen garden and people use platforms of the Public Fountains for giving bath to domestic animals also.

The state of affairs with regard to HSC holders is that in almost all the villages they get more than the standard norm of 55 lpcd. Many Village Panchayats use more than 110 lpcd, which is the water service norm for the Metropolitan cities in India or double the amount of the standard quantity. The average quantity of water supply to HSC holders works out to 112 lpcd.

Thus, in all the study villages the water made available through public fountains is more than the standard norm of 40 lpcd. They have already reached the dream target of the RGNDWM of providing 55 lpcd to PF users. Similarly, HSC holders in almost all the study villages are already getting the RGNDWM dream target of 70 lpcd and more.

In some of the Villages where HSC users can do with 70 lpcd are doing with more than three times of the quantity, for instance in Keerapalayam—a popular Village Panchayat in Tamil Nadu which Dr. Kalam visited—HSC holders are getting almost 223 lpcd. This definitely reflects in the Electricity Bill (Current Consumption Charges) these Panchayats are paying. Surely, the amount of water being wasted is very high in these two villages. Over use or wastage of water, apart from bringing a hefty E.B. Bill to the Panchayats leads to the danger of the source drying up soon.

Quantity-wise if both PF users as well as HSC holders are getting more than the standard norms recommended by the Government of Tamil Nadu, another question arises, if the *Swajaldhara* Project intervention was required at all in the first place. The service level in almost all the villages has been sufficient. That is PF users even before the Project intervention were getting sufficient quantity of water. In the ultimate analysis it appears that many of the villages under study did not require improvement in service levels, as they were already getting enough water or more compared against the standard water supply norms. This fortifies our hunch if the project implementing officials were looking for Panchayat presidents who would take steps to fulfil the community contribution norm instead of identifying Panchayats that were water-starving.

MEASURE TO REDUCE COST OF SERVICE

The amount of water wasted in the study villages is found to be very high. All the Village Panchayats studied put together, on an average 34 per cent of the water is either excessively used or wasted. Merely by being judicious in the use of water, each Panchayat has the potential of saving several thousand rupees. The cost of wastage crosses Rs. one lakh per annum at least in eight Panchayats. It is possible that these Village Panchayats are unaware of the cost of water wasted every year unnecessarily without anybody benefiting, for which the Village Panchayat is footing the bill. More so, the water users in these Panchayat might be unaware of the cost of water wasted every year. It is astounding to recollect here that most water users have remarked that the water supply is inadequate. This gives a strong case for why water should be charged, including the users of the public fountains. It looks, without a speck of doubt that cutting down on the wastage can dramatically bring down the cost of operation.

In a community-managed water supply system, technical management of the system depends on proper operation and maintenance of the physical infrastructure. The study has found that there is excessive physical infrastructure available for water supply in almost all the study villages. Hence, while implementing concepts like Demand Driven Approach, making the community contribute financially seem to give financial matters the overriding priority. It blinds all other realities such as actual requirement as per technical standards, and responsibilities of Operation and Maintenance, etc.

With regard to coverage, all the households get drinking water either through House Service Connection (HSC) or through Public Fountain (PF). Hand-pumps are used as standby service only. There is hardly any village where they walk more than 200 metres to fetch water. Both PF users as well as the HSC holders are getting water supply more than the standard water supply norms of the Government of Tamil Nadu. The problem has been one of 'proper management, regulation and distribution' and not inadequacy of facilities. On an average 35 per cent of the water pumped is either excessively used or wasted. It means merely by being judicious in the use of water, each Panchayat has the potential of saving approximately one-third of the expenses incurred on water service delivery.

The Project has ended up providing technical infrastructure that are more than the standard technical requirement. This results in Panchayats finding it difficult to mobilize the funds for maintenance. A water supply scheme should study the real technical requirements *vis-à-vis* population before offering to install additional technical infrastructure. Ability and willingness of a community to pay the financial contribution towards capital cost alone should not qualify a Village Panchayat to get Project assistance. It has unintentionally caused increase in the quantum of burden that these Panchayats have to bear in terms of Electricity bill and maintenance expenses.

There is excessive draft of water in almost all the Panchayats. Both HSC holders as well as the PF users, use more than the standard norms set out by the Government of Tamil Nadu. Consequently, pumping charges are more than what these Panchayats should be paying if they had actually used only that quantity of water which they should use as per the standard norms. On an average these Panchayats should reduce wastage/excessive use by at least 30 per cent to be able to contain the Operation expenditure—to a significant extent. Steps should be taken to orientate the local Power Pump Operators, as well as the user community with regard to the financial consequences of wasting water.

Identification of villages for implementation of Swajaldhara Scheme seems to have taken place based on Village Panchayat Presidents who would come with community contribution—no matter if that Panchayat was really undergoing drinking water crisis or not.

DECENTRALIZATION IN PRACTICE

Reform in drinking water sector has placed the responsibility of rural water supply squarely on Village Panchayats. There is also a G.O. of the Government of Tamil Nadu (GoTN. 1999, Ms. No. 168) that specifically states that Village Panchayats should constitute Village Water and Sanitation Committees (VWSC). It also stipulates the powers and functions of such a committee in water service delivery. The organizational structure laid down states that the VWSC would be the focal point in establishing community-managed water supply system. It is embedded within the framework of Panchayati Raj System. VWSC has the status of functioning as an auxiliary body (standing committee) of the Village Panchayat. Creating VWSC within the framework of the Tamil Nadu Panchayats Act, 1994, Rules 1999 and the Constitutional 73rd Amendment Act, 1992 enables motivating the Village Panchayats to constitute VWSC, not as an agenda of the *Swajaldhara* Project, but as an overall vision of the Government of India and local self-governance in Tamil Nadu.

The Village Water and Sanitation Committee formed by the Village Panchayat when approved by the Gram Sabha is deemed to have got both legal as well as social sanction. Going by the institutional structure established, the VWSC should deal with all decisions pertaining to drinking water management of a given Panchayat. This can be taken as a kind of administrative decentralization or devolution of power at the lowest appropriate structure in the sphere of water supply management in Tamil Nadu.

In a community-managed system institutional arrangement for the delivery of water services is critical particularly from the stand point of sustainability. The institutional arrangement is adopted depending upon local situation such as from Village Panchayat system and/or VWSC with necessary policy and technical support from the State Government. The capacity of the local institution identified or created needs to be built up properly for the success of the system. The *Swajaldhara* project stresses that community management is not merely a concept to increase the effectiveness of water supply systems; it is also based on a belief in participation and democracy. It is otherwise called democratization of water service delivery.

A well-designed organizational structure, when it really becomes functional with certain institutional norms, would be able to put in place 'equitable distribution' and bring about 'autonomy' in community based water management. It can also ensure a system in place. The regulatory and social control mechanisms administered by VWSC with the support of the Village Panchayat would systematize domestic water supply and ensure uninterrupted supply.

Awareness about the purpose of VWSC was enquired across districts wherever *swajaldhara* scheme was implemented. It indicated that the VWSC is known only to the Panchayat functionaries. Hardly any user community knows about it. It is indicative of how active the VWSCs are in the study villages. No effort has been made to orient the VWSC members on matters pertaining to water management. They were selected in a Gram Sabha and their names announced. The reason stated by some of the respondents for opining that the VWSC was ineffective was 'hardly any decisions made in the VWSC meeting are implemented'. The response regarding the attendance in VWSC meeting suggests that there is a possibility that the VWSCs could be made to function still better by improving the attendance in meetings.

Matters that concern women can be addressed effectively only when women representatives find place in VWSC. Seats are reserved for women in VWSCs; but women often do not participate. Even if they physically participate, they do not participate in the discussions. In order to assess the participation of women in decision-making process related to water supply, an FGD was conducted with the functionaries of Village Panchayat. As required by the VWSC by-law in some of the Panchayats women representatives have been included. But in many of the Village Panchayats women representatives do not attend the VWSC meetings. And in a few Village Panchayats where women participate, they have no voice in decision-making. They attend and remain as passive participants watching the proceedings. There is no Village Panchayat where women have influenced the decisions. The advantage of the VWSC by-law reserving seats for women has given place for women in many of the VWSCs. However, in reality women do not participate in decision-making process relating to water service delivery.

An important responsibility of the *Swajaldhara* Project is to gear up the Village Panchayats to establish a functioning O & M system. However, the interest of the user community declines, once the work execution is over and the water starts flowing on tap in sufficient quantity. Any effort on the part of the Project to make prescriptive intervention on Operation and Maintenance is considered uninteresting and bothersome. As far as the Village Panchayat functionaries are concerned it is either a political promise or social accountability that they should provide potable water to the local community. This makes the VWSC members, most of whom are functionaries of the Village Panchayat, to soft-pedal establishing 'a functioning Operation and Maintenance system or the community-managed system'. As a result, provisions of the water supply by-law such as collecting water charges from user community, restricting the hours of water supply, waste reduction, etc. become only a moderate success, and not to the level envisaged or visualized by the *Swajaldhara* Project.

Community management is based on a belief in participation and democracy. But, little effort has been made to orient the Village Water Committee members on matters pertaining to water management. They were selected in a Gram Sabha meeting and their names got announced.

FINANCIAL PARTICIPATION

One of the significant prescriptions of the sector reform arrangement is cost recovery from users of service. The cost involved in providing water services to the rural community include: (i) creation of physical facilities, (ii) Operation and Maintenance, and (iii) replacement due to wear and tear. Financing the capital cost, and recurring costs such as Operation and Maintenance (O & M) of rural water supply installations are major expenditure items of Village Panchayats. Currently, the government finances all capital and recurrent costs. It recoups little of these expenditures from water charges. The annual estimated cost of Operation and Maintenance (O & M) alone works out to Rs. 6,000 crore, which the government considers heavy for the Government alone to bear.

Therefore, there is a growing trend with several State governments to encourage rural communities to manage their own water supply schemes, with support from the government. This trend, often, runs parallel to the government decentralization process which gives local government more responsibilities and is aiming for greater efficiency, effectiveness and sustainability of public services. This study made an attempt to ascertain the source of money for community contribution, viability of the financing mechanism instituted for cost recovery, and adequacy of funds generated for sustainable financing of Operation and Maintenance of the technical installations.

The study revealed that hardly 20 per cent of the respondents have made some capital contribution. Majority of them have not paid anything financially to get the scheme implemented. As it is mandatory for the Village Panchayats to pay the community contribution to become eligible to avail project assistance, the Village Panchayats seem to have managed the 10 per cent contribution amount by mobilizing funds through other sources such as using the temple fund/common fund etc. Common Fund of the Village has been another major source of community contribution. The next major source has been regressive in nature. That is the contractor who was to implement the scheme has paid on behalf of the community, and it has been recorded for official purpose that 'the community paid'. There is hardly any door-to-door collection of community contribution towards capital cost. It was not that the efforts to collect money locally failed. Rather no effort has been made by the Village Panchayat functionaries to collect money from households. That was, perhaps, because although it might be administratively an intelligent step, it might not be, politically, a pleasant step to take. So, the main reason for community contribution not to have flown from the user community is socio-political.

The objective of financial management in any water supply scheme is becoming self-reliant in meeting the expenditure incurred on water service delivery. It was found in the study villages that many of the HSC holders do not pay Caution Deposit, and a considerable number of them do not pay the monthly water charges as well. Some Panchayats have the practice of collecting water charges from PF users also. But that amount is collected very irregularly. Financial discipline is wanting.

It was found in most of the Village Panchayats that the General Funds or popularly known as SFC grant has been used (misused !) for attending to the repairs in water supply systems, rehabilitation of technical installations, or replacement of worn out water supply infrastructure. Officially, such funds are meant for development programmes to increase labour-intensive public works. It does not in principle support Operation and Maintenance of water supply systems. The Government of Tamil Nadu has created a favourable policy environment issuing the required Government Orders in order to enable Village Panchayats to take up the responsibility by collecting water charges (annually a minimum of Rs. 360) from each HSC user. This is a promising way to considerably reduce the State's financial burden, which not many Panchayats put into practice.

Similarly, many Panchayats do not fully follow the G.O. relating to collection of Caution Deposit from the HSC holders. It was found at least 50 per cent of the households that own HSCs did not pay Caution Deposit. Around one-third of them paid the full amount. The rest paid a portion of what they were actually required to pay. One of the obvious reasons is the amount fixed as Caution Deposit looks too high for the rural HSC holders to pay in one lump sum. Hence, the Village Panchayat has permitted them to pay in instalments. Apparently, many Panchayats have not made proper follow up to effect full collection. And so, the task of deposit collection stands half done. It puts across that the Village Panchayats have not shown seriousness in collecting, caution deposit from the HSC holders.

An analysis of income generated by Panchayats providing water showed that the major share of the income (71%) comes from HSC holders, followed by the provision made from the house tax collected (19%) from the residents. The income earned through caution deposit (by way of bank interest) is absent in all the Panchayats as no Panchayat keeps the caution deposit in the bank. The money collected from HSC applicants as Caution Deposit has been spent on maintenance expenses, as many of the Panchayats run into the problem of paucity of funds when it comes to maintenance of water supply installations. Further many HSC holders did not pay the HSC deposit. Collecting water charges from PF users is considered unjustifiable in several Panchayats. And so, water charge collection from PF users is too meagre. Hence, out of the four sources visualized, only three are real sources of income, as interest on caution deposit is zero in all the Panchayats. House tax is one of the well-known sources of income to the Village Panchayats. However, the house tax collected in all the 17 Panchayats under study was very meagre. The house tax collected in most of the Panchayats (13 of the 17) was less than Rs. 6,000 per annum. It is a very insignificant amount compared to what these Panchayats incur in terms of O & M expenditure.

The major expenditure (66 per cent) incurred is on pumping charges, which is paid to the Electricity Board of the Government of Tamil Nadu. The second main expenditure incurred (22 per cent) is on maintenance expenses such as setting right pump repair, motor repair, arresting leakages, controlling bursts in the pipe lines, and so on. The third expense is the salary paid to the Pump Operators (12 per cent). The lion's share of income goes towards paying the pumping charges.

Box 3.1: Drinking Water Service Delivery Options

The reform initiatives in water supply sector have helped the Panchayats to think about and learn drinking water management at the local level. The Panchayat Presidents tend to think of service delivery options such as: (a) providing all the houses with House Service Connections (HSCs) so that all households pay the

(*Contd.*)

Box 3.1 : (*Contd.*)

activation charges that is the 'Caution Deposit; (b) providing 'only common water collection points' so that although the income to the Panchayat might be reduced so also the expenditure on water wasted; (c) providing a combination of House Service Connections as well as common water collection points, where the rich get yard taps for which they pay, and the poor get water free from common water collection points. There should also be regulated brought about in terms of timings of supply.

The total average income (from both HSC holders and PF users) generated per household is Rs. 54 per annum whereas average expenditure per household is Rs. 233 indicating a wide gap between income and expenditure. In other words, there is a deficit of Rs. 179 per household. No Panchayat earns income from HSC and PF sufficient to meet the full expenditure on Operation and Maintenance of water supply.

The proportion of expenditure on electricity bill was more than 50 per cent in almost all the Panchayats. In certain cases it was more than 80 per cent due to reasons such as providing water for local schools, women sanitary complex and allowing the community to wash clothes etc. in common taps (Case: Sakkankudi, and Keerapalayam, Cuddalore district). Efficient management of finance warrants improving the income or reducing the expenses. If avenues for promoting the income are too narrow, then attention needs to be paid on reducing the expenditure. Payment of electricity bill is a major item of expenditure. The Panchayat has to initiate measures to bring it down. Technology-wise invariably all these Panchayats have gone in for piped water supply which depends on electric power. Over use or wastage of water was one of the reasons for fat electricity bill. Apparently, this came out during analysis of use of technical management of water supply system.

There are political as well as socio-economic reasons that have together caused the slack in the deposit collection from HSC holders. This has caused the HSC holders take it easy when it comes to paying the annual water charges. That the HSC holders are not paying the water charges has caused the PF users to resist payment of water charges. Because the main sources of income from water supply that should be forthcoming did not come, the Panchayat failed to pay the EB bill that came as pumping charges. Failure of payment of EB bill has caused the District Collectors in almost all the districts to divert (a significant portion of) the SFC grant towards the payment of EB bill so the TNEB does not run into debts. The indifference of collection of water charges by the Panchayats have ultimately resulted in development funds being diverted for paying EB bill by the District Collector without seeking the consent of the Panchayats concerned. This is a typical Catch 22 Situation.

(*Contd.*)

Box 3.1 : (*Contd.*)

The first and foremost reason reported by the respondents for non-payment was that the Panchayats did not consistently persuade the community members to make payment. The Village Panchayats are not very keen on generating sufficient income from water users to be able to manage water supply related expenses locally. This has made diversion of funds meant for development purposes (SFC grant) to pay the EB bill. This in effect means money received from the Department of Rural Development being handed over to the TNEB instead of putting it for useful purposes at the Panchayat level.

Box 3.2: Payment of Power Charges

No Panchayat pays the EB bill directly to TNEB. As per an existing Government Order, the District Collectors deducts EB bill out of the funds allotted by the State government to Village Panchayats for development purposes, and pays directly to the TNEB. The balance is routed to the Panchayats. The Panchayats are not even consulted about this being deducted. As a result the Panchayats are, often, unaware of the extent to which EB bill has been cleared, the amount due by them to TNEB etc. This practice of deduction of EB bill without even consulting the Panchayats is seriously condemned by the Village Panchayat functionaries. This practice has serious repercussions which include: (i) funds meant for development purposes being diverted; (ii) the Panchayat functionaries have developed a tendency that payment of EB bill is not their concern; (iii) the Panchayat loses its legitimate democratic power of deciding how funds allotted to it would be spent; and (iv) the bureaucracy taking decisions on behalf of Panchayats.

The scheme implementing officials need to discover that the problem is in their trying to invent short-cuts to show community participation. The Panchayats need to realize that it is their indifference to the water wasted that cause heavy financial burden on them.

MAJOR FINDINGS

The problems with regard to establishing village level Operation and Maintenance are manifold. The first and foremost among them is, there is TWAD's free water scheme that is being implemented in parallel lines with *Swajaldhara*. The TWAD's Scheme does not require people's contribution nor community commitment to O & M, whereas *Swajaldhara* wants the user community to take responsibility in contributing to the capital investment, and also to the O & M expenditure. This creates a discrepancy. The Panchayats show interest in getting free scheme of the TWAD rather than the *Swajaldhara*'s that require a lot of commitment on the part of the community and the Panchayats.

The community contribution required for capital cost is usually paid from the common fund of the community, where common fund is not available; the arrangement is made in such a way that the contractor-to-be pays the contribution on behalf of the community. This is a short-cut that has been adopted in many Panchayats, wherever *Swajaldhara* has been implemented. The Panchayat functionaries strongly feel that they would become unpopular if they started collecting community contribution for augmenting infrastructure.

The logic put forth is that any service user—be it HSC holder or PF user or user of a hand pump—should pay towards Maintenance (O& M). Recovery of this O & M expenditure from each household rests with the Village Panchayat President. However, taking poverty into view the users of common water collection points should not be charged is the contention of many of the Panchayat functionaries.

The Panchayat Presidents strongly feel that it is unbecoming for an elected representative to go round asking for user charges, especially for drinking water. In order to justify their stand or corroborate their statement, they start questioning the populist schemes of the State government as politically attractive, but economically unviable. Asking people to pay for water is not a politically favourable decision as far as Village Panchayat Presidents are concerned. Poor people in the villages should not be asked to pay for water.

In many of the Panchayats visited, the size of the OHT is larger than the requirement by more than 100 per cent. more the facilities, the more the expenses on maintenance; similarly, the more the facilities, the more the chances of water being wasted. All these result in higher operational expenses for the Village Panchayat. The State may provide the facility. But, when the O & M burden rests with the community, the officials involved in the planning exercise do not offer prudent advice to the community on right choice of technology and facilities to reduce the expenses on O & M.

Field visits and calculations of standard water supply norm *vis-à-vis* population strongly suggests that the Panchayats as well as the scheme implementing officials have given overriding priority to matters related to finance. They have not paid adequate attention to technically assess the adequacy or inadequacy of the physical infrastructures that existed, and that which would be additionally required. Making the community contribute financially is taken as an achievement, which blinds all other realities such as actual requirement as per technical standards, and responsibilities of Operation and Maintenance etc.

Quantity-wise if both PF users as well as HSC holders are getting more than the standard norms recommended by the Government of Tamil Nadu, another question arises, if the *Swajaldhara* Project intervention was required at all in the first place. The service level in almost all the villages has been sufficient. That is PF users even before the Project intervention were getting sufficient quantity of water. In the ultimate analysis it appears that many of the villages under study did not require improvement in service levels, as they were already getting enough water or more compared against the standard water supply norms. This fortifies our hunch if the project implementing officials were looking for Panchayat presidents who would take steps to fulfil the community contribution norm instead of identifying Panchayats that were water-starving.

The amount of water wasted in the study villages is found to be very high. All the Village Panchayats studied put together, on an average 34 per cent of the water is either excessively used or wasted. Merely by being judicious in the use of water, each Panchayat has the potential of saving several thousand rupees. The cost of wastage crosses Rs. one lakh per annum at least in eight Panchayats. It is possible that these Village Panchayats are unaware of the cost of water wasted every year unnecessarily without anybody benefiting, for which the Village Panchayat is footing the bill. More so, the water users in these Panchayat might be unaware of the cost of water wasted every year. It is astounding to recollect here that most water users have remarked that the water supply is inadequate. This gives a strong case for why water should be charged, including the users of the public fountains. It looks, without a speck of doubt that cutting down on the wastage can dramatically bring down the cost of operation.

In terms of enhancing women's participation in local level decision-making bodies such as VWSC, the community-managed system through reservation of certain number of seats for women has made a mark. However, it has helped only to the extent of enabling women to physically participate and observe proceedings in the VWSC meetings, and not to contribute anything towards the decision-made.

As per the reform guidelines, the District Water and Sanitation Committee (DWSC) is supposed to audit the accounts of the VWSC. In practice the District Water and Sanitation Committee remain on paper only. They never meet, nor they do anything concerning the village water supply accounts.

As far as contribution towards capital cost is concerned no effort has been made by the Village Panchayat functionaries to collect money from households. That was, perhaps, because although it might be administratively an intelligent step, it might not be, politically, a pleasant step to take. So, the main reason for community contribution not to have flown from the user community is socio-political.

The Government of Tamil Nadu has given out a Government Orders in order to enable Village Panchayats to take up the responsibility by collecting water charges (annually a minimum of Rs. 360) from each HSC user. This is a promising way to considerably reduce the State's financial burden, which not many Panchayats put into practice, due to socio-political reasons. Moreover, this is against the trend of development that the State is promoting in general.

No Panchayat pays the EB bill directly to TNEB. As per an existing Government Order, the District Collectors deducts EB bill out of the funds allotted by the State government to Village Panchayats for development purposes, and pays directly to the TNEB. The balance is routed to the Panchayats. The Panchayats are not even consulted about this being deducted. As a result the Panchayats are, often, unaware of the extent to which EB bill has been cleared, the amount due by them to TNEB etc. This practice of deduction of EB bill without even consulting the Panchayats is seriously condemned by the Village Panchayat functionaries. This practice has serious repercussions which include: (i) funds meant for development purposes being diverted; (ii) the Panchayat functionaries have developed a tendency that payment of EB bill is not their concern; (iii) the Panchayat loses its legitimate democratic power of deciding how funds allotted to it would be spent; and (iv) the bureaucracy taking decisions on behalf of Panchayats.

The first and foremost reason reported by the respondents for non-payment was that the Panchayats did not consistently persuade the community members to make payment. The Village Panchayats are not very keen on generating sufficient income from water users to be able to manage water supply related expenses locally. This has made diversion of funds meant for development purposes (SFC grant) to pay the EB bill. This in effect means money received from the Department of Rural Development being handed over to the TNEB instead of putting it for useful purposes at the Panchayat level.

ACTION POINTS

The reform initiative has ended up providing technical infrastructure that are more than the standard technical requirement. This results in Panchayats finding it difficult to mobilize the funds for maintenance. A water supply scheme should study the real technical requirements *vis-à-vis* population before offering to install additional technical infrastructure. Ability and willingness of a community to pay the financial contribution towards capital cost alone should not be taken as qualification for Village Panchayat to get assistance for water supply. Otherwise, it results in crowding of infrastructure.

There is excessive draft of water in almost all the Panchayats. Both HSC holders as well as the PF users, use more than the standard norms set out by the Government of Tamil Nadu. Consequently, pumping charges are more than what these Panchayats should be paying if they had actually used only that quantity of water which they should use as per the standard norms. On an average these Panchayats should reduce wastage/excessive use by at least 30 per cent to be able to contain the Operation expenditure—to a significant extent. The VWSC should take action to orientate the local Power Pump Operators, as well as the user community with regard to the financial consequences of wasting water.

Even if all the households pay water charges, unless the wastage of water was reduced, and the expenditure on maintenance expenditure was brought down the Panchayats would not be able to meet the Operation and Maintenance expenditure. Monitoring the efficiency of financial management should include not only the income generated to be able to meet the expenditures incurred on water supply, but also the measures taken to reduce expenses such as 'waste reduction'. Therefore, besides realizing the entire amount of the potential income, two important measures that the Panchayats need to take to be able to recover from the heavy expenditure on water supply are: (a) reducing wastage; and (b) bringing down the expenditure on break down maintenance by taking up preventive maintenance.

Another necessary but politically sensitive policy decision to be taken by the GoTN is to instruct the village Panchayats to charge for the use of public fountains and hand pumps. Levying a surcharge on property as water tax from PF users (G.O. 136, dt. 3.10.2002) would not serve the purpose. As long as the PF users and the Panchayat presidents know that the government through the Panchayat will foot the bill and that the services can be kept on an acceptable level the resistance of the PF users to pay for water is quite logical. Therefore, payment of any sizeable amounts on regular bases can only be expected if there is a G.O. Hence, a proactive decision by the GoTN to introduce mandatory payment for all domestic water use needs to be taken. The tariff system should have enough flexibility to allow differentiated rates to be developed depending upon local conditions, as to what the users are prepared to pay for. This will make it possible to introduce modalities for revenue collection. Full support of the district and Block administrative set up of the government will be required to implement such a policy decision.

Reform measures should always begin when new office bearers assume office of the Village Panchayat. During their tenure of five years, they would be persistently followed up in order to make this dream a reality. All that it lacks is precedence. Once the precedence of collecting water charges and full recovery of house tax are achieved, it would become easy for any successive Panchayat functionary to implement it as a practice. The requisite is taking it from the status of concept to the stage of practice. However, as long as the State government has the practice of announcing populist schemes one after another, the demand of the people to get free water supply would remain valid. It must be emphasized, however, that the tariff is only one of several components of a management system and should not be allowed to overshadow or prevent the others from being implemented, viz. institutional management and technical management. The full cost recovery is nowhere near sight. It is neither feasible nor admirable for a welfare state to attempt.

CONCLUSION

The Village Panchayats are to provide uninterrupted drinking water to rural households has become a burden on the Panchayat administration. Given the excess infrastructure in water supply many Panchayats find it difficult to maintain the technical installations, and pay the electricity bill. Excessive use of water is prevalent in most of the study villages. Pumping hours are on the higher side, and simultaneous pumping (meaning letting water flow through the distribution line, when the water was still being pumped to the Overhead Tank), was taking place. This results in not being able to quantify the amount of water pumped/distributed. The amount of money collected as user charges is meagre that it cannot meet the entire expenditure. Therefore, the funds otherwise to be use various development purposes within the village have to be used up in paying the EB bill and in the maintenance of the water supply installations. The Panchayats require capacity building on management of drinking water supply system. Wastage needs to be reduced. Instead of entrusting responsibility to private water providers, it is good the Panchayats have been entrusted with this responsibility. However, Panchayats require technical guidance and capacity building to handle this task of uninterrupted water supply in rural areas.

REFERENCES

Attanayake *et al.* (1996). "System Development for Future Sustainability," 22nd WEDC Conference on *Reaching the Unreached: Challenges for the 21st Century,* New Delhi.

Ben Page (1996). Ergonomics and Human Water Carrying, 22nd WEDC Conference on *Reaching the Unreached: Challenges for the 21st Century,* New Delhi.

Danida (1992). *Water Supply and Sanitation: Sector Policies,* Ministry of Foreign Affairs, DK-1448, Copenhagen.

Danida (1996). *Project Document for Danida GoTN Water and Sanitation Demand Project,* April, Chennai.

Danida (2001). GoTN/*Danida Resource Book—Vol. III,* "Implementation of Water Works", December 2001, Cuddalore.

Danida (2001). *Project Resource Book, Volume 1,* Overview and Planning, Government of Tamil Nadu/Danida, 2001, December, Cuddalore.

Danida (2004). *Management of Water Supply and Sanitation: A Guide to Village Panchayats,* March 2004, Danida: PMG, Cuddalore.

Durgaprasad, P. (2003). 'Drinking Water: Management Strategies and Future Agenda', *Kurukshetra,* Vol. 51, No. 12, New Delhi, pp. 12-15.

Francois Brikke (2002). *Operation and Maintenance of Rural Water Supply and Sanitation Systems: A Training Package for Managers and Planners* (Vol. 1), WHO, Switzerland, p. 45.

Ganapathy, C. (2003). *Possible Remedies to Minimise Contamination of Groundwater in Cuddalore and Villupuram Districts in Tamil Nadu,* Danida: PMG, Cuddalore.

Ganapthy, C. (2006). Personal discussion the researcher had with Mr. Ganapathy, Deputy Hydrogeologist, TWAD Board, December 2006, Salem.

Government of India (2004). "Accelerated Rural Water Supply Programme", *Rajiv Gandhi Drinking Water Mission, Annual Report,* Chapter 7, New Delhi.

Government of Tamil Nadu (1992). GoTN: Danida, *Block Groundwater Potential and Stage of Groundwater Development*—as on January 1992, Cuddalore district.

Government of Tamil Nadu (1998). GoTN: TWAD Ms. No. 231/Circular on *Rural Water Supply Norms* dated 14.5.1998, Chennai.

Government of Tamil Nadu (2004). Groundwater—*Estimation of Groundwater Resources as per GEC Methodology,* PWD, G.O. (Ms) No. 51 dated 11.2.2004. Chennai.

Government of Tamil Nadu (2005). GoTN, *Tamil Nadu Economic Appraisal, 2004-05,* Chennai.

IRC (1995). *Making Yours Water Supply Work: Operation and Maintenance of Small Water Supply Systems,* IRC, The Hague, The Netherlands.

Jeremy Ockelford, Jan-Willem Rosenboom and Bent Kjellerup (1996). "A VLOM Framework for Cambodia", 22nd WEDC Conference on *Reaching the Unreached: Challenges for the 21st Century,* New Delhi.

Kulasekaran, A. (Chief Water Analyst) (2001). *Contamination of Water Sources and Rectification Methods,* TWAD Board, Chennai.

Lennart Nilsson (2002). "Village based Management of water supply and sanitation in Tamil Nadu", 28th WEDC Conference, Kolkata.

Madeleen Wegelin (IRC) (1998). "Community Management Models for Small Scale Water Supply Systems", paper prepared for the workshop on: *Public-Private Partnership in Service Provision for Community-managed Water Supply Schemes*, Kakamega; 7-10 December 1998, Kenya.

Ramesh, R. (2003). "Domestic Water Supply System in Rural Tamil Nadu" paper presented at the AICTE Sponsored National Conference on *'Interlinking of Indian Rivers—Problems and Perspectives'* Organised by the Mahendra Engineering College, 20-22nd October 2003, Namakkal.

Ramesh, R. and Manivel, S. (2005). "Demand Driven Approach—A Development Imperative" Paper presented at the *National Seminar on Community Outreach Methodologies* held at Gandhigram Rural Institute from 27th to 29th January 2005. Gandhigram.

Samuel Paul, Suresh Balakrishnan *et al.* (2004). "State of India's Public Services", *Economic and Political Weekly*, February 28, 2004.

TWAD (2002). MD-TWAD Circular/*Design Criteria*, Lr. No. 1202/AE3/PM/R/2002/ dt. 21.02.2002, Chennai.

WHO (2000). *Operation and Maintenance of Rural Water Supply and Sanitation Systems—A Training Package*, WHO, Geneva. p. 86.

World Bank (2003). *Sustainability, Planning, and Monitoring in Community Water Supply and Sanitation*, The World Bank, New Delhi.

World Bank (2006). *Approaches to Private Participation in Water Services: A Tool Kit*, The World Bank, Washington DC.

Yadava, J.S. (1998). What People Know & What They Practice (KAP Study Findings), Research paper presented at the National Seminar on Rural Sanitation, organized by Rajiv Gandhi National Drinking Water Mission, 9-10 July 1998, Vigyan Bhavan, New Delhi.

CHAPTER FOUR

Primary Health Care

INTRODUCTION

Announcements from the health care sector make headlines in Tamil Nadu almost everyday; about new facilities and equipment being unveiled; and about the potential of health care tourism as the new sunshine industry. Facilities for health care are shining like never before. It is very much noticeable that the private sector involvement in health care is commendable too given the proliferation they make and the advertisements they give on matters like complete health check-up to health insurance etc. With the size of population in India crossing 113 crore, and most of them living in rural areas and in urban slums, the Indian health care system, especially that offered by the government machinery required revisiting. The news that appear on National Rural Health Mission (NRHM) are encouraging. The guidelines are such that it should benefit the rural populace and it should largely involve the local self-government system in service delivery. There are also Patient Welfare Societies formed at Primary Health Centres (PHCs) and Health Sub-Centres (HSCs) with a view to increase the accessibility of the health care facilities and visibility of health services. There is also private health care service thriving alongside.

The questions of accessibility, affordability and acceptability of these reform measures and services to the rural poor required to be analysed. There is also reference to be made about the private partnership in the delivery of health services, although on commercial lines.

The study has used mixed methodology meaning both qualitative and quantitative methods. Two check-lists were used for collecting primary data. One check-list was used for collecting PHC/HSC level information; and the other for collecting individual patients (service-users) responses on health services. The check-lists are given in the Annexure. Besides this, the study mainly involved Direct Observation and On-the-Spot Analysis of situations and responses of the stakeholder groups.

RURAL HEALTH MISSION

Recognising the importance of Health in the process of economic and social development and improving the quality of life of our citizens, the Government of India has resolved to launch the National Rural Health Mission (NRHM) to carry out necessary correction in the basic health care delivery system. The mission adopts a synergistic approach by relating health to determinants of good health, viz. segments of nutrition, sanitation, hygiene and safe drinking water. It also aims at mainstreaming the Indian systems of medicine to facilitate health care. The Plan of Action includes increasing public expenditure on health, reducing regional imbalance in health infrastructure, pooling resources, integration of organisational structures, optimization of health manpower, decentralization and district management of health programmes, community participation and ownership of assets, induction of management and financial personnel into district health system, and operationalising community health centres into functional hospitals meeting Indian Public Health Standards in each Block of the Country (GoI, 2005).

Over the last several years in India there has been a dramatic change in the national government's approach to the health sector. New national schemes, under the banner of the National Rural Health Mission (NRHM), were launched in April 2005. The goal of the mission is to improve the availability of and access to quality health care by people, especially for those residing in rural areas, the poor, women and children. Providing health services is essential responsibility of a welfare state. In India or in Tamil Nadu specifically, there are private hospitals, clinics and medical practitioners offering health service on payment to the governments.

Box 4.1: Summary of Mission Flexible Pool (MFP) PIP 2008-09

	Amount approved (Rs. in Lakh)
Patient Welfare Society Grants—PHC	1421.00
Annual Maintenance Grants for PHCs	880.50
Annual Maintenance Grants for HSCs	635.80
Untied funds to PHCs	355.25
Untied funds to HSCs	870.60
Village Health and Sanitation Committee	1515.80
Mobile Medical units	834.00
Health Melas	312.00

(Contd.)

Box 4.1 : (*Contd.*)

	Amount approved (*Rs. In Lakhs*)
Establishment of new PHCs	4259.75
Training and Capacity building of Health staff	299.55

Specifically, the NRHM has three-pronged strategy of (a) community involvement, (b) decentralization to Panchayati Raj Institutions—Zilla Parishads, and (c) programme management units in each district.

As with all centrally-sponsored schemes, the NRHM relies on the States to implement existing and new initiatives. For example, earlier schemes of the Department of Family Welfare such as reproductive and child health programme (RCH), immunisation, contraception, information, education and communication (IEC), training and research, area projects and other family welfare services are all included in the NRHM. The new initiatives under the NRHM are mostly financed through what is called the 'mission flexible pool' which provides for activities like selection and training of a new cadre of community health workers called Accredited Social Health Activist (ASHA), upgradation of health facilities (community health centres—CHCs and public health centres—PHCs) to first referral unit (FRU) and facilities meeting the new Indian Public Health Standards (IPHS), constitution of patient welfare committees, and mobile medical units, untied funds for sub-centres, preparation of district action plans and so forth. These activities would continue upto the end of the Eleventh Plan (2012). Over 60 per cent of all Central Government health allocation is now routed through NRHM. Under the new RCH, the pooled funds of external funding agencies such as the World Bank and Department of International Development (DFID) are also incorporated.

The entire mission has a provision of Rs. 12,000 crore in the 2008-09 national budget and more is expected each year till 2012, presumably to a level of about 2 per cent of the gross domestic product from the current level of 1.2 per cent. Ending December 2008, the NRHM has completed three years of existence and a lot of ground to cover. The village will have a Health and Sanitation Committee (VHSC) and a fund of Rs. 10,000 as untied funds. The NRHM also mentions private sector regulation and health insurance in its guidelines.

NRHM IN TAMIL NADU

There are 1,421 Primary Health Centres in the State. Government of Tamil Nadu has announced that there would be 116 new PHCs established within the next one year, making a total of 1,537 PHCs. There are 1000 PHCs in Tamil Nadu that have the staffing and facilities to run 24 hours a day/7 days a week. There were only 780 PHCs at the time of commencement of the Mission. The government has given out plans for equipping the remaining PHCs with such facilities. There are additional nurses and sanitary workers to be appointed states a government notice. The District Collector is the Chairperson, and Deputy Director of Health Services is the Mission Director. In order to ensure community management of hospitals, the Mission envisages forming local committees in each PHC, and at Panchayat levels. One factor that can contribute to better success of health service efforts in Tamil Nadu, in addition to NRHM, could be implementation of World Bank assisted Tamil Nadu Health Systems Project. It was implemented in selected districts, viz. Kanyakumari, Dharmapuri, Vellore, Thiruvallur, and Perambalur.

Box 4.2: Vital Data—Health, Tamil Nadu

Vital Indicators	*Tamil Nadu*	*India*
Birth rate (SRS 2004)	17.1	24.1
Death rate (SRS 2004)	7.5	7.5
Infant mortality rate (SRS 2004)	41.0	58
Under 5 mortality rate (SRS 2002)	50.0	80.0
Maternal mortality ratio (2005)	90	400
Total fertility rate (SRS 2003)	1.9	3.0
Child sex ratio (Census 2001)	942	933
Life expectancy at birth (2001-06)	(M) 67.0	(M) 64.1
	(F) 70.0	(F) 65.4

PERFORMANCE

Even as the State averages an infant mortality rate (number of deaths per 1000 live births) of 37, well below the national average of 57, the recently released statistics from the Sample Registration Survey (SRS) show that there are pockets in Tamil Nadu where the IMR is as high as 54.

Public health experts have expressed concern about the patchy performance of the State in controlling infant deaths. High IMR in north western and southern districts of the State going by the SRS data for the survey year 2006 has goaded the government into considering the introduction of certain special schemes for these pockets.

District-level figures were provided for the first time by the SRS, which usually only provides statistics up to the State level. Western districts including some notorious for female infanticide and foeticide: Dharmapuri, Salem, Namakkal, The Nilgiris, Coimbatore and Erode have an IMR of 54, close to the national average. In the southern districts of Dindigul, Theni, Madurai, Sivaganga, Virudhunagar, Ramanathapuram, Tirunelveli and Kanyakumari, the IMR is 52.

Districts around Chennai including Tiruvallur, Vellor, Kancheepuram, Villupuram, Cuddalore and Tiruvannamalai are better at 32. The best performances are in the east, including the delta districts, Nagapattinam, Thanjavur, Thiruvarur, Ariyalur, Perambalur, Tiruchi, Pudukottai and Karur with an IMR of 28, bringing down the State average. 'We are concerned about the high IMR in some districts. The State government reports that it has plans to intensive campaigns in these areas. The strategy would include IEC activities and infrastructure and staff upgradation at the PHCs, in these specific districts.

The facility augmentation that has taken place in most of the PHCs in Tamil Nadu has made way for increasing the inflow of patients to Government PHCs. The average OP (Out-Patient) inflow in PHCs of Dindigul which was 160 has gone up to 210. The average number of in-Patients at any given time of a month was 37, and it has increased to 45. The average child birth for a month that was 6 has gone up to 11, reports the Assistant Director of Health Services, Dindigul.

Box 4.3: Health Infrastructure—Tamil Nadu

District Headquarters hospitals	30
Taluk Hospitals	155
Non-taluk hospitals	80
Women and children hospitals	7
Primary Health Centres	1537
Health Sub-centres	8683

ACCESSIBILITY

A rapid assessment was made in the PHCs and HSCs of Dindigul, Madurai, Virudunagar, Dharmapuri and Coimbatore districts. As far as Dindigul and Madurai districts are concerned a rapid assessment of 4 PHCs and HSCs were visited, interactions held with Medical Officers, the VHNs of HSCs and patients on chance encounter. In Dindigul district, Chinnalapatty, Athoor and Sithayankottai, and in Madurai district Chekkarooni was studied. As per the Indian Public Health Standards (IPHS), there should be one PHC for 30,000 population. An assessment of the existing PHCs in these districts were made and it was found that the population that each PHC is supposed to cover exceeds the norms. For example, the PHC in Chinnalapatty (Athoor

Block) in Dindigul district covers a population of 41,163. Chekkanoorani PHC in Thirumangalam Block covers 49,141 population from eight Panchayats with 45 hamlets.

The State government has announced that it has sanctioned six PHCs for Madurai district based on the proposals received from the Director of Public Health and Preventive Medicine. The six PHCs to be established include Villur (Kallikudi Block), Kaitharinagar and Thanakkankulam (Thirupparankundram Block), Sakkimangalam (Madurai East Block), Nattapatti (Chellampatty Block) and Muduvarpatti (Alanganallur Block). The interaction with the staff in the PHCs revealed that Kappaloor hamlet in the same Block covers more than 10,000 population being an industrial area.

INVOLVEMENT OF LOCAL SELF GOVERNMENT IN RURAL HEALTH CARE

NRHM has contemplated three ways of integrating local self-government and local government health service institution, especially the Primary Health Centre. They are: (a) micro level health planning at the village level in consultation with the local body members; (b) formation of Village Health and Sanitation Committee that is expected to function as a subsidiary body of the Village Panchayat; (c) untied funds (Rs. 10,000 per year) to VHSC for implementing health promotion, and cleanliness activities in the Village Panchayat area.

Thus, the Government of India under NRHM, in order to involve the Village Panchayats in health care activities and in the development of primary health centres and health sub-centres has made Panchayat level committees, and provision of untied funds for general development of health facilities in the locality. Each Primary Health Centre (PHC) gets Rs. 75,000 per year (Rs. 50,000 as development fund, and Rs. 25,000 as general fund). Each Village Panchayat gets Rs. 10,000 as for the Village Health and Sanitation Committee to decide and spend for health related activities. Similarly, each Health Sub-centre gets Rs. 10,000 as general fund for the Patient Welfare Society to decide and spend. The VHNs, with the guidance of the MO of PHC are supposed to develop a micro plan in consultation with elected leaders. This is an admirable portion of the NRHM that it recognises the local government system, and places health as a basic service should be done in collaboration with the Panchayats. But in reality it is found that Village Panchayats are referred to only as a requirement of certain specific steps in the NRHM, and not recognising the place of Panchayats in promoting general health of community in a given geographical area.

VHSC: It is reported that each Village Panchayat has formed a Village Health and Sanitation Committee. The Village Panchayat President is supposed to be the Chairperson of the Committee. When probed about the existence of VHSC, it was reported that it was one of the several committees formed under various schemes like water committee, education committee and so on. However, the funds are not being misused in many of the Panchayats. This is used for paying the transport cost of pregnant women in most of the villages, with the approval of the VHSC. The Village Panchayats make use of the funds for paying the sweeper's salary from out of Rs. 10,000 the Panchayat receives. Even the Village Panchayat functionaries are unaware of the Village Health and Sanitation Committee. The Panchayat Presidents have a sigh of relief that they have a source of money to pay the salary of the local sweeper, who otherwise had to: (a) either pay through some other account where it could not be accounted, (b) or choose to keep the village unclean for want of funds for paying the sweeper. It has become a way of managing general cleanliness of the village.

PWS: Each PHC has formed a Patient Welfare Society. The names have been put up on a board in a prominent place in each PHC this team visited. However, meeting of PWS rarely takes place. The amount allocated (Rs. 10,000) for PWS is spent by the VHN with the knowledge of the Medical Officer concerned. This is mostly used for maintenance of the Health Sub-centres such as meeting out electrical repairs, gas cylinders. In many districts, it has also been spent for paying the transport expenditure of patients from remote rural areas to the PHC for delivery, and travel cost of referral cases. It is also used for paying the shortage of money in paying the ambulance hire charges. There is also permission for the VHNs to use this money for recharging their mobile phones so as to enable the public contact them whenever their services are required.

There is nothing democratic or committee ish about it. It is a decision made by the VHN in consultation with the Medical Officer concerned. However, the money helps the patients who travel to the hospital for delivery. There are places where the money given to the PWS is used for providing meals to expectant mothers who come to the hospital.

PHCs: The Primary Health Centres in most of the places in the study districts were found have got a face lift. There are PHCs with tiled labour ward, clean place for patients to sit and wait. The number of beds has increased, and other facilities and equipments have increased; new Siddha Unit has come up in several hospitals. The amount of money allotted, i.e. Rs. 75,000 per

Box 4.4: Objectives of the Patient Welfare Society

- Improve the hospital, upgrade the equipment and modernise the health services.
- Ensure discipline in the institution and supervise the staff.
- Establish affiliations with private institutions to upgrade services.
- Undertake construction and expansion in the hospital building.
- Ensure optimal use of hospital premises.
- Improve participation of the committee in the running of the hospital.
- Ensure scientific disposal of hospital waste.
- Ensure proper training for doctors and staff.
- Ensure subsidized food, medicine and drinking water to the patients and their attendants.
- Ensure proper implementation of National Health Programme.
- Ensure proper use, timely maintenance and repair of hospital equipment and machinery.
- The PWS can levy user charges, raise funds additionally. PWS can take over and manage canteens, ambulance services and other facilities.

The core activities for decentralised management of the health systems like untied grants to Village Health and Sanitation Committee, Health Sub-Centres, PHCs have to be fully provided for and it is not permitted to divert any savings from these core activities under NRHM.

PHC per year has enabled the Medical Officers to spend it on providing a face lift to the hospital. Some of the hospitals have even set up a garden at the entrance, or on the path way.

Box 4.5: PHC—Morappur, Dharmapuri District, Tamil Nadu

Morappur PHC at Dharmapuri district could be cited as a model for one of the best PHCs in the State. In fact, this PHC has got award for rendering best services, and clean maintenance of hospital premises and the environment. There is garden maintained outside that make one enter without any inhibitions. There are tiled floor all over. There is in-patient room, and there is a spacious waiting hall, where people can watch TV while waiting for their turn to consult the Medical Officer. With facilities such as Surgical room, labour room, X-ray room, blood test room, ECG and Scan facility, and Siddha Unit the PHC looks like a district hospital. There is solar water heater for patients to take hot water, which otherwise in many PHCs one has to get from the nearest tea shop. There is also a place for children to play with swing, slides, and see-saw. There is information board on

(Contd.)

Box 4.5 : (*Contd.*)

various health schemes displayed for information of the public. When there is child birth, it is announced immediately over a loud speaker for everyone waiting to come to know. This hospital also encourages men to take tubectomy operation. In a camp conducted, a little before this team visited, Morappur PHC has conducted a family planning camp where 97 birth control operations were performed. It has got award for best health services in the district three times from the district collector. It is also marching towards obtaining ISO certification.

Box 4.6: PHC—Athoor, Dindigul District, Tamil Nadu

Despite the fact that there are government PHCs improving on a par with private hospitals and rendering modern services, and facilities, there are PHCs like the one in Athoor where there is constant complaint by the user community from villages. PHC at Athoor is supposed to serve around 20 hamlets in the neighbourhood including Athoor, Mallayapuram, Akkraipatty, Parapatty, Palayasempatty etc. Patients start flowing in starting from 7.00 am. It often happens that the Medical Officers do not turn up, or the pharmacist in whose custody medicines are kept, do not turn up and so people have to come the following day, or approach private clinic. The local community reports that at times, the hospital is kept open. But, there would be no employee of the PHC around. The respect people have about hospital do not allow people to enter and misuse. There are times, people rush emergency cases to the hospital at Chinnalapatty or to Dindigul not willing to try their luck waiting for the doctor to arrive at Athoor PHC. This has created a kind of mistrust among the community if they are really provided with right kind of drugs, or the ones available. Incidentally, Athoor is a Block headquarters and a constituency and, a little interior though.

Rural Health Service: One of the basic emphases made by the NRHM is that VHN and the Health Inspector (HI) together should be in a position to cure all kinds of small ailments in villages, and guide people on matters that they should really consult a physician at the nearest PHC. An FGD conducted with VHNs revealed that each VHN is officially supposed to cover 5000 population that might consist of 4-5 villages. But in practice they cover more. They cover villages on a weekly rotation basis. They need to skip villages for one week or two weeks at a stretch if there were official meetings. VHN is the main source of health related data in the State. If the data compilation works were there then again they have to skip going to villages. This, often becomes the reason for them to earn the displeasure of the community.

As per the NRHM norms, one additional ASHA—Accredited Social Health Activist is supposed to join the VHN for assistance. This ASHA would be paid on contractual basis, and that a salary of Rs. 1000 was fixed. But, it is being implemented only in a very few places. In most of the places in Tamil Nadu VHNs are not aware of the provision available for ASHA.

All these efforts have resulted in increasing the patient in-flow into government hospitals, and the number of institutional deliveries has increased as well. However, there are no local level health plans prepared as contemplated by the Mission, nor are there any active involvement of VHSC in the affairs of Health Sub-Centre. That the contemplation of making the people own up the government hospital is yet to come. Similarly, when asked about District Health Plan that is supposed to be a collection of plans received from several PHCs reflecting Panchayat plans, it was understood that District Plans are in place, but they are not based on any micro level panchayat plans. In fact, there is no plan prepared at Panchayat level on health. The Panchayat Presidents are also unaware of such a plan. They do not seem to realise the need for such a plan either.

Dindigul district has been divided into two Health Districts having Dindigul and Palani as two headquarters. At the rate of one PHC for 30,000 population, there are 27 PHCs in Dindigul health district, and 22 PHCs in Palani health district. There immunisation is given on Wednesdays. The facilities in almost all the PHCs have improved, and so the average out-patient in-inflow per day in the district has improved from 160 to 210, the in-patients have improved from 37 to 45, and the number of child births has improved from 6 to 11. Similarly, the Health Secretary reports that the number of women approaching the PHCs has improved from mere 80,000 to 2.5 lakh in the last two years. However, there are PHCs without Medical Officers in districts like Nagapattinam and Thiruvarur. Government of Tamil Nadu reports 100 per cent immunisation whereas the national average in utilisation of immunization is only 44 per cent.

INDIAN PUBLIC HEALTH STANDARDS

Immediately after the launch of the NRHM in December 2005, the Government of India has come out with a guideline for ensuring quality of services in HSCs and PHCs. These guidelines are known as Indian Public Health Standards. There is a set of IPHS guidelines for HSCs. There is also a similar one for PHCs as well. These guidelines besides standards on facilities, space etc. it also provides the job descriptions of health personnel involved.

Box 4.7: IPHS : Population *vis-à-vis* Health Centre Ratio

One HSC for 3000-5000 population
One PHC for 20,000-30,000 population
One CHC for 80,000-1,20,000 population

HEALTH SUB-CENTRES

The ANMs and the VHNs are the kingpins of the rural health service in Tamil Nadu, and manage the HSCs in the State. They manage the entire health related fieldworks, and data collection in the service area of HSCs they are the incharge. They are supposed to get assistance from Health Inspectors, who are not so well known as VHNs are. The following Boxes 4.8 and 4.9 provide the expectations of IPHS out of VHNs, and the facilities they need to have for carrying out job as effective fieldworker. The IPHS are prescribed to provide basic primary health care services to the community and achieve and maintain acceptable standards of quality care.

Box 4.8: Minimum Requirement (Assured Services) a HSC should offer

The manpower indicated for a HSC is two or three at the maximum. There would be two health workers (one male and another female). In addition there could be one voluntary worker to keep the HSC clean. This also includes an indication of services an ANM/VHN is expected to carry out.

- One sub-centre for every 5,000 population; one VHN for 3,000 population in hilly areas.
- Early registration of all pregnancies.
- Minimum three antenatal check-ups, and associated tests like height, weight, BP, anaemia, abdominal examination, breast examination, folic acid supplementation, injection tetanus toxoid etc.
- Minimum laboratory investigation like haemoglobin estimation, urine for albumin and sugar, and referral to PHC for blood grouping.
- Identification of high risk pregnancies.
- Malaria prophylaxis.
- Counselling on diet and rest.
- Promotion of institutional delivery.
- Appropriate and prompt referral.
- Breast feeding advice, post natal hygiene, care of new born, registration of birth.

(Contd.)

Box 4.8 : (*Contd.*)

- Use of untied funds for HSC maintenance.
- Arranging for JSY scheme for the beneficiary to get Rs. 6000 + Rs. 700.
- Full immunisation.
- Prevention and control of childhood diseases.
- Family planning and contraception.
- Follow up services to eligible couple.
- Adolescent health care.
- Control of local endemic diseases, and disease surveillance.
- Organising health day at anganwadi centres.
- Training and guiding traditional birth attendants and ASHAS.
- Records maintenance.

Box 4.9: The HSC Physical Facilities

An HSC is supposed to have the following facilities as per IPHS

- Waiting area
- Prominent display boards
- Visit schedule of ANM
- Suggestions/complaints box
- Labour Room
- Clinic Room
- Examination Room
- Toilet
- Residential Accommodation for the Health Workers with two rooms, kitchen, WC, and bathroom.

Besides these, there would be waste disposal arrangement, adequate furniture, equipments, drugs, a small lab, electricity, water, phone, transport for staff movement.

Given the IPHS standards, the facilities in Tamil Nadu HSCs are nowhere near. The condition and the facilities available with the existing HSCs (in Madurai, Dindigul, Virudhunagar, and Dharmapuri districts) is not even one-fourth of what has been prescribed under the IPHS. Although these sound too big a kind of facilities, it is good to have such a dream so that villages get such health care facilities in the days to come. The expectations in terms of job execution from an ANM or a VHN is voluminous. They strongly feel they need assistance. But, appointment of ASHAS on contractual appointment would not serve the purpose. Although records are maintained at the PHCs level, the source of data is only the ANMs and VHNs. The health care of around 5,000 population and health information this size of population entirely vests on these grassroots level health workers, who are surely overloaded.

Box 4.10: The Minimum Requirements (Assured Services) at PHCs as per IPHS

- Typically a PHC is supposed to serve a population of 20,000-30,000 population.
- One PHC acts as referral unit for 6 sub-centres. It should cover all preventive, promotive, curative and rehabilitative health care.
- OPD services: 4 hours in the morning and 2 hours in the afternoon/evening.
- 24 hour emergency services for dog bites, snake bites etc.
- Referral services.
- In-patient services.
- Maternal and child health care.
- 24 hour delivery services/post natal care/new born care.
- Family Planning and medical termination of pregnancies.
- Management of reproductive tract infections/STIs.
- Disease surveillance and Control of epidemics.
- Collection and reporting of vital health events/statistics.
- Basic laboratory services.
- AYUSH.

Box 4.11: PHC—Essential Infrastructure as per IPHS

- Own building of 375-450 sq. metres plinth area.
- Waiting area (with seating arrangements, notice boards, health pamphlets, toilet, drinking water, suggestions box).
- Out Patient Department.
- AYUSH doctors, besides the allopathic doctor.
- Wards with 4-6 beds (clean).
- Labour room (with clean linen).
- Arrangement for nutritious and hygienic food.
- Operation theatre (with equipments and furniture).
- Minor dressing room/injection room.
- Laboratory (with equipments and furniture all over).
- General store and dispensing-cum-store.
- Office room (with generator, electricity all over, water supply, toilet).
- Dirty utility room/laundry and diet facilities for in-patients.
- Accommodation with a Boundary wall around the hospital area.
- Transport arrangement.
- 15 staff including medical officer, pharmacist, lab assistant, Nurse mid-wife.

PROBLEMS REPORTED

The following are the general problems reported by the community in the service villages of PHCs, and during the exit interviews conducted outside PHCs in the following districts: Dindigul, Madurai, Virudhunagar, and Dharmapuri.

Timings and Absenteeism of Staff: At PHCs, the timings as per the IPHS is four hours in the morning and 2 hours in the evening for out patients. But, the doctors and the pharmacists in many sample PHCs conducted in this study do not stick to timings (Athoor in Dindigul for example). People need to enquire if the doctor and the staff have arrived to get a consultation. If they go at specific timings if possible they should be waiting for long hours. Although there is a fixed timing put up on the notice board, the time of staff visit do not often go with it. However, one solace is that doctors or the staff do not go off when there are still patients waiting, although it is only a rare occurrence. Absenteeism of PHC staff puts patients to inconvenience. Moreover, it causes poor maintenance of medical records, and basic health statistics, which should flow from PHCs upward. There are also local people visiting the doctor to get attestation for various schemes.

Drug Availability: In the opinion of the doctors and pharmacists, the drug availability in PHCs have improved considerably to the requirements to that extent that expired medicines are sometimes destroyed (Chinnalapatty in Dindigul for example). But, to manage occasional non-availability, the doctors prescribe medicines and advice the patients to either come the day medicines arrive or buy them from the open market. This is viewed with discontent by the patients.

Facility Improvement: The facilities in PHCs in the past three years have improved to a considerable extent. However, they cannot be said to be in line with the standards prescribed by the IPHS. Aspects such as boundary wall, waiting hall, beds and labour wards have really undergone improved in many of the PHCs. Certain laboratory facilities have improved to the extent that Morappur in Dharmapuri and Chekkanoorani in Madurai could be quoted as best examples witnessed. However, the PHC at Chinnalapatty does not have a separate drug storage room. Drugs are kept at labour room and drugs for delivery are kept in OP check up room. These have really helped in building the image of the public health service in Tamil Nadu. An interaction with a group of SHG members in Kalikkampatty revealed that many of them have stopped going to private clinics and that they have started using PHC service in Chinnalapatty recently.

Vaccination: It has been made a regular practice in Government PHCs to provide immunization on all Wednesdays. The authorities have found during a review that people living in hilly and remote areas (in Madurai district Poondi, Kaunji, and Pookal in Kodaikanal) that has no transport facilities hesitate to take their children to the PHCs, so as not to forego a day's wage. This has made setting up of mobile teams to go to such far-flung villages that had no transport facilities to reach the nearest PHC. Vaccination programmes are serving a dual purpose as a complete health check up is also done. Where children are found to be sick, vaccination is postponed.

Treatment: The community members make two different references to treatment—medical treatment of patients who visit the PHCs under study, and the emotional treatment. Although the medical treatment has improved considerably in many PHCs, the emotional treatment requires considerable improvement. Health as a matter of right of the people is spoken in the NRHM documents, but the way people are made to wait with no information about the time of arrival of the medical officer, or the pharmacist; about prescribing medicines to patients without explaining to them about the diagnosis made, or what was understood in the diagnosis; people are blindly asked to take the medicines prescribed not knowing 'what was diagnosed'.

Involvement of Local Self-government: The contemplation of the mission document is that local hospital is part of Village Panchayat. The healthy development of citizen in a given village depends on how PHCs work in collaboration with Panchayats and *vice versa*. However, in practice there are hospitals (PHCs) that complain that they do not get even water line connection from the Panchayat. Similarly, when the medical officers are asked about the relationship between the PHC and the Panchayats, they looked blank. The Village Panchayat President's designation/signature is required for releasing the JSY scheme money, and for releasing the untied funds allotted to the VHSC. Otherwise, there seems to be no working relationship between the Panchayats and the PHCs. This is an area that requires improvement. Especially the idea of preparing micro level health plan, involvement of Panchayats in immunization, child nutrition programme etc. can prove positive results.

Involvement of Local School: The local school children are provided health education covering sanitation, hygiene and cleanliness habits. They are also trained in identifying the sources/causes of malaria, and how to prevent/ control malaria. The school children have been trained in destroying the sources of mosquito. They have done it as a game or play. There are health committees, and school sanitation committees formed to keep the school environment clean. The expectation is that they would do it continuously. This has been done successfully in some villages in Dindigul, Madurai and in Dharmapuri districts. However, from the reports of teachers, children and Medical Officers it is understood that this has been done as one-time affair, based on some official communication received from DDHS. It was not followed up, nor was there any recurrent activity pertaining to it later on.

Staffing: There are also vacancies in many of the PHCs not filled. For example, Chinnalapatty PHC in Dindigul reports that out of the 42 postings sanctioned for that PHC, 11 postings are vacant; out of 35 staff in Athoor 5 positions are vacant; out of 42 positions in Chekkanoorani 5 positions remain vacant. These vacant positions are of pharmacists, male nursing assistants, drivers, hospital workers, and Health Inspectors. One of the serious problems could be absence of lady doctor, and absence of staff nurse/Nursing mid-wife has resulted in poor admission of delivery cases. Even the appointment of ASHA is not fully implemented in Tamil Nadu.

Keeping positions vacant increases the work burden of the existing employees. This in turn is shown in carrying out jobs resulting in poor attendance of patients. This is reflected not only in patient care and health service, but also in data management. For example, facility improvement at Chekkanoorani PHC is said to have improved the OP in-flow, and number of deliveries conducted. However, the data they provide do not reflect it convincingly (in fact, there is fluctuation and in the year 2006 the number of deliveries conducted has declined by 20 numbers) because there is no staff in place for maintenance of data. Perhaps, data entry has not been properly done.

The Government of India is making efforts to provide quality health care for all by 2025. A study was conducted by FICCI. The country would require 17.5 lakh additional beds by 2025 to achieve this target. In the context of a huge shortage of qualified doctors, the study has found that against the requirement of 7,00,000 doctors by 2025, there was a net addition of just 17,000 doctors a year. This would come nowhere near the requirement.

Institutional Delivery: The public health records of the government of Tamil Nadu have it that 94 per cent of the deliveries take place in hospitals only. There is only 6 per cent of domiciliary deliveries taking place as of 2005-06. An institutional delivery that was hardly 57 per cent in 1991 has come to 94 per cent in 2005-06 is a good show. The efforts of the NRHM is expected to realise the dream of making 100 per cent institutional delivery.

Moreover, out of the 94 per cent reported as institutional delivery, as much as 40 per cent of the deliveries take place in private nursing homes. Only the rest is with the government run hospitals, PHCs, and in HSCs. At least half of this 40 per cent could be families from poor families going to private clinics for want of labour wards and other facilities in the PHCs.

The scheme of paying Rs. 6,000 (plus Rs. 700 for institutional delivery) for women who enrol themselves for anti-natal care has evoked a lot of interest among the newly married young girls. They invariably register with VHN, and periodically keep in touch with VHN so as to become eligible to get the scheme-money. The Janani Suraksha Yojana provides Rs. 700 for pregnant women financial assistance for the second delivery also to facilitate institutional delivery. This scheme enables rural women to keep using government health care services. This process helps the VHN to provide ANC and PNC as well. There is almost none in villages who is unaware of this scheme. Coupled with the general trend of awareness on anti-natal care and post-natal care, this scheme has successfully brought down the maternal mortality and infant mortality rate in Tamil Nadu, which was 39 in 2005-06 has come down to 37 in 2006-07. The VHN pays visit for one week after the child birth and offers advice on breast-feeding, and general cleanliness of the new born baby. These are matters that take government health service delivery to the door steps of rural people. This is for rural people to enjoy health as a matter of right.

The expectant mothers who come for scanning are provided with one time meal so as to avoid their remaining hunger until they reach home after getting the scan report done. The expectant mother that has been admitted for delivery would be provided with three-time nutritious meal for three days. In order to encourage institutional delivery and to reduce the possibilities of risks during delivery, the expectant mothers would be given admission in PHCs one week before the expected delivery date. There are hospitals that celebrate '*valaikappu*' for expectant mothers to keep them in good humour.

INDIAN SYSTEM OF MEDICINE

With a view to revitalising the local health traditions and mainstreaming AYUSH infrastructure, including manpower, and drugs, or to strengthen the public health system at all levels, there is alternative of providing Indian System of Medicine provided in all the PHCs, with a qualified Siddha doctor in place. There is also supply of 50 different kinds of siddha medicines prescribed and supplied to the patients who opt for siddha medicines. This is slowly catching up especially among the elders in villages. However, in many hospitals the position of siddha doctor is vacant and so it remains non-functional.

Private Practice: Private medical practice in PHC or CHC areas is quite very minimal. In some places (e.g. Chekkanoorani, Chinnalapatty, Morapur) even if there are private clinics opened the consultancy fees charged is only very minimal ranging from Rs. 10 to Rs. 30. These private practices are generally made use of by the moneyed in the villages, and at times of emergency by the poor. Otherwise, the poor always go to PHCs only. It could be clearly understood from the chain of interviews conducted that the poor still depend on PHCs and CHCs only. They get medicines also from PHCs only. The relationship referred to is more personal and informal, rather than a rural citizen approaching a government hospital for health service as a matter of right.

If there are major ailments, the poor get referral from the local PHC doctor and approach the CHC or a Medical College Hospital in the town, and do not attempt to step into a town based clinic or private multi-speciality hospital. They are fully aware of the expenditures involved. One discontent of the poor when they approach the district hospital or medical college hospital for some major ailments is, it often happens they are asked to buy medicines from the open market. They state short supply as a reason.

PUBLIC PRIVATE PARTNERSHIP

The Mission is open to make use of the private hospital and ambulance services operated by NGOs, and other parallel schemes of the government such as TNHSP. For example, the government reports that many PHCs hire private specialists (anaesthetists and obstetricians) for the provision of caesarean operations. It is reported that 15 per cent of the emergency caesarean surgeries are performed in the government hospitals with the help of private anaesthetists which has contributed in the reduction of maternal deaths by 36 per cent.

The TNHSP has handed over fully equipped ambulances to NGOs for operation. The idea is collecting the ambulance charges from patients at rates determined by the State. It is usually Rs. 5 per km, which falls short of the cost involved. Therefore, it was found in most of the places the idea is falling apart because of the poor planning on the operation and maintenance of ambulances done by the scheme. Even in Dharmapuri district, which is hailed as one of the successful places among those implementing the ambulance services, the NGOs have either handed over the ambulances to the DDHS or they are almost at the verge of handing over. In the experience of the NGOs, the cost of operation and maintenance of the vehicle that is permissible does not hold up to the practicalities.

MAJOR FINDINGS

- The National Rural Health Mission (NRHM) has successfully provided a platform for community health action at all levels. Besides merger of the Department of Health and Family Welfare in all the States, NRHM has successfully moved towards a single State and District level Health Society for effective service delivery at grassroots level.
- The impression the poor rural community have about the PHCs and HSCs is not so poor as one thinks. The poor still depend on the government for health services. That the government health services are not made use of by the public is a myth. Even at secondary level the poor do not approach the private clinics because of the money factor. They go to district level hospitals on referral by the medical practitioner of the PHC.
- Several fold improvements have come in terms of facilities at PHCs. However, compared to the standards prescribed by the IPHS, there is still a long way to go.
- There are positions of statisticians, health workers, and pharmacists vacant in some of the PHCs visited. The become burden to the existing staff, and it reflects in service to the patient, and in data management system. There is shortage of staff including male health workers for controlling the communicable diseases and emerging new diseases.
- Successful PHCs show that it is more in the hands of the DDHS concerned and the Medical Officers of PHCs rather than any other factor to augment the facilities or to render better facilities. This holds good for involving the Panchayats as well.
- The district level health plans are prepared. But, they are not consolidation of village level/Block level plans. In fact, there is no micro level health plan made in consultation with Panchayats. The sectoral convergence referred to in the NRHM do not take place because Panchayats are not involved.

ACTION POINT

- The number of PHCs and CHCs are less compared to IPHS. The postings in many of the PHCs remain vacant rendering hardship to the existing staff. The number of PHCs that work 24 hours × 7 days should be increased. The vacant positions should be filled in so that the poor health as a matter of right.

- People unlike the impression they have about government schools, do not have a very poor impression about PHCs. Both accessibility and the money factor make the people approach the PHCs rather than the private clinics. This should be maintained with good impression that the PHC staff make amidst people.
- While the government has granted a five year tax holiday to health sector to encourage private entrepreneurs to set up hospitals in Tier I and Tier II towns, there is an urgent need for rapid expansion of quality health care besides efficient use of allocations made by the government for health care. This could be a suggestion for making health care reach all.
- The infrastructure in PHCs requires to be enhanced in line with the standards of the IPHS. Ensuring such standards for HSCs may take time. But, PHCs may be given priority in setting up the facilities so that the poor do not have to be referred to district hospitals and to private clinics.
- Private clinics require to be regulated, and their services can be made use of in delivery etc. on payment.
- The State has plans to take up a massive capacity building exercise of Village Health and Sanitation Committees and PRIs at all levels. The district level plans are prepared. But, there is no micro level plan prepared at village level.
- The field level health workers are insufficient to perform all the functions expected of them as per the IPHS. The State would ensure appointment of ASHAS and performance based payments to ASHAS/Community Health Workers.
- Quality of services for deliveries at public health facilities is monitored; private sector facilities are accredited and monitored.
- The Public-Private model (with NGOs and private hospitals) could work in rendering health service, whereas the private clinics require to be monitored for facilities, competence, and on fees collected.
- The school children could be effectively used for eradication of mosquitoes and mosquito breeding sources. But, this is done as one time affair. This should be done periodically so as to sustain the interest of the children, and to offer them health tips, and health education constantly.

- Like the waiting hall of PHCs have been made to have charts and boards containing health tips, there could be wall writing, and posters pasted in the villages on health related schemes, and health tips.

CONCLUSION

With the introduction of NRHM and TNHSP Tamil Nadu has moved to a better stage in providing primary and maternal health care services especially for women and new born babies. The service of PHCs have improved could be seen from the increasing patient in-flow, and the general opinion community pass when there was a series of exit interviews conducted in PHCs, and HSCs. To testify this statement, the *India Today* survey of Primary Health in the country has placed Tamil Nadu on first rank. Compared to IPHS and the facilities in the existing HSCs, and PHCs, only very few of the PHCs in the State are in that stage. As far as HSCs are concerned we are nowhere near the IPHS standards.

REFERENCES

Arun Gupta & Navdeep Singh Khaira (2008). Flaws in Child Nutrition and Health Governance, *Economic and Political Weekly*, April 26, 2008.

Government of India, National Rural Health Mission (2005-2012). *Mission Document*, GoI, New Delhi.

Government of India (2006). *Guidelines on Indian Public Health Standards (IPHS) for Primary Health Centres,* Director General of Health Services, Ministry of Health & Family Welfare, GoI, New Delhi.

Government of India (2006). *Guidelines on Indian Public Health Standards (IPHS) for Sub-centres,* Director General of Health Services, Ministry of Health & Family Welfare, GoI, New Delhi.

Government of India (2008). *Economic Survey 2007-08,* Ministry of Finance—Economic Division, Oxford University Press.

Jeffery Hammer, Yamini Aiyar, Salimah Samji, Understanding Government Failure in Public Health Services, *Economic and Political Weekly*, October 6, 2007.

Peter Berman & Rajeev Ahuja, Government Health Spending in India, *Economic and Political Weekly*, June 28, 2008.

Pia Malaney (2000). *Health Sector Reform in Tamil Nadu: Understanding the Role of the Public Sector*, Centre for International Development, Harward University, London.

Shyam Ashtekar, The National Rural Health Mission: A Stocktaking, *Economic and Political Weekly*, September 13, 2008.

V.B. Annigeri, District Health Accounts: An Empirical Investigation, *Economic and Political Weekly*, May 17, 2003.

ANNEXURE

ASSESSMENT ON THE RURAL HEALTH SERVICES

District
Block
Location of the PHC
Population covered
Number of Panchayat/Habitations covered
Is the PHC providing 24hrs and 7days delivery facilities?
Number of Beds available

SERVICES

- Average number of Out-Patients daily
- Average number of Out-Patients Monthly
- Average number of In-Patients daily
- Average number of In-Patients Monthly
- Average number of Delivery Per Month
- Separate ward for In-Patient and Out-Patient cases
- Availability of Specific services
- Mother and child health services
- School Health Programmes/National Health Programmes/Health Camps.
- Deviation of work/disturbance in the routine work/work load.
- Field visit of Male Health Workers and Lady Health Workers to Sub-centres.
- Is AYUSH available?
- How about the use of AYUSH by Patients.
- Is ISM&H available?
- Duty timings of Doctors.

MANPOWER

Sl. No.	Position/Designation	Number of Staff
1.	Medical Officer	
2.	Health Inspector	
3.	Block Health Extension Educator	
4.	ANM—Auxiliary Nurse Midwife	
5.	Senior Treatment Supervisor (STS)	
6.	STLS	
7.	Health Visitor	
8.	Sector Health Nurse	
9.	Village Health Nurse	
10.	Multi-purpose Worker	
11.	Pharmacist	
12.	Assistant	
13.	Statistician	
14.	Sanitary Inspector	
15.	Staff Nurse	
16.	Hospital Worker	
17.	Sweeper	
18.	Male Health Worker	
19.	Driver	

Total Staff

Staff Availability for Emergency services

Is facility (and staff) for delivery available all the 24 hours

Training given to the ANM, Female Health Workers, Male Health Workers, Doctors etc.

Job Description, In-service training, Skill upgradation.

ESSENTIAL LAB SERVICES

- Routine urine, stool, and blood tests
- Sputum testing for TB
- Blood test for malaria parasite
- Rapid test for pregnancy
- Rapid Test for HIV
- Blood Grouping, Blood Sugar, Cholesterol,
- Vidal Test for Typhoid, Filarial, HB
- Diagnosis of RTI/STD

PHYSICAL INFRASTRUCTURE

- Location of the PHC
- Building
- Availability of Ambulance Services
- Labour Room Available
- Room for Drug Storage
- Compound wall (or proper fencing), gate
- Cleanliness of the toilets
- Distance from the district hospital
- Drinking water
- Rest room for the nurses or staff/waiting room for patients
- Telephone facility (Is the Number put up visibly for local people to note)
- Power supply
- Waste disposal arrangement
- Display Boards for the information with regard to the services available in local language
- Record maintenance (manual or computer records)/Information Back up

COMMUNITY PERCEPTION

- If user Charges collected
- Benefits under Janani Surksha Yojana
- Quality of services

CHAPTER FIVE

Special Economic Zones

I. THE PREMISE

The Government of India has announced setting up of Special Economic Zone (SEZ) in vast tracts of (supposed to be barren) lands for foreign as well as domestic companies set up manufacturing and service providing establishments. It would be a foreign territory within the country. The idea is that it would bring in a lot of private, and foreign direct investment resulting in employment generation and economic growth. Controversies over SEZs have erupted in several places of India, and Tamil Nadu is no exception to it.

> *Farmers agitate in front of the District Collector's Office at Tuticorin against a government proposal to acquire over 2500 acres of land for setting up of Special Economic Zone.* —*Dina Malar* (Nellai Edition), 11.6.2008

> *The farmers in Bairamangalam in Krishnagiri district along with Dr. Ramdoss, the PMK Founder, have expressed voice against the government's move to acquire 3,600 land in Bairamangalam (and in a few other villages) for setting up of SEZ.* —*Dinakaran* (Salem Edition), 1.11.2005

> *We shall not part with our land—which is our source of livelihood.*
> —*Dina Mani* (Madurai), 24.8.2008

> *Acquiring cultivable land for any other purpose—be it for industries or for service sector is objectionable.* —*Tamil Osai* (Coimbatore Edition), 3.3.2008

> *The villagers in Raycot district of Maharashtra vehemently oppose Reliance Group from setting up SEZ in the State.* —*Dina Malar*, 29.9.2009

> *Will Cheyyar be Tamil Nadu's Nandigram? Government puts 10 villages on notice over land acquisition [for setting up SEZ]; eight of them oppose SEZ move.* —*The New Indian Express*, October 4, 2008

The research questions that this study posited are:

- What is the basis of the Policy Guidelines Act and Rules put to use for setting up of SEZ and for land acquisition. What is the tenor of those instruments?
- Is land acquisition for SEZ promotion taking place as per the Act, Rules and Policy Guidelines of the government?
- How about acquisition of agricultural lands, and how is acquiring agricultural land, if taken, justified/compensated?
- How about the other livelihood assets of the poor, common facilities of the community, and the lands in possession of the local governments including pasture land, lakes, ponds, waterways, temples, dwelling houses, drinking water sources and so on viewed and dealt with.
- How about the resettlement and rehabilitation arrangement of the poor whose houses are evicted, lands are taken, and their source of income crumbled for the purpose of SEZ?
- How deep or shallow is the employment promise that the SEZs make?
- What does it hold out ultimately? And what are the poor doing with (the compensation) money with no land in possession?

OBJECTIVES OF THE STUDY

The objectives of the study are:

- To record the voices of the community in general and the poor in particular about the land acquisition for setting up of SEZ in various districts of Tamil Nadu.
- To find out if development of SEZ affects the private property resources of the poor, and the common property resources of the community, which have a bearing on their sources of livelihoods.
- To make a social cost-benefit analysis in terms of loss of lands and other resources, and the benefits the community members are likely to get in terms of employment, and more, if any.
- To determine if the acquisition of land and the process of setting up of SEZ goes as per the Act, Rules and Policies of Government India and Government of Tamil Nadu including the resettlement and rehabilitation arrangements.
- To make out the place of various stakeholders such as the State, the companies setting up business in SEZ, and the local community in general.

The objectives extend beyond one another, meaning each of the five objectives is not distinguishable by nature or content. This is deliberately so, because of the methodology of research that this study intends to use—case study of each village where SEZ is coming up, case study of select individuals (especially the poor) who have parted with their lands, and a chain of interview with the stakeholders including the general community and the functionaries of Village Panchayats. However, one characteristic that would run across all the five objectives is 'the place of local community and local institutions after the SEZ proposal got shaped'. How are the indigenous people treated in the process? What is happening to local people, their livelihoods and local democracy in the process?

METHODOLOGY

This study intends to use case study method coupled with chain of interviews. Case studies are done of: (i) the villages that have faced major land acquisition due to setting up of SEZ, and (ii) select individuals (especially the poor) who have parted with their lands for SEZ. Besides case study, chain of interviews are held with the stakeholders including the general community and the functionaries of Village Panchayats.

Data Sources: The study has used both primary and secondary sources of data. The study has primarily attempted to investigate through multiple sources of evidences. Chain of evidences have been collected in order to verify the validity of information. Anecdotal evidences have also been collected from people and Panchayats affected. Primary data have been collected from the Village Panchayat functionaries, people affected by the establishment of SEZ, or those who find themselves vulnerable to the fallout of SEZs in Tamil Nadu. The districts covered are: Krishnagiri, Thiruvannamalai, Kancheepuram, Thiruvallur, Trichy, Tuticorin, and Tirunelveli. Case studies of communities prior to and after the establishment of SEZ; the way Panchayats were involved in the land acquisition deal; compensation negotiations; resettlement and rehabilitation arrangements etc. have been collected from primary source. Oral histories, situations and observational methods have been employed as well. Secondary sources of data have been collected from websites of the Government of India, Government of Tamil Nadu, and from published literature on SEZs.

Data Analysis: We have conducted multiple case studies and analysed them on replication logic. Therefore, the analyses made are primarily from case studies. Sufficient time and efforts have been put in to understand each case, and to verify relevant policy papers etc. with a view to put things in proper perspective. Evidences collected from the field have been used for corroboration of the arguments made.

Scope of this Study: The study primarily covers aspects pertaining to land acquisition, issues of compensation, resettlement and rehabilitation, employment generation and the benefits to the local people, the social externalities caused by SEZs, and the place of grassroots level democracy in SEZ deal. The main focus of the study has been communities. There are several districts in Tamil Nadu where SEZs have been announced or commenced. This study deals with only a limited number of districts, viz. Thiruvannamalai, Kancheepuram, Perambalur, and Krishnagiri in detail although references are made to other districts as well.

Limitations of this Study: This is a single State study of Tamil Nadu only. The references made of policies often pertain only to Tamil Nadu. Officials in charge of promoting SEZ has a standard statement of response to any question they are asked about SEZ: 'You look up our website. It is all there. That is all there'. So, for information relating to governmental procedures etc. only websites (see references) of Government of India and Government of Tamil Nadu were used. The study, as its purpose is confined to people, their land resources, and other livelihood resources it does not intend to bring out the economic growth it has enabled the State Government to report about.

CHAPTER ORGANISATION

This chapter is presented in four parts. Part I deals with the premise of this study along with methodology; Part II presents the case studies conducted of villages and people affected at various stages of SEZ development; Part III makes an analysis of the cases presented in Part II with a view to bringing out the fallout of establishing SEZs in the study areas; Part IV summarises the findings, and presents action points for reducing the social externalities caused by SEZs.

Box 5.1: What is Special Economic Zone ?

Special Economic Zone (SEZ) is a geographical region or notified zone that has economic laws that are more liberal than a country's typical economic laws. It aims mainly at attracting capital in the form of Foreign Direct Investment (FDI), and providing an internationally competitive and hassle-free environment for export production—be it goods or services.

Source: SEZ Policy Paper, GoI.

II. CASE STUDIES ACROSS DISTRICTS IN TAMIL NADU

The case studies presented below were conducted in six selected districts of Tamil Nadu, where establishment of SEZ are either apace or units have even started functioning. The six districts covered are: Kancheepuram, Thiruvannamalai, Perambalur, Tuticorin, Tirunelveli, and Krishnagiri.

CASE 5.1: ORAGADAM—KANCHEEPURAM DISTRICT

At Oragadam SEZ, like in many other SEZs things flared up very seriously at the start of land acquisition to the extent that 37 people went to jail opposing the acquisition of lands, especially the agricultural lands. Much soon the SEZ developers put money into mouth so that voice of resistance and opposition become feeble and unheard. Agricultural lands are lost, water bodies such as lakes and ponds are lost, water ways (drainage) are lost, trees are lost, school buildings are lost, temples and places of worship are lost, and even dwelling houses are lost to SEZ in Oragadam. All that the people get in return is 'cash compensation'.

The Area/Demographic Characteristics

Oragadam, at a distance of 45 km away from Chennai on Thambaram-Kancheepuram Road, is emerging as the new industrial belt. The State Industries Promotion Corporation of Tamil Nadu conceived the idea of setting up an industrial part in Oragadam in 1999 and a total of 1905 acres from Oragadam and 8 other villages located around it were acquired subsequently.

Special Economic Zones, and SEZ units are booming in the surrounding area of Chennai since the time SEZ started getting pronounced in Tamil Nadu. Oragadam Panchayat with 463 households has two hamlets, namely Oragadam and Chennanguppam, with a population of 1,150. Majority (about 80%) of the households belong to Scheduled Castes, and the rest of them belong to Backward Community, especially *Naidus* and *Vanniyars.* Agriculture, coupled with wage employment through agricultural operations, were the main stay of the people. The small number of Caste Hindus held large acres of agricultural lands, and large number of SC households held small acres of land—portraying the typicality of land possession pattern in the State in general. It also implies that the size of holdings of SCs was small, and the size of holdings of the Caste Hindus was bigger. Although the SCs were involved in cultivation of paddy in their own land, the practice of working for wage in others' lands prevailed as well.

The District Administration and SIPCOT in 2007 acquired 1,642 acres of land in Oragadam and Chennankuppam areas and in the process developed what is now known as Oragadam Module—floated by the State Government of Tamil Nadu as a much accepted method for future land acquisition across the State. The State Government emphasises that more than Oragadam Module has provided a firm basis to negotiate and fix land price in Oragadam area.

The District Administration and the SIPCOT mooted a 'fair price' method wherein the guidelines value, last registered value and the market value of land transferred during the first quarter of 2007 were considered for the calculation. The 'fair price' thus arrived was approved by the State Government. The area of the complex is 1935 acres, with the saleable area of 1,642 acres. The salient feature mentioned about this is that it is located very close to Chennai. A maximum price of Rs. 20 lakh per acre (i.e. Rs. 20,000 a cent) was fixed for lands abutting the road and a minimum of Rs. 14 lakh (i.e. Rs. 14,000 a cent) was fixed for lands located in interior areas.

The talk about SEZ at Oragadam came up as early as 1999. The process of land selection, negotiations with land owners, followed by community unrest, land acquisition and plans of resettlement and so on went on until 2005-06. The proposal came to a complete shape at the fag end of the year 2006 only. The compensation for almost 90 per cent of those who parted with their lands has been settled in the year 2006 and in 2007. There are a few cases of land owners whose lands are in litigation within the family members or clarity of ownership is indistinct in the documents they produce. Such lands have yet to be compensated and acquired by the SEZ developer. In total, 950 acres have been acquired from Oragadam landholders. As of now (2008), there are hardly two, three industries that have started construction works such as Apollo Tyres for one.

The normal rate of lands in Orgadam area was Rs. 2000—Rs. 3000 per cent at that time (2005-06). The farmers demanded Rs. 50,000 per cent from the companies. The District Collector who negotiated the deal found it to be too high a demand. After negotiations it was agreed that price for lands would be fixed at three differential rates based on the category it belongs to, viz. (i) barren, (ii) agricultural land with one harvest a year, and (iii) agricultural land with two harvests a year. For the purpose of records it was noted as lands close to the road, and lands inside the village. The one that was giving two harvests a year was fixed at Rs. 20,000 per cent; the one that gave single harvest was fixed at Rs. 16,000 per cent; and barren lands were fixed at Rs. 14,000 per cent. The farmers made up their mind to sell.

CASE 5.2: PRAKASH (PAP), ORAGADAM

Prakash appears very much disappointed, since location of SEZ in Oragadam has caused him to lose the land that was supposed to inherit him from his father. This 26 years old bachelor—born in Oragadam village—drives the Village Panchayat President's Tata Sumo vehicle at the moment. He, along with another ward member (Ammavasai), is being used by the Panchayat President on all his (the President's) business related errands. Prakash started narrating his experience and views about the land acquisition for SEZ that just got completed recently, and about the real estate business that is flourishing in Oragadam village in the past three years. He, at once, started chiding his father who shattered his dream—naively though—of owning a car, which could be let out for hire.

He recollects his school days when his father sold some two acres of land at a very meagre price in order to meet some domestic urgency. He remembers the year 1993-94, when he was studying in seventh standard, his father sold some two acres of land for Rs. 15,000. It works out to hardly Rs. 200 a cent. Now, after announcements of SEZ in Oragadam village, the land value has scaled up to unimaginable level. The operation of realtors have scaled up tremendously. The government rate for a cent of land (that is approximately one hundredth of an acre) was Rs. 14,000, when the compensation was paid to those who sold land for the SEZ, two-three years ago. His father had to sell the remaining 80 cents of land that he had been left with. But then it was a joint *patta* (land deed) with his paternal uncles. So, a scarce little of the money was given to his father. Prakash regrets that if his father had been a little thoughtful and kept those 2 acres of land now, his dream of buying a car would have come true. He adds immediately that in the hands of the realtors the land price has gone further upto Rs. 1.5 lakh/ cent now.

Prakash, who has completed only his Primary Education, worked in Chennai for more than 9 years as a labourer in different places. Now, as a driver to Panchayat President's vehicle and also as a labourer involved in loading and unloading of building materials brought for construction works at the SEZ area, he earns a good money upto even Rs. 1,000 per day. His innocence made him unthinkingly reveal that the Panchayat President took up supplying building materials to the companies involved in construction works for the past three years, and that the Panchayat Presidents in and around Oragadam have created a cartel that they should deal in all the building materials supply, and nobody else should be allowed entry into such business in SEZ area without the Panchayat President's knowledge. Informally, the construction-companies have also seemed to have agreed to this deal, for all that they want is to complete the work smoothly without crossing sword with people who seem to be locally influential or powerful. Taking advantage of the situation some wise Presidents like Oragadam's are involved in real estate business as well.

He revealed that the Panchayat President during the start of the land acquisition process stood along with the community against the cultivable land being taken up for SEZ purpose. He met the District Collector, Project Officer—SIPCOT, and took part in an agitation organized by the local farmers against the acquisition of farm land. He took matters to the media also. He was in prison for almost a week along with 36 others in connection with the agitation organised. But, when he realized that nothing worked out against the will of the government machinery, he gave up all his fight, and found good business opportunities in it. Moreover, the personal money he used from his pocket in taking poor farmers to officials at Kancheepuram, Chennai and so on, also deterred him from all the negativities against SEZ. His title as Panchayat President served as spring board wherever needed, when got down in his new business. He stopped all his moves against the farm land acquisition and started afresh with his new business of supplying building materials, and dealing in real estate business in Oragadam area.

It was then a section of the people who voted (in the local body election) for him joined the people who voted against him in spreading gossip that he has been bribed by the companies. Prakash says it strongly that he knew and people who work closely with him knows that the President realized at some point of time that the community's expression of discontent was not going to help reverse the Government's decision of land acquisition. It was that which made him gave up the fight. Then in the process he also, perhaps, calculated the business gain he would get if he got down to supplying building materials creating a cartel with other Panchayat Presidents in the neighbourhood villages. Now, he is almost a full time building materials supplier as well as real estate dealer. He does patchy work as President of the Village Panchayat including giving dole money from his pocket to satisfy a complaining locale.

Prakash opines that SEZ has no benefits for the local people except for a few who can influence the companies and deal with the government officials. He adds that a retired local Revenue Inspector's son has gathered a group of people and formed "Village Protection Committee". He gives hopes to a group of people that he would get back the land taken for SEZ or at least get a higher compensation amount—all for a done deal. There are ignorant poor farmers who listen to him and go behind not knowing that they are trying to putting up a dead dog.

He adds that the current Panchayat President (Mr. Anandan) was the first one to buy a car (Tata Sumo) in the village. He has taken a bank loan for it with the new found hope in the new business he has ventured now. Prakash already knew how to drive a car, which he learnt like how one learns to ride a cycle little by little stealthily. The President later helped him get a driving licence. Now, he is a known driver.

Coming back to what he started narrating, he said that finally he got some Rs. 80,000 from his father out of the money his father got as his share of the 80 cents of land sold, after paying a portion to his paternal uncle. With the Rs. 80,000 in hand, Prakash hopes that with a word of mouth of the Panchayat President he would be able to borrow a bank loan and buy a car to drive as his own for rent. But, then he is afraid if for some reason, he failed to repay the monthly instalment on time, the bank would take away the car. He would lose the car, his Rs. 80,000 money in possession, and whatever status he lives within Oragadam. This does not allow him to go for a bank loan. He keeps the money safe, and his car dream alive, thinking that some day he would revive it and make it a reality, he concludes.

CASE 5.3: SUKUMAR (PAP), ORAGADAM

M. Sukumar (35) lives with his wife and two daughters in Chennankuppam hamlet of Oragadam Panchayat. Sukumar is a school dropout and his wife (Manjula, 30) has studied upto School final. Their two daughters (Monisha, 13 and Sylaja, 9) are studying in the local school. Although Sukumar is a trained electrician, his primary income flew from cultivating 40 cents of land that his father owned.

Sukumar's is a Hindu undivided family. He and his elder brother made a living cultivating paddy in the 80 cents of land that their father owned in Oragadam village. Manjula [Sukumar's wife] works in Nokia Electronics Company[1] near Shri Perumbudur and earns Rs. 2,500 a month. But, Sukumar does not know the nature of job she is engaged at Nokia (or he does not want to reveal to us that she is involved in unskilled manual labour).

Sukumar used to cultivate paddy in 40 cents of land, and his elder brother cultivated 40 cents of land, for which the title deed remained with their father. A local lake was the source of irrigation for his, and many others' land in that area, which is also at stake now. Every year Sukumar used to harvest 20 bags of paddy from his 40 cents of land. He used to retain 10 bags for the family consumption, and sold out 10 bags for managing the year's expenses. Once land acquisition for Oragdam SEZ started, Sukumar—like many other farmers in that area—was under the impression that agricultural land would not be taken. It did not take too long for Sukumar to realise that lands including agricultural lands that gave two harvests a year would also be taken, if required. The then District Collector, Kancheepuram and the DRO-SEZ who came to Oragadam to show lands to the private companies (SEZ-developers), confirmed that agricultural lands would also be taken and that the farmers would be financially compensated. That sent shock waves among the farmers. They started getting organised—informally though—and refused to part with agricultural lands.

Sukumar, of his own volition, joined the group of farmers who raised voice against the land acquisition. The opposition was so strong that around 200 of them sat on a day-long token fasting, with information to the officials, police and to the local press. Sukumar along with 36 others were arrested by the police and put in remand for almost one week. Sukumar and other farmers in the jail felt that the officials would somehow defuse the opposition and, that at any cost, land acquisition would go ahead. The statement from the officials promoting SEZ including the District Collector sounded: 'sell your lands—no matter if it is cultivable or not—but bargain for differential rates, meaning cultivable lands to get a premium price over the barren lands'.

By that time many farmers had made up their minds to sell their lands, provided the government helps negotiate with the company to get good compensation money. Sukumar's father (in whose name the title deed for 80 cents of land was possessed) decided to sell the land to the SEZ developers. Sukumar's and the one his brother ploughed—80 cents both put together—was fixed at Rs. 14,000 a cent. Obviously, Sukumar's father got a cheque for Rs. 11,20,000, an amount he had never imagined in this life. His father assured Sukumar a portion of the money for him to open a petty shop at the Oragadam cross road.

Sukumar who thought his life would go on ploughing and cultivating the land that he would inherit from his father, has totally changed now. He has rediscovered his hope by running a petty shop at the cross road, and to continue to sell his skills as electrician in the locality, as an off-time occupation. Asked: 'What does he think life has to offer for him as a petty shop owner?' He has only a smile in reply. About the future of his two daughters, he is determined to send them to college and help them study as long as they want to.

CASE 5.4: MS. SATHYAVATHI (PAP), ORAGADAM

Sathyavathi (41) and her family members at Oragadam village opine that no amount of protest, outcry, and community action could prevent the government from grabbing our farm lands for setting up SEZ for companies here. All the lands, both cultivable and uncultivable, have been acquired by the government. The only area that has been left with is the portion where the dwelling houses are located, perhaps for two reasons. One is that evicting people from dwelling houses might intensify the community agitation to uncontrollable levels, which the government did not want to face; and secondly, once the factories start letting out effluents and smoke, people might quietly pack up and quit the place without the companies or the government having to evict them.

Mrs. Sathyavathi—a Scheduled Caste woman by community has a family of 6 members including her husband, mother-in-law and the sons whose livelihood depended on 4 acres of paddy cultivation. The family was earning about Rs. 50,000 per yield, and had two crops a year. All the four acres have been acquired by the government. But, a handsome money of Rs. 14 lakh per acre was paid. The family has a mixed feeling, in the sense, when they think of the money they got as compensation, they are happy. When they think that they have lost the land which served as a source of status, livelihood and confidence, the family looks worried. Asked if they would get anything other than the compensation money, like employment to any member of the family in the factories being set up, she responds: '*nothing would be given, not even sweeper's work to us*'.

Mrs. Chandra (62), illiterate woman farmer, Sathyavathi's mother-in-law who intervened the conversation seemed to be a daring character. She narrated that all their efforts against the land acquisition were systematically put off even before it found expression in full form. Things, all the time, moved in favour of the companies only. She found no use talking about a gone case. What she was worried of at the moment was that the District Administration was spreading word that the local middle school (Natesan Government Middle School located in Manivakkam village) would be closed down—the reason the companies require the land where the school is located. She added that there was a mention about it earlier also. But, people were told that a new school would be constructed in another location close by. But, of late, why should the District Administration covertly motivate people to take their children away and admit at Velankanni School in next village. Perhaps, the company that would be located there did not want to bear the cost of constructing a new school. Similarly, a woman sanitary complex is being demolished as well. But there is no talk about constructing a new one anywhere nearby. An understanding government machinery facilitates all these meticulously.

Chandramma, seemingly illiterate, is able to read that it is their indirect strategy to reduce the number of children at this school to be able to say finally that the school was closed down because there was not enough strength to run it as per government norms. Plainly, this is 'state-market collusion', where the community has been left alone. What is visible is our (farm) land—private property resource acquired, or that we are prevented from using the grazing land which we liberally used as a common property resource of the community. What goes unnoticed is the basic infrastructure such as school, sanitary complex, bore well sources, supply channels to water bodies, our temples, and even the cremation ground. She explained that though the villagers contended against the farmland grabbing, demolishing women sanitary complex etc. and raised questions to ensure their rights to the Government, nothing has happened in favour of them. The original plan contained that the entire village, including the dwelling area, would be relocated in another place. But as the villagers protested the Government withdrew and stopped moving further.

Asked about Chandra's opinion about the compensation money collected—a heft amount that the family would not have imagined to see in their life time, she snaps immediately that any amount of currency money can be used up in this consumerist world today. Land was an asset that was a source of livelihood for our family for generations. Agriculture can give hold for generations. But, cash can give hold for current generation for a limited period of time. We knew how to multiply seeds, and how to create a bag of paddy from ten paddy seeds. But, we are not trained in multiplying money, or creating money through money. At the most all that we know is keep it in a bank and use up little by little. The next generation must study, get some employment in the town and forget agriculture. Otherwise, they have no hold to live on this earth. They have nothing to fall back as ancestral property. Finally, she shares her imagination of how Oragadam could have been chosen as SEZ area. They saw from one end of the road at Oragadam, and discovered vast sheet of land barren. But, they did not guess that beyond what is immediately visible to their bare eyes there are several acres of irrigated land being cultivated and that people are dependent on it for years as a source of livelihood. Chandra does not want to blame the government. She is only worried: (i) why is the government not as much after agriculture as it is after setting up of industries; and (ii) that why is the government not bothered about poor people losing their livelihood resources and basic infrastructure in the villages, which the companies want to wash their hands off, leaving it to the government to deal with.

The 'nature' of the thing we have lost (the land) is something that appreciates in value year after year. But, the thing that you (the company or the government) has given in exchange is, by nature, depreciates in value as days go by. When we cultivated our own rice and vegetables, we were not bothered about price rice. Land acquisition has put us in a situation where we have to buy our rice, oil and vegetables from 'the market'. Earlier, we were not worried about price rise. We did not want to know what inflation meant, nor what caused inflation because our land, our farm gave us the food we ate. But, with the money in hand and no farm in possession we have to go to the market to buy rice. As money rolls in hand in plenty and farm products are in short supply, the price of all essential commodities has gone up, whereas your money value is spiralling downwards. Soon we will be left with no money. With neither money nor land in hand, we shall have no source of livelihood.

Land, labour, capital are the main factors of production in rural areas. The entrepreneurial skills to till the land and cultivate is with them inherent. Capital they managed through credit either through institutional agencies or through non-institutional agencies. Now, they have capital (which renders them not to borrow), and labour available with them. But, the most essential of the factors production, i.e. land for tilling is not in their possession. It is only the dwelling habitations that have been left. The way the SEZ units are coming up is such that it is encircling the people's habitation, and so, people are of the opinion that they might have to quit the place selling off the land to companies. The way land acquisition is taking place, it is reversing land reforms and Bhoodan Movement.

CASE 5.5: BHOODAN LAND (PAA)

Villagers of Chennankuppam near Oragadam (about 22 km from Thambaram) said even their five acres of burial ground was taken away for the Nissan Project. Houses, hutments, the village lake, ponds, temples and schools were also in the process of being demolished to pave way for the new companies. Most villagers were Dalits who have nothing other than their lands. Lands gifted by caste Hindus under the Vinoba plan many decades ago were being taken away by the state. Even the 2.5 cents of land given for the Dalits under the *kudimanai* patta category was also taken away for Oragadam SEZ. About 86 families are affected.

SEZ takes over apparently anything, even land donated under the Bhoodan movement. Padmanabhan remembers the day in 1954 when Acharya Vinoba Bhave came to Sriperumbudur. Padmanabhan was in his thirties. He stood in line hopefully, and proudly accepted what was due to him—land to the tiller. He shows a crumbling sepia-coloured paper that certifies his right to the land. Today he is in his eighties. Padmanabhan's pride remains. In his starched white shirt and *dhoti*, he leans on his cane as he looks to the far end of a barren expanse that has just been filled in. A few months ago it was green. It was this land that he had cultivated since 1954. "They told us that was not my land", says Padmanabhan, "This is Bhoodan Board's land, so they said we have not right over it." Today, tall metal girders span the horizon. There is no trace of Padmanabhan left on it. The SEZ has it all.

CASE 5.6: ADHI DRAWIDAR WELFARE LAND

The government had allotted 2.5 acres each for 87 Adhi Drawidar families in the year 1997. Those families did not occupy that land, for want of funds to construct a house. Those 87 families stand high chances of losing the land they got free from the government. They are negotiating with the SEZ developers and the District Collector not to acquire it. The District Collector has assured another place of the same size.

There was a traditional common land in the village called '*thatchan maniyam*'. It was meant for poor artisans such as carpenters to set up a hut and work to earn a wage. Around 13 families in Oragadam village lived in such lands, those 13 families have been asked to resettle in a place that the government would allot 2.5 cents of land with a small house to live.

CASE 5.7: IRUNKATTUKOTTAI NEAR SRIPERUMBUDUR—KANCHEEPURAM DISTRICT

The workers of *Hundai* car manufacturing plant near Sriperumbudur had affixed wall posters all over Sriperumbudur town pointing out the maltreatment given to workers by the *Hundai* Administration. Many of the issues in wall poster spoke about the raw deal given to workers. The workers go on strike on rotation basis outside the company's unit at Irunkattukottai near Sriperumbudur, Chennai. The workers point out specific labour hostile policies which include: (i) terminating or suspending employees with no valid reason; (ii) transferring employees to far off places like Mumbai, Kolkata so as to punish them for they spoke labour rights, or dignity of labour; and (iii) employing contract labourers in huge numbers and getting down to massive outsourcing to be able to economize on the workers who would have to be made permanent.

At the outset, it has all started when the workers assembled for *Bijoya Dasami Pooja*—a Hindu festival, when the workers worship all the work-tools keeping them in front of the god. The works manager at *Hundai,* in Irunkattukottai has insulted the workers for assembling in one place, and has thrown the photo of a goddess they had kept for worshipping. It strongly hurt the sentiments of the workers. Any works related circular, thereafter, started getting interpretation by workers with a negative tone. The workers started giving interpretation to whatever the management said or did. The management started viewing the workers with hostility. Meanwhile, the workers were disenchanted that none of their problems could be solved through the Works Committee (from among the workers) which the company had formed. So, they made move to form trade unions under the Indian Trade Union Act holding hand with the AITUC—a national level trade union connected to the Communist Party of India. Some workers who were instrumental in assembling the workers for union activities were transferred to *Hundai's* units at Mumbai and Kolkata.

The workers sitting outside the *Hundai* unit has become almost an annual occurrence now. Some workers remain suspended, some terminated. Those terminated get active in trade union activities, and because those inside the company also have grievances they join hands with the trade unions and continue their work as well as fight against the *Hundai* Management. The view of *Hundai* Management is that it is the discretion of Management to decide on the number of employees, and to make or outsource and so on. Moreover, employees working in a SEZ unit are not allowed to form Trade Unions as per the SEZ Act, Rules and Policy of Government of India. Workers problems go on.

Set up business in a place where there is huge economic benefits like the SEZs which are duty free/tax free zones. Buy raw materials from where they are available at the cheapest price; bring labourers for employment from places where they are available for the lowest wages. Mobilize capital from cheapest sources. Sell in places where the products sell at highest profit. There should be 'no problem' of land, workers, capital, effluents, environmental laws, or whatever that is existing they are not put to use.

CASE 5.8: MATHUR PANCHAYAT—THIRUVANNAMALAI DISTRICT

Will Cheyyar be Tamil Nadu's Nandigram? Government puts 10 villages on notice over land acquisition; eight of them oppose SEZ move. This piece of news appeared in *The New Indian Express* in October 2008, regarding a Gram Sabha resolution passed against land acquisition in eight Village Panchayats near Cheyyar about 15 km from Kancheepuram.

Eight Village Panchayats near Cheyyar in Thiruannamalai District passed resolutions at their Gram Sabha meeting on Gandhi Jayanthi day (October 2, 2008) against the government's move to acquire 2,200 acres for the expansion of the Cheyyar Special Economic Zone (SEZ) indicated that trouble was indeed brewing. The eight Village Panchayats were: 1. Mathur, 2. Karanai, 3. Mahajanampakkam, 4. Malkaal, 5. Cholavaram, 6. Ukkamperumpakkam, 7. Azhinchilpattu, 8. Kunnavakkam. Those eight Panchayats together passed a Gram Sabha resolution that no land would be given for SEZ got flashed in the newspapers. Dr. Ramdoss, who read the news items visited the village on the 31st October, 2008, and has enquired the goings on. He told the press who gathered that if the local people were willing, let the land acquisition go ahead, but people should not be forced to part with land.

These villagers have expressed their objections orally and in writing to the District Collector when they were called for a meeting (on September 4, 2008). Of the 2,200 acres the government intends to acquire, most of it is agricultural land that was under one crop cultivation. Besides that, there were ponds, tree crops, water ways and so on.

In 1997, SIPCOT acquired 650 acres of land in Cheyyar area, especially in Mathur for its industrial estate. The Lotus Footwear manufacturing company located its production facilities in a sprawling factory built on 275 acres—manufacturing Nike brand sports shoes. In order to expand the SEZ, the government decided to acquire more land measuring 2,200 acres. The notice served to individual land holders about land acquisition for SEZ, and a letter from the District Administration directing the concerned Village Panchayats to send a Gram Sabha resolution passed for No Objection from the community side erupted problems. The Panchayat headmen had been asked to send (to the District Administration) a Gram Sabha resolution stating that the Panchayats have no objection in parting with the common lands (including common resources such as water ways, ponds etc.). Simultaneously notices have been served to individual land owners as well. All the Panchayat functionaries joined together and decided that they would influence the Gram Sabha to raise objection against land acquisition for SEZ.

The nature of land as stated by the Panchayat President and as confirmed by the local people is:

- 10 per cent barren land,

- 30 per cent Tree crops,
- 40 per cent Single-crop, and
- 20 per cent Government/Panchayat land.

One of the issues that earned the wrath of the villagers (from Mathur) was that they have given 100 acres of land to SIPCOT in 1997. But hardly anybody from the locality was employed. The Movement has pressurised the companies to employ local people also. Their argument was that if (approximately) 100 acres that they parted with remained with them, it would employ at least 200 persons at the rate of 2 persons per acre. But, the companies are recruiting staff, and workers from all over the State and beyond, but hardly anybody from the locality is employed. Since then the company has employed at least about 120 youth from the locality. The number of people employed in Mathur keeps mounting (crossing more than 500) due to the pressures the local Village Panchayat functionaries exert on the companies, under the banner Anti-SEZ Movement.

Another contention of the Panchayat functionaries is that a land remains a single-crop land because it does not have irrigation facilities. But, if the government assisted to dig bore wells and pump water, it has the potential to become two-crop or three-crop land. That a land is single crop land cannot be a pretext for giving it to private companies. It only depicts the industries and service sectors getting the priority of the government, and agriculture and agriculturists being neglected.

When the land acquisition was about to commence, people have had the practice of buying and selling land in the locality of Mathur as usual. The Sub Registrar (for Land Registration) and had issued a notice stopping buying and selling of lands in the notified area. The farmers of the concerned villages have made a protest against the Sub Registrar's Office (shouting slogans) that refusing the registration of land is illegal, and it is baseless because as all of them have proper documents and that they have the discretion to sell their land to anybody they like to. The matter has been flashed in the media. It has gone to the notice of the Registrar, who immediately vacated it. Lands are being bought and sold freely at the moment.

The DRO, Thiruvannamalai through the BDO has sent a letter to the Panchayat Presidents stating that the Panchayats should send a resolution passed stating that they have no objection from the government taking over local ponds, water ways, *porambokku* lands, etc. for a public cause. It has created all the trouble, when people started questioning 'what is meant by a public purpose'. The Presidents have been pressurised to pass such a resolution. This is enough evidence to put across working of grassroots level democracy under the control of the BDO—the market through the government machinery demanding a resolution passed and sending a draft as to how they want it. It totally undermines the autonomy of the local democratic institution. It has happened in some of the States of India (Maharashtra) that public willingness voting should be conducted for buying land from an area, or setting up of SEZs. People of the ten village Panchayats in Cheyyar area (Thiruvannamalai) also demand such voting be conducted. However, the market won over democracy, and the lands including the common lands have been acquired for the purpose of SEZ. Finally, all that the Village Panchayat could save because of the struggle was a local pond (*Kaveripakkam* tank of about 4 acres water spread area). They got employment for the youth in that area.

Out of the 275 acres taken in this area so far, about 100 acres belong to Mathur Panchayat. Out of these 100 acres about 72 acres belong to private people. The remaining 28 acres belong to Panchayat. The Panchayat after a struggle with the officers in-charge of land acquisition could save 4 acres of pond area, but the remaining 24 acres went into the hands of the company setting up unit. The government takes away all kinds of *porompokku* land for handing it over to the companies. When private lands are taken assessment is made, and compensation is paid. When common lands are taken they are taken lightly. The Panchayats are not paid any compensation for they maintained those common assets so long. These lands that are in possession of the VPs are taken back. What are the VPs given? Why not a portion of the sale proceeds of Panchayat *porompokku* given to VPs is a question of the Panchayat functionaries? The VPs are expected to give resolution—NOC. The government can consider to give a compensation to the respective Panchayats for local area development.

650 acres was the total land taken in this area. Lotus was given 275 acres. Forts India—conveyer belt company, Takata American automobile company, Loyats Installations—roofing sheet manufacturing company, Ashok Leyland. Loyats have started manufacturing. Forts (15 acres) and Ashok Leyland—are in construction stages. Takata (225 acres) only the name board is there, neither work, nor construction started. Ashok Leyland, Nokia joint venture construction are also coming up. Although people are happy about several companies coming up. Their concern is how does it help them. Their concern is it would stripe them off their lands and marginalise them instead of involving them in the plan for development of those who parted with land. The very fact that no public hearing was made, and that notices are served on

the decisions taken about land acquisition sent to them hurts the local people. The directive asking the Village Panchayat to pass a Gram Sabha resolution stating that the Panchayat has no objection in offering the common lands hurts them. At the initiative of President of Mathur Panchayat (Mr. Thamiliniyan), these Panchayats demanded employment for local youth in the units set up within SEZ area. The officials in the SEZ Units witnessed the power of Panchayats in transacting the deal, and so they provide employment to local youth as well.

The Hindu (2nd November, 2008) reports that as many as 1,112 persons belonging to villages in and around the Cheyyar Special Economic Zone (SEZ) in Thiruvannamalai district have been recruited by companies that have established their units there. This news was also confirmed as a fact by this research team. Mr. Thamiliniyan, Village Panchayat President of Mathur near Cheyyar confirms that it was true. He added that it was because of the struggle the local people waged against setting up of units without providing employment to local people. The recent development with regard to recruitment is encouraging. They consider local job applications also. This was verified in the field and got confirmed is especially in Mathur and other Panchayats in the vicinity.

Case 5.9: Kanniyappan and Family—Mathur

Kanniyappan (47) lived as a farmer cultivating groundnuts, and pulses in his 2 acres of farm land that he owned in Mathur, along with his family of five in his own house. Five of his brothers also lived there in small hutments. Now, he is one of the victims of land acquisition that the government machinery carried out for setting up SEZ in Mathur Panchayat near Cheyyar in Thiruvannamalai Distict. Kanniyappan lives in a rented house, and earns his living doing odd jobs including agricultural labour. His brothers' families have all gone scattered living in rented houses in various places in the vicinity.

It was late on a Friday evening (a day before Pongal) in 2007 Kanniyappan was asked to vacate his house and quit the 2 acres of land he used to plough along with his brothers. The notice was served in 1997 itself, he was told. The compensation money to be given was Rs. 32,500 per acre which now remains in the court. He is fighting a losing battle. He has filed a case in the court. The only hope is if the provisions of the Rehabilitation and Resettlement Policy, 2007 would be put to use in order to help him, which is very much unlikely from the way he narrates the turns the case is taking. Kanniyappan changed lawyer for he found his own lawyer was trying to convince him to withdraw the case, and accept whatever compensation amount the company had handed over to the Cheyyar court.

When eviction was being carried out by the officials of the government, he laid down in front of the bulldozer refusing to allow it move. His brother seems to have taken a sabre in anger not knowing how to prevent the huts being pulled down. Kanniyappan, his brother and the entire family was to be arrested. The officials responded that they are executing an order, and so whatever fight he wants to put up he could do it only through court. Then, upon request only Kanniyappan and his two brothers (Dharman and Markabandhu) were taken to police custody, and then to Vellore prison at about 2.00 am the next day. Saturday and Sunday the brothers had to be behind the bars. On Monday, when they were produced in the court, they were taken for 15 days judicial custody. Meanwhile, his family through some local lawyer appealed for release on bail. As the cases filed were preventing government officials carrying out their duty, and attempted murder it was not possible to get bail. Then after five days on a cash deposit of Rs. 10,000 for each, they were released on a conditional bail that they should sign at Dusi Police Station daily.

The Manager of the Lotus Company seems to have said that he felt ashamed to walk in the court premises. Kanniyappan has retorted that he (and his brothers) were in jail, and has been loitering in the court premises having lost their land, and houses, all because of the company. Otherwise, he had no business to be around in any court or police station

It was then (on the 5th day) Kanniyappan filed a court case against the Lotus Footwear Company on land acquisition and forced displacement. There is hearing called for, and adjoined. His time is wasted. His money is wasted. He has borrowed almost 1.5 lakh from the local pawn brokers pledging all the jewels in the family's possession. The family that was walking on farm field, is loitering in court premises. A lawyer on behalf of Lotus Footwear Company is attending the hearing. But, every time hearing is called for Kanniyappan has to go, foregoing his daily wage. From being a farmer he has become a wage earner, and lives in a rented house. His family pays Rs. 700 monthly rent. It is said he can accept from the RDO through the court Rs. 79,938 for the two acres the family lost to SEZ. Otherwise, keep fighting this losing battle pledging whatever jewels they have. His brother who was running a fruit stall has been pull down as well. The education of the children is affected. Family peace is lost.

All that he demands now are: (i) a reasonable compensation for the land at prevailing market rates; (ii) resettlement in terms of dwelling house; and (iii) education of his children.

CASE 5.10: DHARMAN—MANGAL KOOTTU ROAD

Dharman (61) had two acres of land in Mangal Koottu Road in Mathur, where Lotus Footwear Company has set up its manufacturing unit. His two acres of land got levelled along with the lot purchased from others for developing SEZ, Cheyyar. Dharman's is a six-member family, with two sons, three daughters plus his wife. Dharman and his wife were agricultural wage earners. Dharman often went to Chennai to do odd kind of works and saved some money with a dream of owning a piece of cultivable land. Dharman has worked for nearly twenty years (since 1965 until 1985) in Chennai as a manual labourer in various odd kinds of works. With this hard earned money he put ten pawn jewels that his wife owned, and purchased two acres of land at Mangal Koottu road, which now he has lost for SEZ. Dharman and his wife felt proud when they purchased two acres of land, that it would give them the source of livelihood, and their sons can inherit this land as a permanent asset. The happiness did not last. The notice of land acquisition came in less than ten years time 1996. He had to work for 20 years to own 2 acres of land, and in less than 10 years since he started cultivating it, he had to lose it for SEZ.

His possession of land and the income from it had given him the impetus to go in for a bank loan for house construction. He raised Rs. 80,000 from the Cooperative Housing Society, Cheyyar and constructed a house in another piece of land he had at Mathur main village. As land got into land acquisition area, he could not repay the loan. The loan amount became almost Rs. 2.91 lakh as on 1.12.2003 and the Housing Society started serving notice for attachment of property. He requested SEZ developer to settle the house loan to the Housing Society, so that at least he could be relieved of the loan, though the land slips away from his hands. It did not materialise despite court orders.

Then, he settled the entire housing loan raising private loan, with the hope that he would be able to settle the private loan from the compensation amount he would get for his land from the SEZ developer. But, he felt a bomb shell exploded when he came to know that his compensation amount was only Rs. 70,338 and that it has been deposited in SBI, Cheyyar in his name. With all the relevant papers, Dharman is loitering in the Cheyyar court premises almost daily.

CASE 5.11: S. MARGABANDU—MANGAL KOOTTU ROAD

S. Margabandu (47) lived in Mangal Koottu Road in Mathur. He had constructed a small house (350 sq.ft) in his own land, where he lived with his wife and two daughters. The daughters are doing school final, and higher secondary level of education. His two acres of land along with a hut the family was living in, got acquired for SEZ Cheyyar. He was allotted a piece of land for constructing a house. When he got down to put up a hut there, another local person raised objection. Margabandu realised that the land allotted to Margabandu was under encroachment. Since then he keeps sending petitions to various offices such the SIPCOT, District Collector etc., including the Chief Minister's Cell. He has filed a court case also. Nothing seems to work. He is living in a rented house paying Rs. 500 every month. He is a tailor, and earns just enough to meet the family expenditures and the education of his daughters. He is worried about the expenditures he is incurring on court case. He is fighting with the hope that some concerned government officials would do him some good, and that he would get his piece of land for constructing a house.

CASE 5.12: PERAMBALUR DISTRICT

Perambalur is one of the districts in Tamil Nadu where land acquisition for setting up of Special Economic Zone has been completed very recently. Contrary to the stories of land grabbing and bureaucratic compulsion that reeled off about land acquisition in many other districts of Tamil Nadu, people in Perambalur had altogether a different story to narrate, when this research team landed there. The entire process of land acquisition was smooth, and the local community had no discontentment—not even a speck of disapproval, about having lost the land. In fact, the community expressed that if land identification and acquisition were done in the manner it was done in Perambalur, it would be completely hassle-free, and industrialisation process can take place with complete support of the local people. How was this possible? What was different about Perambalur?

Perambalur is on the National Highway (45) of Trichy-Chennai. The land acquired belonged to four Village Panchayats, viz. Thirumandurai, Penakonam, Erayur, and Ayanperayur in two Blocks of Perambalur District. Nearly 3,500 acres have been acquired for SEZ purpose from around 2,800 farming families. These lands have been identified as falling in really dry or arid zone. The only thing that the land owners were getting from those lands was title as 'landowner'. Otherwise they had hardly a little in terms of crop or leasehold income. Most of them were barren or lands meant for rain-fed crops. The land was not fertile, nor was there any lake or irrigation facility. Striking at ground water through boreholes would not be a viable proposition in the opinion of the land owners. Hence, land was not giving them the prime hope of life. They had other means of livelihood such as animal husbandry, wage employment in the stone quarries close by, and so on. This is reason number one, how the officials and the GVK Infratech Private Limited—the SEZ infrastructure developer in Perambalur have been able to convince the community for Rs. 3 lakh per acre.

The other attractions to the community have been the assurance given about employment for one person in each family; and one house plot, measuring 2400 sq. ft. for each farmer who has parted with less than 2 acres, and 2 to 3 such house plots for those who parted with more lands. These have been given in writing to the community. Another good thing that has happened with regard to providing employment is that job will be offered depending upon qualification, and if a given number of youth do not have the required skills, they would be provided relevant training and then be absorbed.

There has been a special committee formed for the purpose of land acquisition, with District Collector as Chairperson. The other members in the committee included relevant Panchayat Presidents, Panchayat Councillors, PO-DRDA, District Revenue Officer, VAO of relevant villages, and farmers' representatives. This committee has held three rounds of meeting with the land owners where the district collector explained about the benefits of setting up SEZ, and sought to know the compensation amount the demand. Besides this, the Panchayat Presidents have also had separate sitting with each land owner and convinced. The community has started demanding upto Rs. 10 lakh per acre, and then after discussions and negotiations, they have settled at Rs. 3 lakh per acre. After almost everyone accepted, land transfer and registration has taken place in batches at Valikandapuram Sub-Registrar's Office.

All said and done, six of the land owners have opposed upright that they would not part with the land. They have demanded higher compensation. Being big land owners, they have raised severe objections, and have stated that they would rather file a court case, if they were forced to part with land. Taking cognizance of their minds, the GVK group has heeded to pay Rs. 6 lakh per acre to those six big farmers for finalising the land deal. All the six of them have got Rs. 6 lakh per acre. By that time, all the others' lands had been already handed over to GVK. Despite the majority who gave land came to know about six others being paid higher compensation, they were perplexed if they would be able to raise an objection, after all the paper work was over and done with. This differential payment—less to those who are easily convinced and double the compensation amount to those who raise objections—is a socially erroneous strategy. To the fortune of the GVK Limited, no political party or local organisations pitched in to create a hullabaloo.

Now what is on the surface of the mind of the people here is the employment hope. The units might be set up in about a year's time, and the people are looking forward to get jobs—as per the promise of employment for one person per family. They have also been told that only an IT Park would be established there, and so the negative externality such as pollution or smoke would not be there. The compensation money that they got remains largely in the local Indian Overseas Bank, State Bank of India, and PACL Insurance Limited. Some of them have used the money for house repairing; others have invested in gold jewellery.

The case of land acquisition as Perambalur can be taken as a good way of identifying barren land for acquisition, and a good deal for those who parted with lands. The idea of giving house plots inside SEZ, for which SEZ Act provides, and appropriate employment for local people after capacity training could be stated as good aspects of land acquisition for SEZ in Perambalur.

CASE 5.13: VALASAMUDRAM, TUTICORIN DISTRICT, TAMIL NADU

People of Valasamudram in Tuticorin district went on continuous agitation at the Office of the District Collector and resorted to blocking the road requesting the State government to drop its plan of acquiring land for setting up of second SIPCOT (in the lines of SEZ). The village has a total of 1,300 acres of which, the announcement is, that the government wants to acquire 990 acres for the second SIPCOT. When the matter came to light people started showing their discontents.

Valasamudram is one of the two hamlets (the other being Venkatachalapuram) that together make Valasamudram Village Panchayat in Oddapidaram Block of Tuticorin district (Tamil Nadu). Valasamudram has a population of 765. People are involved in rain-fed agriculture. Although agriculture is dependent on seasonal rainfall, the main stay of the people is farming only. They do one crop a year. They cultivate brinjal, chilli, onion, sunflower, millets and black gram. During agriculturally peak seasons labourers from neighbourhood villages (Sidalaikottai, Arasaradi, and Kumarapuram) are also called for agricultural works. Except two, three big land owners who own around 20 acres, all the others have on an average 1.5 to 2 acres only. The number of people employed in industries or service sector in the town is a countable few. Almost everyone in Valasamudram is dependent either on agriculture or on animal husbandry. Given the small number of households here, the number of cattle population is fairly considerable. There are around 40 cows, and 1,200 sheep and goats.

On a sunny afternoon, cars and jeeps painted 'Government of Tamil Nadu' a little above the front windscreen came into the village. Those who got off the vehicle—seemingly government officers—walked talking among themselves towards the land where we had sown black gram and millets. Local people were only staring at them, not knowing the goings on. When the same 'bunch of missionaries' visited the second and the third time, people came to know that they were government officials including the Project Officer SIPCOT, Tahsildar and others from the office of the district collector making a visit to acquire lands for setting up 'second SIPCOT'. SIPCOT is a more familiar expression than SEZ in this area because there is already one SIPCOT in Veerapandiyapuram area near here. On hearing about the intention of the government regarding land acquisition, people developed antipathy. They would not let their land go into the hands of the companies was the general feeling of the community. But there was no official communication—either to the Panchayat Office or to the land owners, regarding the proposed SEZ that 'the community members heard' about.

The Panchayat President wanted to confirm the truth behind the 'hearsay' and so enquired officials known to him at the District Collector's Office. He could get only a hazy picture of the goings on that it is possible; they might take; and that there is a proposal being discussed; and how much land would be taken is not known yet and so on. But, the responsible persons that he thought would be in a position to give him the 'correct information' did not reveal anything significant. As a last resort he made a move on the 26th May, 2008 by putting to use the citizen's weapon: Right to Information Act. He wanted to know the details of land being proposed for acquisition in the jurisdiction of Valasamudram Panchayat. He got a reply on the 5th June, 2008 from the Public Information Officer that there is a proposal to acquire 928.30 acres of land in Valasamudram Panchayat. The people got confirmed information from the Panchayat President.

Since the time people came to know of the land acquisition proposal, they gave out petitions to the District Collector, Political Party leaders at the district and State levels, MPs, and MLAs known to them, Secretaries of Government Departments and so on. There seemed to be no action from any of them. With the support of the locally important people, the Panchayat

President sought the support of all the political parties in their support to shout slogans in front of the Office of the District Collector against the proposed SEZ. They got considerable support from parties like CPI, CPI(M), BJP, DMDK, and the local farmers associations. They staged two demonstrations—one on the 10th June and the other on 16th June, 2008. They resorted to blocking the road between Tuticorin and Madurai on 11th August, 2008. The protests called the district administration to hold discussion with the local people at Valasamudram. The District Collector had asked for three months time to settle the issue and for shifting the location for new SEZ. The matter stands there as of now when this team visited on 20th October, 2008.

The stand of the people is that lands are their prime source of income and employment. They cannot give up agriculture and search for wage employment in the town. Incidentally, there is another related issue that has come up against the district administration to handle simultaneously. That the people who handed over lands for setting up the 'first SIPCOT' in Veerapandiyapuram, Samynatham, and Gayaloorni areas have not got their compensation money fully settled yet. Many of the farmers have filed court cases that the government was delaying payment of compensation for the land they handed over several years ago. And they are also fighting in front of the Office of the District Collector for the remainder money that is due to them. People of Valasamudram is worried that they would also be left high and dry after land acquisition is over to hang around in the government office premises to get the compensation money. Then, they would neither have the land for cultivating nor the compensation money in hand. Although they are not prepared to part with the land in the first place, this factor of delaying payment that happened in the case of first SIPCOT is also a factor that is scaring them.

Secondly, most of the lands acquired for the purpose of SIPCOT-1 is lying there unused. The compensation money has not even been paid to many of the land owners. The government could allot those unused lands to the new companies that want to set up business and offer all the concessions offered to SEZ units. Instead of doing it, acquiring 930 acres anew is uncalled for. It chokes the source of income of the people in Valasamudram. This is the general impression of the local people.

Thirdly, people also suggest alternative location that is really barren and lying unused. They have suggested in their petition to the District Collector that barren lands between Gulppur and Vaipparai villages where thousands of acres of barren lands are lying without putting into any use. The Panchayat

President is of the opinion that farmers who are supposed to till the land, have to be alerted also these days that their lands should be properly fenced and shielded from being grabbed.

CASE 5.14: BAIRAMANGALAM, KRISHNAGIRI DISTRICT, TAMIL NADU

The idea of acquiring lands at Bairamangalam, and Kundumaranapalli villages of Kelamangalam Block, and Anchettipalli and Sanamavu villages of Hosur Block has been put on the back burner after the community manifested its discontents in multiple ways. The community has very strong reasons for not allowing establishment of SEZ in their village, and they have also meticulously built up a strong case to prove to the district administration and to the State government why they are in opposition to part with their lands.

Any outsider who goes into Bairamangalam is viewed with suspicion. No one—neither the farmers at Bairamangalam nor the Village Panchayat functionaries—opens up to talk to you, until they make it doubly sure, who you are. For them any outsider who opens up to talk about the land, or SEZ is either from the GMR—the SEZ developers who came with the land acquisition deal in the first instance, or from the district administration shrewdly trying to get a feel of the mind-set of the farmers.

The Government of Tamil Nadu through the TIDCO has made moves to acquire 3,600 acres of land for setting up of SEZ at Bairamangalam, Kundumaranapalli, Anchettipalli, Sanamavu villages in Krishnagiri district near Hosur. Major portion of the areas mentioned are prime agricultural lands for which the Assistant Director of Agriculture, Krishnagiri has vouched. But it has been mentioned in the announcement letter that it is all dry and barren lands. The announcement sent shock waves across the farming community and farmers took to streets. The farmers have given petition to the District Collector in the Grievance Day Meeting at the Collectorate. The District Collector has held a special meeting with 30 local representatives and Panchayat members from Bairamangalam area with a view to convince them.

The farmers have put across their plea that the lands are prime agricultural lands that produce most of the vegetables sold at Hosur Farmers' Market. There are 2 to 3 loads of vegetables (potato, carrot, cabbage, tomato, beans etc.) sent almost daily to places like Madurai, Coimbatore, Erode, Bavani, and Ernakulam. There are rose flowers cultivated in green houses set up with the financial assistance of the NABARD. There are also long crops like manago, sappota, and coconut with drip irrigation facility. There are 15 irrigation tanks, and 410 irrigation pump sets meant for agricultural purpose.

Reportedly, there are at least 5,000 families of farmers and agricultural labourers dependent upon these lands. It is surprising to come to know that this area has been reported as 'dry and barren' until the Assistant Director of Agriculture, Krishnagiri was requested to make a special survey and report. The Assistant Director's report confirmed that the villages proposed for SEZ have large tracts of fertile agricultural lands. Perhaps, the Department still uses the land records handed over to them by the British Administration, when these lands had not been developed for cultivation.

The resistance meant to the TIDCO and the District Administration that it is a strategy of the farmers to gain a good bargain. They have approached some of the farmers individually who really have lands not in use, or wanting to give up agriculture for there is no one to look after the land in the current generation. They (about 5 to 10 of the farmers) have got into the bargain and have demanded for higher compensation—up to Rs. 25 lakh per acre. The price per acre that started at Rs. 5 lakh by GMR representatives has been gone upto Rs. 8 lakh. Besides this, the District Collector has also got into the bargain to convince the people with employment for one person in the family, and agreed to give one plot per acre of land given to SEZ. But, the people did not give in.

The Village Panchayat wrote to the Central Minister for Agriculture explaining the fertile nature of the area, annexing the survey report of the Assistant Director of Agriculture. Mr. Sarad Pawar, Minister for Agriculture seems to have written to the Mr. Kamal Nath, the Minister for Commerce, who in turn has sent a letter to the State Government, and the District Collector to drop land acquisition in Bairamangalam. The Panchayats along with all the functionaries and community if they can talk in one voice and take appropriate measures, it is able to make the Central Ministries to turn and look up.

CASE 5.15: HOSUR, TAMIL NADU

Hosur has one of the oldest SIPCOTs in the State of Tamil Nadu. Following this, there are SEZs announced in Blocks such as Kelamanagalam extending beyond the vicinity of Hosur town. Those who watch the industrial development and setting up of SEZs in Hosur have many interesting things to share. The first and foremost of them all is, even a hear-say or supposed hunch of setting up of SEZ in Hosur or in any district of Tamil Nadu for that matter cause tremendous inflationary tendency on land prices. Real estate business comes with a bang in that area.

The state of land in Hosur town and in the vicinity after the establishment of SIPCOT, and announcement of SEZs can be explained thus: (a) the first circle of land were acquired by SIPCOT (Phase 1 and Phase 2) for its industrial units; (b) the second loop of land (outside the first circle) went into the hands of real estate business people; and (c) the third loop, beyond the first and the second circles, were purchased mostly by Non-Resident Indians (NRIs) or hefty moneyed people who build small farm houses and keep it fenced for purpose best known to them. Ultimately, there is no land in the possession of the aboriginal people who originally belonged to this place. They have been systematically evicted in a phased manner virtually to the margins. They are struggling to find an identity for them.

The Electronic City (Bangalore) begins at hardly 18 km from Hosur. After the establishment of Electronic City (SEZ) at Bangalore, the land price, the house and room rent, and general cost of living at Bangalore are much higher compared to what it is at Hosur. The normal tendency is to rent a house in Hosur and commute to Electronic City for work. This brings new in-flow of population into Hosur. Another factor is buying a land or flat in Bangalore or getting it officially registered is almost a Herculean task. Moreover, in many of the areas in Bangalore construction of new houses has been prohibited. The immediate alternative for such people is to buy a land/house in or near Hosur. This spillover of population and demand for housing and other facilities has caused further escalation of the land/flat prices at Hosur. Besides other things, one of the environmental fallout is that Ramanayakkan lake at Hosur town that had a water holding area of 22 acres has been encroached from all the four sides, and hardly 10 acres remain at the moment.

This is about land grabbing and marginalization. But, what happened to the units that set up business in the SIPCOT area. The fact is except a countable few like the TVS, Titan, Ashok Leyland, and a few others, hundreds of smaller units and ancillary industries set up have all withdrawn from the SIPCOT area stating reasons including recurrent loss, labour problems, unit runs sick or not being able to adhere to the ISO standards and so on. There are units that have merely abandoned everything and vanished in thin air (e.g. Uma Maheswari Textiles, ELCOT, Alif, Tafco, Allied Foundries, Asian Bearings Limited, Kothari Electronics, Orient Vision, Tools International etc.) The banks that lent money to such units have appointed security guards at the gate of such units not knowing how to recover the money lent to them. There is also this clever strategy of units shifting to new SEZs when the concession period nears the finishing point that you have to start paying all your duties/

taxes if you continue to run your unit there. So, systematically show that the unit is sick and wind up, then start with a modified name in a new SEZ (e.g. English Electricals, Indo-Swiss Jewellers, have shifted to Bangalore's Electronic City). This goes into the question of employment generation the SIPCOT/SEZ units cause, and the condition of the employees, and their families. Some of the units (e.g. Lakshmi Mills) gave VRS and reduced the workers. Lakshmi Mills Foundry shuttered down.

One thing is that many of the employees especially at foreman and supervisory levels recruited are from States like Bihar, Orissa, Andhra Pradesh, Chhattisgarh and so on. They come through some manpower agency or labour contractors. They are ready to work for more than 8 hours for Rs. 80 to Rs. 100 a day. As they are only contract labourers there is no need for payment of any social security measures, including accident benefits. They are often relieved of work after 179 days, and are recruited as new employee after one or two days gap so that they are not covered by any of the labour laws. There are several names given to them—contract labourer, temporary worker, apprentice, house-keeping people, and so on.

The workers, who raise voice for getting social security benefits or higher wages, would be transferred to units in Perundurai or elsewhere, which deter workers from questioning, and be contented with what is offered. The constant call for new recruits/employees in SIPCOT area does not mean new jobs are created. It only means that the same workers would be recruited again with a break in service or it is the time to lay off workers who question and to recruit new ones instead.

There was a fire accident at Micro Labs (a medicine manufacturing unit in 1996), Hosur. There was no confirmed report of the number of people who died in that accident. This is because many of the workers were from States like Bihar, Maharashtra etc.—nobody insisted on enquiry or details. Perhaps, the victims' parents or family thought this person forgot the family and settled down in Hosur. But, the reality could be the person died in an accident and nobody informed about it to the family at Bihar or Chhattisgarh, reports Mr. Adavan Deetchanya, Editor of *Puduvisai*. He adds that it is not only in Tamil Nadu we get workers from States like Bihar, workers from Tamil Nadu also migrate and work in the stone quarries of Bangalore, Vijayawada etc. in conditions no better than this. When people are away from their native place, and when travelling to native place involves money earned for several days, the tendency would be not to go home frequently. This is a strategy adopted by owners to make workers concentrate only on work.

Another thing that happens to young girls is, some of the spinning mills (e.g. Premier Mills, Baghanur) and garment units in Hosur have a scheme called *Sumangali thittam*. There are labour contractors involved specially in this kind of recruitment. They travel into the remote villages in the backward district of Tamil Nadu like Thiruvannamalai, Pudukottai, Dindigul etc. and bring young girls for employment with the consent of the parents. The arrangement is that these girls in groups have to reside in a house given by the spinning mill owner and work for three years. Of course, they are allowed to go home on Diwali and Pongal days. The food and clothing for three years would be taken care of by the owner. At the end of the third year, the girl would become eligible to get a lump sum amount (Rs. 30,000-Rs. 35,000) towards her marriage. There are also employers, who at the maturity of the third year, give bad name to girls and terminate them from work, so that they do not have to pay the terminal benefit promised (lump sum) that they would be given at the end of 'successful completion' of three years period.

It is evident that making the landholders as landless labourers is taking place, further marginalization of those who were dependent on agriculture is witnessed also. The employment promise is not long lasting. The circumstances are such that those who are disenchanted with the non-remunerative nature of agriculture are selling off their lands, and they find no incentive to continue pursuing agriculture. Those who still find agriculture remunerative fight back that they would not part with land. Although pursuing agriculture gives them dignity and status as land owner, they find selling farm land for real estate purpose, or for industrial purpose gives them the money they were, perhaps, longing to find. But, with money in hand and no land in possession, they understand as well that their future is at stake and the next generation would curse them for what they are doing today.

III. ANALYSIS AND DISCUSSION

Tamil Nadu is one of the frontline States in establishing Special Economic Zones (SEZ) in the country. The State Government of Tamil Nadu reports that so far 32 SEZs have been approved in the State, many of them in the northern districts of Tamil Nadu that lie close to Chennai which is the State capital. There are many industrial corridors, and industrial parks being announced under SEZ in the southern districts of Tamil Nadu as well where industrial development is relatively slow compared to northern districts such as Thiruvannamalai, Kancheepuram, and Thiruvallur. Taking cues from the Central Government's policy note on SEZ, the State Government of Tamil

Nadu provides plenty of concessions and facilities to those who establish units at SEZ areas. The Industrial Policy of Government of Tamil Nadu has also been revised in 2007 to be in favour of industrial development providing concessions, loans, and subsidy to those who commence units at SEZs.

The SEZ area is otherwise known duty-free enclave for investors. The units in SEZs are 100 per cent exempt from corporate income tax for the first five years; 50 per cent exempt for the next five years and, for the final five years, 50 per cent of the profits ploughed back is exempted from tax. It has been revised again that the tax exemptions would be applicable for 15 years. Besides this, there are other things like simplified procedures for development, operation and maintenance of SEZs, and single window clearance for setting up of an SEZ or for setting up a unit in the SEZ, plus self-certification in documentation. Similarly, there are also imperative that only barren land be acquired, and single-crop land be taken if needed, and acquisition of double-crop land should be limited to 10 per cent of the total land required.

Box 5.2: Quality Infrastructure and Attractive Fiscal Package

The SEZs are virtually deemed to be a foreign territory within the country free from all the rules and regulations governing the import and export (www.sezindia.nic.in). The SEZs are specifically treated as duty free enclaves for the purpose of industrial, tariff, service and trade operations with exemption from customs duties and a more liberal regime on levies, foreign investment and other transactions. The domestic regulations, restrictions and infrastructure inadequacies such as road transport, rail transport, air service, power, water etc. are sought to be removed for creating an investor and industry friendly environment. In a nutshell, SEZs are supported by quality infrastructure, attractive fiscal package, both at the Central and the State levels, with minimum possible regulations.

Source: www.sezindia.nic.in

Three important considerations of the State in trying to attract large-scale private investment to commence manufacturing and service industries, as put across by officials involved in promoting SEZ are: First, employment generation through additional economic activities for which the State does not have to find funds; secondly, the State would be able to report growth of industrial and service sectors for which the investment required from the State is only policy facilitation; and thirdly, politically, there would be widespread activities taking place in terms of production, employment, consumption, export and so on for which the government can take credit. Establishment of industries and service sector units can generate large scale employment. It also has high potentials to contribute towards State/national income. In brief, the view of the State government is that SEZs bring dividends to the State in terms of economic and industrial development and generation of new employment opportunities.

A recent report of the Government of Tamil Nadu states that SEZs in Tamil Nadu has brought in Rs. 2462.4 crore as investments and 29,195 direct employment in the State during 2007-08 alone. Special Economic Zones bring up several contentious issues of serious nature. It includes land acquisition, loss of agriculture and local employment, issues of resettlement and rehabilitation, employment generation in the SEZ units, employment conditions, issues of grassroots level democracy, and so on. This report is built upon a series of field visits and direct observations made to find out if development of SEZ affects the private property resources of the poor, and common property resources of the community. The role of the State, the proportion of the companies that set up business (i.e. the market) has assumed, and the position of the local community.

Two main oft-repeated benefits uttered about SEZ are: it generates large scale employment, and augments the income of the State. This statement also needs to be analysed in this context. This report does not deny the additional employment the SEZs have generated. It only views the benefit accrued in terms of employment and the cost incurred to bring about this benefit. This is discussed besides other vital issues already mentioned such as land acquisition, compensation, support to agriculture, and resettlement and rehabilitation. The place of grassroots level democracy, private and common property resources in a context SEZ is emerging fast need to be observed and reported closely, which this study has done. The analyses that emerge below are from the case studies conducted across districts in Tamil Nadu—of villages and people affected by SEZ development.

1. LAND ACQUISITION

Land is an important factor of production. So far as rural Tamil Nadu is concerned it is land that provides livelihood to majority, and it is the size and nature of land one possesses that determines the status of a family in the society. It is closely associated with the power one assumes or ascribes in common forums. One of the main users of land in India especially as a livelihood asset is the farming sector—reportedly about 54 per cent. It remains mostly for agricultural purposes with private farmers. There are also considerable amount of common land in possession of the Village Panchayats. The common land of the Village Panchayats mainly includes *porombokku* lands of various types, water bodies, and paths. Some Village Panchayats maintain common land with proper demarcations, and there are Panchayats that use ponds for fish cultivation and common land for raising tree crops. By and large, excepting the agricultural sector, other sectors, viz. industry and service did not claim any significant portion of land for their use. Of late, the SEZs have come about to acquire several hectares of land—not less than 1000 hectares—in one enclave contiguously.

The social benefits of SEZ, as alleged by the Government of India (www.sezindia.nic.in), are:

- Land that cannot be used for agricultural purposes could be made use of for setting up of industries, and for building infrastructure that would render services of economic value.
- Additional economic activity shall help generate more (private sector) employment and income earning capacity of individuals and families.
- Enhanced purchasing power shall push many people above poverty line. The overall poverty levels shall significantly come down over the years, with the enhanced participation of the private sector.

Therefore, the first concern is of *land acquisition*. This is not only for SEZs, but also for other things such as power plants, airports, highways, dams and housing projects. As India is in the development mode, more and more instances of this will happen in the future. So, the time is already overdue that we rethink the land acquisition laws and policies currently operating in the country. Unfortunately, we are still operating under the legal shadow of the colonial-era, namely, the Land Acquisition Act of 1894. Under this Act any public body can acquire a person's property and it can unilaterally decide the compensation to be paid and can simply override any objection from the owner. A key solution, therefore, would be overhauling the Land Acquisition Act which is out of step with modern day requirements as well as protecting the individual's property rights. Can we still be in the colonial mindset that gives no weight to the welfare of the poor?

The Question of Economic Efficiency: This often results in competing claims between sectors, especially because SEZ lays hand both in private lands (including agricultural lands), and common land of the Panchayats. This brings into question the superiority of one sector over the other, or evidently the dominance of industry over agriculture. That the government gets down negotiating deals with land owners on behalf of the Zone Developer exposes the government's preference for industry over agriculture. The situation with regard to agriculture in India is 52 per cent of the workforce engaged in agriculture using 54 per cent of the land area contributes to 16 per cent of the GDP. The remaining 48 per cent of the workforce in the industry and service sectors contribute to 84 per cent of the GDP, where the share of service sector alone is 55 per cent. This is spoken as deficiency or inefficiency of the agricultural sector. Sure enough, industries are important.

Economic efficiency questions sound fine, when national level figures are statistically analysed using a computer system. But, listening to the voices of the poor engaged in agriculture through participatory studies carried out at the micro level, interacting face to face with farmers is something entirely different. What immediately comes to mind is economic efficiency cannot be set as the only criterion in determining if a sector deserves to own such a big land area. And does it require grabbing cultivable land and handing it over to the Corporate Houses, who make tall claims about corporate social responsibility? Can not they or the government find barren land elsewhere for industries? Or can not the government take SEZs as an opportunity to bring to use the barren land that remains unreached so far? Why lay hand on cultivated land? Moreover, whether the Sovereign Socialist Democratic Republic of India should do it and hurt the poor by grabbing the only livelihood asset in their possession. They know nothing else than farming, after all. Can not we find barren land that is unobjectionable?

Cultivable Lands Taken: Oragadam is located hardly 45 km away from Chennai city on a four-roads-junction, and also the road expansion works are going on. This is perhaps, the main reason for the SEZ developers laying eyes on acquiring the major portion of lands from Orgadam Panchayat. But, Oragadam and the adjacent hamlet, viz. Chennankuppam that which together make the Oragadam Panchayat are agriculturally predominant villages. But for a small portion of barren land that was being used as pasture land for the cattle population, the remaining lands were cultivated once a year and some twice a year. The policy of the government safely reads that 'as far as possible' only barren land should be acquired for SEZ purpose. That is mainly waste and barren land, and if necessary single crop agricultural lands alone should be acquired for the SEZs. If perforce, a portion of double cropped agricultural land has to be acquired to meet the minimum area requirements, the same should not exceed 10 per cent of the total land required for the SEZs.

In reality, one apprehension expressed since the start of the SEZs which has been witnessed in reality is that cultivable lands are also taken in order to get a contiguous area delineated for the zone (SEZ). In Oragadam village near Chennai out of the 950 acres acquired so far, at least 300 acres of cultivable lands that used to give two crops a year have been acquired. This holds good for Bairamangalam near Hosur in Krishnagiri District also. But, at Bairamanagalam the farmers' vehement opposition to part with the cultivable lands (about 220 acres) has made the authorities and a private SEZ developer (company) to hang up land acquisition. At Valasamudram in Tuticorin district the Panchayat has used RTI Act to get information on the number of acres to be acquired for SEZ.

Undo the Land Ceiling and Bhoodan Efforts: The efforts made through land reform measures, Land Ceiling Act, Bhoodan movement etc. obviously, were attempts to make sure that even a poor household should hold at least one or two acres of land for farming, which would be a source of livelihood and confidence. Ironically, SEZ is undoing the efforts made through Land Ceiling Act and Bhoodan movement. Lands gifted by caste Hindus under the Vinoba plan many decades ago were being taken away by the State. Even the 2.5 cents of land given for the Dalits under the *kudimanai patta* category was also taken away for Oragadam SEZ. About 86 families are affected. It is acquiring small pieces of land from the poor to be consolidated for the need of big industrialists. The farmer who knew nothing else than farming, is thrown out of his village snatching from him his only livelihood asset—the land at terms determined by the State.

SEZ takes over apparently anything, even land donated under the Bhoodan movement, says a resident of Chennankuppam hamlet in Oragadam. Similarly, Padmanabhan remembers the day in 1954 when Acharya Vinoba Bhave came to Sriperumbudur. Padmanabhan was in his thirties. He stood in line hopefully, and proudly accepted what was due to him—land to the tiller. He shows a crumbling sepia-coloured paper that certifies his right to the land. Today he is in his eighties. Padmanabhan's pride remains. In his starched white shirt and *dhoti*, he leans on his cane as he looks to the far end of a barren expanse that has just been filled in. A few months ago it was green. It was this land that he had cultivated since 1954. "They told us that was not my land", says Padmanabhan, "This is Bhoodan Board's land, so they said we have not right over it." Today, tall metal girders span the horizon. There is no trace of Padmanabhan left on it. The SEZ has it all.

Thus, SEZ grabs land from the poor, and the voiceless and evicts them to urban areas in search of wage employment, or further marginalise and distance them from accessing the benefits of growth. A farmer who owns one or two acres of land with pump set for irrigation has some kind of confidence that he would be able to maintain a family hunger-free. But, lands that came under *thatchan maniyam* (a place provided for traditional artisans by local community in olden days) has been acquired. For those who used land given by the government are expected to part with it with no questions. The promise is they would be given 2.5 cents of land after finding appropriate resettlement area. Perhaps, Perambalur (near Trichy) is the only place in Tamil Nadu where lands that were completely barren have been acquired. The people who parted with the land are contented that they arrived at a fairly good deal as compensation.

Of course, there are policy prescriptions that barren land only should be acquired, and if for the purpose of contiguity, lands with single-crops are required they may be acquired, and that if lands with two-crops ought to be acquired, it should not exceed 10 per cent of the total land. For those who part with land and/or are under displacement there should be rehabilitation plan carried out to resettle them and provide the basic facilities. It implies that no matter even a portion of cultivable lands are acquired, no matter if people belonging to a habitation got displaced, SEZ should get established. It indicates clearly industry getting an edge over agriculture. It communicates poor subsistence farming is inefficient, and they had better get further marginalized so that 'something more efficient gets installed in the places they were occupying'.

Those without Private Property Resource: Another pertinent issue is that at least the land owners would be offered some cash compensation. But, the sharecroppers and the agricultural labourers in villages have no room to make any claim whatsoever, except the training on pickle making that might be offered to them as part of the rehabilitation plan. These training programmes most often serve as a strategy in the hands of the Officers in-charge of executing the rehabilitation plan to pacify the evictees until the community get used to the adjustment-difficulties, when the Officer would stop going there for his project period is over. Then he has either been terminated or transferred to implement similar 'successful' rehabilitation plan in some other location.

Already the shift from agriculture to other sectors and the number of farmers who give up agriculture is alarming due to reasons such as shifting from agriculture to horticultural crops, support to cultivate crops like *jetropha* for bio-fuel production, and the annual natural withdrawal from farming due to the drudgery and gamble involved in agricultural pursuits. Besides this if SEZ goes heedless in land acquisition, evicting farmers involuntarily from farming, it is a signal indicating a grave danger in terms of creating agricultural refugees, and food insecurity.

Setting up of manufacturing units, and service provision through IT industries etc. are desirable for an economy to get on the fast track of development. The concern is that this should not create a smokescreen to make everything else obscure or trivial. This is a matter of serious concern when it comes to hit agriculture. Taking cognizance of the soil type and climatic conditions in Kelamangalam area (near Hosur) a District Collector who motivated a group of farmers to get down to cultivation of rose flowers setting up six green houses with the financial assistance of the NABARD, gets down in the next one year to grab lands for SEZ not being able to withstand the pressure from the instructions of the State government. This has happened despite the fact that the local farmers have got a survey done by the State Agriculture Department and come out with a report that the land is 'purely agricultural land and that this village sends 4-5 loads of vegetables almost daily to places like Coimbatore, Erode, Bavani, Ernakulam and Chennai'. Higher level political lobbying by the local farmers, coupled with media coverage have put the idea of land acquisition on the back burner subsequently.

Common Property Resource: The focus is mainly of land being acquired, there are also common property resources such as water bodies, pasture land, places of worship, and burial ground of the local community taken away for SEZ. Villagers of Chennankuppam near Oragadam (about 22 km from Thambaram) said even their five acres of burial ground was taken away for the Nissan Project. Houses, hutments, the village lake, ponds, temples and schools were also in the process of being demolished to pave way for the new companies. Most villagers were Dalits who have nothing other than their lands. All the lands, both cultivable and uncultivable, have been acquired by the government in Oragadam, Mathur and Mangal for example. Only in Mathur the fight of the Village Panchayat President has made it possible to protect a pond with a water spread area of 4 acres. Chennankuppam hamlet (near Oragadam) alone has lost at least five ponds and lakes. Reportedly there are five water bodies being levelled for the purpose of developing SEZ in Oragadam and Chennankuppam areas. They are:

1.	Sennanguppam Lake	42 acres (approximate water spread area)
2.	Alkuttai	3-4 acres
3.	Koduvankuttai	2½ acres
4.	Thimmanthangal	10 acres
5.	Kallukuttai	7 acres

The only area that has been left with is the portion where the dwelling houses are located, perhaps for two reasons. One is that evicting people from dwelling houses might intensify the community agitation to uncontrollable levels, which the government did not want to face; and secondly, once the factories start letting out effluents and smoke, people might quietly pack up and quit the place without the companies or the government having to evict them. Moreover, as of now, with no water storage structures, or waterways, there is no way a rural community can exist in a village depending on agriculture or animal husbandry.

Common Facilities: There are bore wells, water collection points, women sanitary complexes constructed recently, schools, balwadies in Oragadam and Chennankuppam getting levelled for the purpose of SEZ. There are also false information spread around in villages (Chennankuppam) that local school would be closed down for want of children. This is used as a strategy to reduce the number of children at this school to be able to say finally that the school was closed down because there was not enough strength to run it as per government norms. Plainly, this is 'state-market collusion', where the community has been left alone. What is visible is the (farm) land-private property resource acquired, or that we are prevented from using the grazing land which we liberally used as a common property resource of the community. What goes unnoticed is the basic infrastructure such as school, sanitary complex, bore well sources, supply channels to water bodies, temples, and even the cremation ground getting levelled.

People of Manivakkam village are worried that the District Administration was spreading word that the local middle school (Natesan Government Middle School located in Manivakkam village) would be closed down—the reason the companies require the land where the school is located. She added that there was a mention about it earlier also. But, people were told that a new school would be constructed in another location close by. But, of late, why should the District Administration covertly motivate people to take their children away and admit at Velankanni School in next village. Perhaps, the company that would be located there did not want to bear the cost of constructing a new school. Chandramma, seemingly illiterate, is able to read that it is their indirect strategy to reduce the number of children at this school to be able to say finally that the school was closed down because there was not enough strength to run it as per government norms. Similarly, a woman sanitary complex is being demolished as well. But there is no talk about constructing a new one anywhere nearby. Plainly, this is 'state-market collusion', where the community has been left alone.

The Compensation Amount: We need to critically examine the current practices of *compensation*. Sadly, the history of compensation is full of stories of false promises, cheating, bad administration and malpractices of middlemen. This trend should be reversed, and we should bring in more transparency and credibility to the whole process. To make this happen, at least the following key questions need to be raised. What is right and fair amount of compensation? Should it only be limited to current market prices or should we also look at the future value of the land? Who should have claims to compensation? Do we consider only those who have legal titles, or should we not also consider others who are owners for many years but do not have legal titles? What is our moral obligation to sharecroppers and agricultural labourers who lose their tenancy or employment? If we talk about social justice, we cannot be contented answering only the legal question. We need to be morally right as well.

The 'nature' of the thing (the land) the local community lose is something that appreciates in value year after year. But, the thing that the company or the government has given in exchange (cash) is, by nature, depreciates in value as days go by. Moreover, compensation in most of the places is spoken in terms of 'cash' only, except in rarity like Mathur where constant nagging of the Panchayat President has helped nearly 300 youth to get employment in the units at SEZ. This has also been done not with reference to parting with land, but due to the virtue of residing in that area.

With money in hand and no land in possession the one-time farmers have to go to the market to buy rice. They are also afraid that soon they would be left with no money. With neither money nor land in hand, they would have no source of livelihood. This would cause migration to cities and towns like Chennai, Kancheepuram.

Those who happily disposed of their lands for SEZ are the ones who held land in Oragadam, but lived far away in place like Kancheepuram or Chennai. Many of them had purchased them as sites for house construction. The pieces of land possessed by the local people were the ones being used for agricultural purposes. This second category of the people only has resisted parting with their land initially. It is a section of these people who were arrested when they attempted to indulge in a road *roko*. Similarly, Perambalur lands were truly barren and so those who parted with land are happy receiving the compensation.

Land, labour, capital are the main factors of production in rural areas. The entrepreneurial skills to till the land and cultivate is with them inherent. Capital they managed through credit either through institutional agencies or through non-institutional agencies. Now, they have capital (which renders them not to borrow), and labour available with them. But, the most essential of the factors of production, i.e. land for tilling is not in their possession now. It is only the dwelling habitations that have been left from being acquired for SEZ. The way the SEZ units are coming up is such that it is encircling the people's habitation, and so, people are of the opinion that they might have to quit the place selling off the land to companies. The way land acquisition is taking place, it is reversing land reforms and bhoodan movement. It is undoing the Land Ceiling Act. It enables the SIPCOT, the government institution to acquire land and the companies to acquire lands in large quantities. They might temporarily appear to be money locked up. But, it is surely an investment that keeps appreciating. The ones who stand to lose are the farmers who parted with land.

Real Estate Boom: SEZ, basically, is a plan for urban development (township) in rural areas. In all the areas where SEZs have been identified or announced the real estate business takes place in full swing. Once a SEZ develops it creates an artificial inflation in prices in that region, and especially the land price takes a skyward flight. That which was purchased for a few thousand rupees from the local farmers becomes saleable for several lakhs. Nanguneri Multi-product SEZ in Thirunelveli district (Tamil Nadu) was announced but hardly a few units have been set up there. But, the real estate business in the surrounding of about 30 km from Nanguneri to Munanjipatti is so busy, no local people can think of buying a piece of land there. The only people that thrive on the announcement is realtors, who are selling lands at exorbitant rates, reports *The Hindu* (dated 19th September, 2008)—India's National Newspaper. It holds good for Oragadam near Chennai also, where farmers have sold an acre of land for Rs. 14 lakh to the SEZ developer. In less than a year, the price of an acre of land has crossed Rs. 50 lakh.

2. RESETTLEMENT AND REHABILITATION

The Government of India is still discussing the draft bill on Rehabilitation and Resettlement. As there is no R & R policy in place, the only guideline that is useful to the poor people who have to be resettled and rehabilitated is the Central R & R Policy 2007. The policy provides land-for-land compensation for acquisition of land for SEZ purposes, including employment to one person from each family that parts with the land required. Besides this, the policy provides for financial support to the affected families, their cattle sheds, shops, working sheds, transportation costs, comprehensive infrastructural facilities and amenities in the resettlement areas for education, health care, drinking water, roads, electricity, sanitation, religious activities, and other community resources (National R & R Policy, 2007). The recent R & R Policy, 2007 of the Government of India provides for relief of any small number of families, whereas the earlier policies were applicable only if more than 400 families were affected by the land acquisition. The land developer is supposed to take the responsibility for all resettlement and rehabilitation. The District Collector facilitates this process.

Although resettlement and rehabilitation involves a complete process of ensuring that the people who parted with land should not be allowed to fall below poverty line. The stories put down of Dharman & family, Kanniyappan & family, and Margabandu & family (Mathur-Thiruannamalai) presented in Chapter 2 put across the poor attention paid on rehabilitation and resettlement as far as SEZs in Tamil Nadu is concerned. These families are loitering in the court premises fighting to get a reasonable compensation. They are struggling having been disturbed and displaced.

The cash compensation in Oragadam was to some extent reasonable for farmers who had land in acres, rather than those who had only a few cents for subsistence farming. Chandra's is one of the families that sold (though unwillingly), about 4 acres of land for SEZ. Asked about Chandra's (Oragadam-Kancheepuram) opinion about the compensation money collected—a hefty amount that the family would not have imagined to see in their life time, she snapped immediately that any amount of currency money can be used up in this consumerist world today. Land was an asset that was a source of livelihood for our family for generations. Agriculture can give hold for generations. But, cash can give hold for current generation for a limited period of time. We knew how to multiply seeds, and how to create a bag of paddy from ten paddy seeds. But, we are not trained in multiplying money, or creating money through money. At the most all that we know is to keep it in a bank and use up little by little. The next generation must study, get some employment in the town and forget agriculture. Otherwise, they have no hold to live on this earth. They have nothing to fall back as ancestral property.

Finally, she shares her analysis of how Oragadam could have been chosen as SEZ area. They saw from one end of the road at Oragadam, and discovered vast sheet of land barren. But, they did not guess that beyond what is immediately visible to their bare eyes there are several acres of irrigated land being cultivated and that people are dependent on it for years as a source of livelihood. Chandra does not want to blame the government. She is only worried: (i) why is the government not as much after agriculture as it is after setting up of industries; and (ii) that why is the government not bothered about poor people losing their livelihood resources and basic infrastructure in the villages, which the companies want to wash their hands off, leaving it to the government to deal with; (iii) she is only worried about the poor attitude of the officials on providing alternative livelihood, resettlement and rehabilitation arrangement.

Box 5.3: Resettlement and Rehabilitation

The government has announced the National Policy on Rehabilitation and Resettlement. The policy provides land-for-land compensation for acquisition of land for SEZ purposes, including employment to one person from each family that parts with the land required. Besides this, the policy provides for financial support to the affected families, their cattle sheds, shops, working sheds, transportation costs, comprehensive infrastructural facilities and amenities in the resettlement areas for education, health care, drinking water, roads, electricity, sanitation, religious activities, and other community resources. The land developer shall take the responsibility for all resettlement and rehabilitation. The District Collector facilitates this process.

Source: National R & R Policy, 2007, Ministry of Rural Development (Department of Land Resources—Land Reforms Division)

Apart from cash compensation paid, resettlement and rehabilitation should come in the form of providing land for land, assisting construction of house for those who part with land and houses, assisting to put shops or work-sheds/workshops, cowshed, training and bank or financial assistance to commence petty trade. If agricultural lands are given land development assistance, and cultivation loan should also be given. Appropriate employment should be provided for members of families whose lands have been acquired for SEZ purpose. These are normal requirements as per the policy of resettlement and rehabilitation. But, these things hardly take place in reality. The only compensation method in vogue is 'cash payment'. That is also paid as per terms determined by the State. The landholders are able to get existing market value only if they showed their collective voice like they did in Oragadam or in Peramabalur.

As per the R & R Policy should be a Resettlement & Rehabilitation (R & R) Committee at the Project level to redress grievances regarding compensation, rehabilitation and resettlement issues. This Committee shall have representatives from local NGOs, Panchayats, local elected representatives including women. This Committee also has the power to take up post-implementation social audits of the rehabilitation and resettlements plans. There is also a National Monitoring Cell at the Department of Land Resources that should monitor if R & R plans are effectively implemented. But, unfortunately it was found in none of the local Project level R & R Committee is formed. Hence, individuals affected by the project has to approach individually with no mechanism in place. The people write petition to all those officials whom they come to know was in-charge of land acquisition.

With regard to payment of compensation, the rates fixed ten years ago are also used (Mathur—Thiruvannamalai). The insensitivity of the officials could be noticed in some of the cases in Mathur, when the project affected families (PAFs) were put in police custody with fabricated cases upon them. This is the reason people call SEZ—Special Eviction Zones. If the 'compensation package' is designed reasonably, especially when agricultural lands are acquired, land acquisition can take place hassle-free. It should be in the interest of the rural economy and food security of the State that agricultural lands should be kept away from being taken for SEZ development.

3. EMPLOYMENT

One of the main arguments given in favour of SEZs and for inviting private investment into India—besides contribution to the national income popularly known as GDP—is employment generation. SEZs do create jobs through manufacturing activities. Many foreign based companies find India as a good destination for outsourcing, and so SEZs bring additional jobs into India. The annual growth rate of 'public employment' in the organised sector prior to 1991 was 1.52 per cent, which has come down in the negative to 0.03 per cent in the year 2000. The growth rate of 'private employment' in organised sector during the same period has increased from 0.45 per cent to 1.87 per cent The SEZ-Fact Sheet of the Government of India—2008 reports that SEZs have generated employment for 3,49,203 persons.

In India the unorganised sector dominates the employment scenario and hardly 7 per cent of the total employed is in the organised sector. That is to say agriculture and allied activities provide the source of income to the rest of the population, which is an awesome number. The government estimate with regard to the land requirement for SEZs is 4,46,600 acres (1,78,632 hectares). Even if we calculate providing employment for 2 persons per acre from families that part with land (plus the sharecroppers and landless labourers) of the respective areas, let the rest of the employment be given to others—it should provide employment for 8,93,200 persons. Would the nature of employment that SEZs provide be in a position to accommodate such a big number of local people? The ones established are IT, IT-enabled services, pharmaceuticals or chemical plants. The skill-set required for such industries are entirely different. Obviously, the employment promise to 'local people' is only a sham. The fact remains that SEZs generate employment—a miniscule proportion could go to the local people. Similarly, one should not dig the service conditions, or the terms of employment.

All industrial units in the SEZs are declared as 'Public Utility Service' under the provisions of the Industrial Disputes Act, 1947. The Development Commissioner has the powers to act as judge as far as the units in the SEZ area are concerned. Therefore, workers, employees would not be in a position to organise into unions or strike work to protest against terms of employment such as wages/salaries, working conditions etc. Inspection requirement with regard to labour at the units in SEZs would be kept at the minimum level. New concepts like paying an all-inclusive consolidated salaries, self-certification, flexi-time (work at any time that is convenient), working time for women etc. are introduced (SEZ, Policy of Government of Tamil Nadu, 2003). Recruitment of employees through one gate, and retrenchment of employees through another gate is a common phenomenon in the units run under SEZs in Tamil Nadu.

Here is a case in point at Kancheepuram district. The workers sitting outside the *Hundai* unit at Sriperumbudur has become almost an annual occurrence now. Some workers remain suspended, some terminated. Those terminated get active in trade union activities, and because those inside the company also have grievances they join hands with the trade unions and continue their work as well as fight against the *Hundai* Management. The view of *Hundai* Management is at the discretion of Management to decide on the number of employees, and to make or outsource and so on. Moreover, employees working in a SEZ unit are not allowed to form Trade Unions as per the SEZ Act, Rules and Policy of Government of India. Workers problems go on.

Box 5.4: Labour Protection in SEZs

All industrial units in the SEZs are declared as 'Public Utility Service' under the provisions of the Industrial Disputes Act, 1947. The Development Commissioner has the powers to act as judge as far as the units in the SEZ area are concerned. Therefore, workers, employees would not be in a position to organise into unions or strike work to protest against terms of employment such as wages/salaries, working conditions etc.

Inspection requirement with regard to labour at the units in SEZs would be kept at the minimum level. New concepts like self-certification, flexi-time (work at any time that is convenient), working time for women etc. are introduced.

Source: SEZ, Policy of Government of Tamil Nadu, 2003.

The workers go on strike on rotation basis outside the company's unit at Irunkattukottai near Sriperumbudur, Chennai. The workers point out specific labour hostile policies which include: (i) terminating or suspending employees with no valid reason; (ii) transferring employees to far off places like Mumbai, Kolkata so as to punish them for they spoke labour rights, or dignity of labour; and (iii) employing contract labourers in huge numbers and getting down to massive outsourcing to be able to economize on the workers who are likely to be made permanent.

The rule of the market economy is that if somewhere has the richest human resources and the cheapest labour, the enterprises and business should naturally go there. Although SEZs bring opportunities for sharing best practices, innovative technologies and capital from all over, the basic drive is availability of trained manpower at cheap labour-cost, coupled with concessions and tax holidays here. Obviously, the basic intent should be earning profit, and not providing employment at ILO standards.

One can witness in Oragadam near Chennai, ever since construction works for setting up of units started many youth and women walk around in Oragadam area speaking languages other than Tamil. They are migrant labourers from States like Uttar Pradesh, Andhra Pradesh etc. The companies have handed over construction work to some construction companies. These construction companies keep away the local people from getting manual labour in construction works. It happens with several companies in construction stage, they get in touch with some labour contractors who supply any number of workers from poorer districts of Bihar, Uttar Pradesh, Andhra Pradesh etc. Hardly any local people are used even in manual labour.

They find several advantages in employing such people from far away districts rather than the local people. Two distinct reasons are spelt out for not employing local people in manual works. First, 'the nativity feeling and the power associated with it' that those who construct the building, in fact, grabbed my land. This feeling comes up to local people often and some quarrel develops if native people were given manual labour work, which, perhaps, the Construction Company wants to avoid. This has happened with companies here one of which is Apollo Tyres Manufacturing Company, at Oragadam Industrial Park. Turning this situation favourable to the Company is best achieved by bringing manual labourers for construction works from far away States, who would not have any feeling of nativity. Moreover, the fear of being thrown out of employment anytime, and the feeling of the workers not belonging to that place become a vulnerable point for the labour contractor to manage their workers from other States without difficulty. Those from far away places are unlikely to organise and raise voice, whereas local workers will have a tendency to raise voice against issues that they do not agree with. Similarly, when it comes to men or women, the companies prefer women to men again to be able to manage easily making use of the vulnerability.

A chain of interview conducted at the SIPCOT in Hosur revealed that several industries have been closed down stating various reasons such as labour problem, the unit runs sick and so on. The reality as reasoned out by experts is that after enjoying the tax concessions of this duty-free zone for nearly eight or nine years, the private units make book adjustments for two, three years and close down unit in one SEZ and then shift to another SEZ start afresh with all the tax concessions again. There are industries shifted from Hosur SIPCOT to the newly developed SEZ in Bangalore. The book adjustments made by the popular Satyam Computers is one of the examples of the proportion at which corruption and malpractices are possible within SEZs. Once the industry closes the employees are deserted. Big business houses adopt the technique of offering VRS to employees, and the smaller ones close down showing themselves as sick units. Big or small—many of these companies adopt the technique of having temporary labourers, and contract labourers only recruited through labour contractors or manpower agencies.

When the employment generation by public sector units are almost in the negative, the private investment in SEZs do develop employment at reasonably good salary. However, the terms of employment, hours of work, and service conditions are surely very much in favour of the investors, and not in any win-win situation. There are also some of the industries like the IT paying a very high salary creating a local inflationary tendency. The fall of house rent in Chennai after the IT industries retrenched employees in thousands could be one of the examples, how SEZs can create a local inflationary tendency.

The Local Labour: Apart from the cash compensation given to the local landholders, one of the huge advertisements made about setting up of SEZ in rural areas is about the potential an SEZ has in generating employment—employment including for those people or members of their families who part with their lands. A recent report of the Government of Tamil Nadu states that SEZs in Tamil Nadu has brought in Rs. 2462.4 crore as investments and 29,195 direct employment in the State during 2007-08 alone.

Whatever might be estimation or potential for employment, one thing, that is, very obvious, is that all (or at least most) of the employment provided in SEZ could not be for local people from where land was acquired. If local people believed so, perhaps, they are at fault. This is based on the premise that the skill requirements for a company might be different, at different levels and at different sections. Certainly, it is absolutely impossible for any village (or set of villages) to be able provide all the employees needed for various positions. However, it might be positively taken by the local institutions or such as NGOs or even Panchayats for that matter might identify some potential youth and arrange for training so that they become eligible for employment. The companies that set up business might also offer to arrange for such training, like it is reported about the Tata's Nano, when it was located in Singur at West Bengal. Except that which is reported about the Tata's arrangement for training of local youth for employment, we have not heard anywhere, any company in Indian SEZs providing training to the educated youth in the vicinity to acquire certain skills so that they become employable. There are companies taking them as apprentices as a business strategy to reduce the full time employees they need to employ.

There are several such strange man management techniques employed when it comes to employing people for construction or running the units. For instance, one can witness in Oragadam, ever since construction works for setting up of units started many youth and women walk around in Oragadam area speaking languages other than Tamil. They are said to be migrant labourers from States like Uttar Pradesh, Andhra Pradesh etc. The companies have handed over construction work to some construction company. These construction companies keep away the local people from getting manual labour in construction works. It happens with several companies in construction stage, they get in touch with some labour contractors who supply any number of workers from poorer districts of Bihar, Uttar Pradesh, Andhra Pradesh etc.

Box 5.5: Grievance Redressal Procedures

There are Resettlement & Rehabilitation (R & R) Committees at the Project level to redress grievances regarding compensation, rehabilitation and resettlement issues. This committee shall have representatives from local NGOs, Panchayats, local elected representatives including women. This committee also has the power to take up post-implementation social audits of the rehabilitation and resettlement plans. There is also a National Monitoring Cell that monitors if R & R plans are effectively implemented.

Source: www.sezindia.nic.in

They find several advantages in employing such people from far away districts rather than the local people. Two distinct reasons are spelt out for not employing local people in manual works. First, 'the nativity feeling and the power associated with it' that those who construct the building, in fact, grabbed my land whereas this land originally belonged to me, to my brother, to my father, or to my uncle; and the person I am working for, cross-folding my hands, is actually an invader bossing over me. This feeling comes up to local people often and some quarrel develops if native people were given manual labour work, which, perhaps, the Construction Company wants to avoid. This has happened with many a company here one of which is Apollo Tyres Manufacturing Company, at Oragadam Industrial Park. Turning this situation favourable to the Company is best achieved by bringing manual labourers for construction works from far away States, who would not have any feeling of nativity. Secondly, the amount of wage paid. The workers from other States are prepared to work even for Rs. 80 a day, and they do not mind working extra hours for extra payment. Whereas the local workers demand higher wages, and they need personal time to take care of other works they might have in Chennai or Kancheepuram. The fear of being thrown out of employment any time, and the feeling of the workers not belonging to that place become a vulnerable point for the labour contractor to manage their workers from other States without difficulty. This view is shared by many Panchayat Presidents who watch them work daily.

There are some Village Panchayat Presidents raised issues such as pressure on the civic facilities, especially the absence of sanitation facility.

These workers who come from other States are made to live in make-shift tin houses, and cook outside on the open area. They defecate in the open and spoil the local water bodies for cleaning, washing etc. When the government makes pronouncements of clean villages the workers from far away States cause insanitation.

Even companies that have started functioning, they prefer to employ women workers rather than men. This is again about the popular feeling that women are easily controllable, obedient and are non-questioning. When it comes to outsider or insider, the companies tend to prefer outsider so as to manage them using the vulnerability. Similarly, when it comes to men or women, the companies prefer women to men again to be able to manage easily making use of the vulnerability. In both the cases there is an economic dimension as well, in the sense, those from outsider can be paid meagre wage and put to work for long hours. The same thing holds good for women also. Those from far away places are unlikely to organise and raise voice, whereas local workers will have a tendency to raise voice against exploitation.

4. DEMOCRACY AT THE GRASSROOTS

The place of Village Panchayats or grassroots level people's institutions is almost non-existent. They have been cut off in many places where it is supposed to play a vital role. These institutions are string-operated by the district administration and the bureaucracy as desired by the SEZ developer, companies that set up business and the government machinery. For example, the SEZ Policy of Government of Tamil Nadu (drawn from SEZ Policy of Government of India and the SEZ Act, 2005) states:

- SEZ area (or the zone) is considered to be a foreign territory within India free from all the rules and regulations. The rules and regulations that is thus far prevalent governing the other non-SEZ areas shall not be applicable to SEZ areas. SEZs are considered as separate townships with self-contained facilities such as road, water, solid and liquid waste management arrangements etc. Neither the zone nor the units in the zone shall seek the local body (Panchayat) to provide any service such as water, sanitation etc. (SEZ, Policy of Government of Tamil Nadu, 2003).

Once the land has been sold to the developer—be it the government, or any private company—the developer shall make all the necessary arrangements for services such as water supply, power, pollution control etc. Therefore,

Panchayats need not provide any service, nor would they need to charge for any of these services within this industrial township. Once the land has been sold by private land holders, and common lands have been handed over the Panchayats have no say over anything.

There are also issues raised by Village Panchayat Presidents that compensation is paid only to private land holders. The land in the possession of the Panchayats, the trees being felled that belonged to the Panchayats are never taken seriously. These were assets of the Panchayats, but taken for granted. The Panchayats are expected to send a Gram Sabha resolution passed stating: 'the community does not have any objection to the common lands being acquired for setting up industries'. This is an official direction received, for which the Panchayats are supposed to pay heed. Many of the Panchayat functionaries wanting to be in the good books of the officials raise no objections, except a few places in Thiruvannamalai. This is viewed as a weakening the power of an elected body of the people, or the market winning over democracy with the assistance of the bureaucracy.

As these units have been exempted from all the existing laws of the land including the Panchayati Raj Act, 1994, Industrial Dispute Act, 1947 etc. The units at SEZ would not get any running licence from the local bodies, nor does it go for licence renewal like it happens in other non-SEZ areas. Panchayats have nothing to do with these separate townships. This is weakening the Panchayati Raj System. If there are any effluents let out, it is for the Pollution Control Board (PCB) to take action. Panchayats can only make a complaint to the PCB.

Under the SEZ Act for ensuring transparency, provision has been made for mandatory displaying of displacement, rehabilitation and resettlement, with names of affected persons, extent of land acquired, compensation/ rehabilitation packages etc. Such information shall be placed in the public domain and shared with the concerned Gram Sabhas of Panchayats by the Project authorities striking a balance between the requirement of land for the zone (for development purposes) and protection of land owners and other displaced people. In many of the places where SEZs have been started, the individual landholders have been sent notice about the decision of the government to acquire his/her land, and Village Panchayats have received information about the common land to be acquired. The Panchayats did not receive full information about the extent of land to be acquired including the private lands. In fact, in Valasamudram (Tuticorin), the Village Panchayat President has used the RTI to get the information regarding SEZ land acquisition in his village.

The basic principle of good governance is to involve the affected people in the decision-making process. If the SEZ Act says that the industry will use local resources such as ground water for example, but the Panchayats will have no say in it. It is not the right way of thinking about what development is or what democracy is.

Another important provision is that a Resettlement and Rehabilitation Committee should be formed comprising representatives from local Panchayats involved, SHGs, NGO working in the area, and the lead bank manager of the area. This committee shall deal with the SEZ developers on behalf of the community or PAFs. This committee shall also take up monitoring of proper implementation of resettlement and rehabilitation. But, this is not implemented in any of the SEZ area visited. The Village Panchayat Presidents are not aware of this. They are not aware of the provisions of the R & R Policy, 2007 either.

SEZ Act puts across that the employees of SEZ units should not form trade unions. The existing Industrial Dispute Act, 1947, the Bonus Act etc. would not be applicable. There would be only a 'work committee' formed and this work committee can pass on their grievances of workers to the Company Management. There would be no union formed or affiliations sought with national trade unions like INTUC, CITU, AITUC etc. The Development Commissioner of SEZ shall be the ultimate authority to decide on any matter relating to labour problems. The right of the employees to form union is denied in the SEZ Act. The 'right to organise' is denied.

5. THE ISSUE OF CORPORATE SOCIAL RESPONSIBILITY

It is important to notice the inherent contradictions and double standards of capitalism and the logic of the free market operating here. On the one hand, advocates of the free market think that concessions and subsidies of any form will distort incentives and the markets and that business will flourish when there is no regulation from external agencies particularly the government. On the other hand, when it comes to acquiring land for industrial projects the very same people are demanding for free or subsidized land. Isn't it paradoxical that almost every major project is situated on a subsidized land taken away by force or persuasion directly or indirectly from poor farmers?

Today, industrialists are talking so much about Corporate Social Responsibility (CSR)—the need of being responsible for social development. CSR is not sitting on cultivable land surrounding towns and cities and then doing some charity to people on whose land you are sitting. What type of CSR is that? A good practice of CSR for companies and businesses would be to invest in rural markets and initiate projects in remote areas. If infrastructure is a problem to have access to these places we should be prepared to create it. This may not pay back in the short-term, but in the long-run it will turn out be beneficial both to the company and society as a whole. There are already best practices that can be stated as models. So, when we talk of efficiency we need to look at efficiency in the long-run in terms of sustainable growth. Moreover, we need to balance economic efficiency with what we can call 'social efficiency'. What is the use of having a skewed type of development—development that leaves out the vast rural areas of the country and sections of population?

In this context, it should be realised that people with more power should take more responsibility rather than pushing it on the weak and the vulnerable. The economic and political power that some of the corporates wield are enormous. This power should not be utilised to exploit the already powerless and weak in order to amass more wealth for oneself. In what way, can this be morally justified? Instead, when you have more power, you should be willing to assume more responsibility to shoulder a larger share of the burden. That exactly is the demand of responsibility.

6. Perception about Development

One tends to be somewhat ideological when it comes to SEZ. Without scrutinizing the problems involved, it is possible to prematurely take sides for or against SEZ, to become a SEZ-mania as if this is the panacea for all our problems or a SEZ-phobia believing that nothing good can come out of this or industrialization in general. There are oversights on both sides and that is one of the reasons why this issue has become so contentious and often leading to a situation of impasse. The government and the businesses fail to take note that land is not just land, but it has more to do with the livelihood, dignity, social esteem, culture and future of farmers and village and tribal communities.

One's view point about SEZ should begin with what constitutes development in one's perception. That is there is a basic question: 'what is construed as development'? The idea of establishing SEZ stems from the western idea that only when you have industries, big buildings and dams there is 'development' taking place. Agriculture and allied activities are construed as indicators of primitiveness or backwardness. This is becoming a popular notion all over. The idea of industrialization started taking root in Hosur town since the early 1970s when the first SIPCOT was established. Land grabbing in the name of setting up industrial units that started then did not stop yet even in 2008.

The notion of 'industry' as an indicator of development, and agriculture as a sign of backwardness is what makes one think that subsidy given to industrial units as prudent and the same offered to agriculture as unwise. Certain basic questions such as: Industry—in whose interest? for whom? with whose resources? are never raised at all. Consequently, the livelihood resources, and the confidence of the poor on life are being eroded. Those who depended on land as a source of livelihood are wiped out of their habitations so as to bring about 'development' in those places. This is an erroneous understanding of development. Industries must be set up, and they should also provide employment, but it should not be at the expense of agriculture, or after hurting a section of population who depended on land for years.

With similar kind of support, infrastructure and subsidies (offered to industries) even agriculture can create unprecedented records in production and employment. Those with money to invest get all support from the government starting from finding land until eviction of or convincing the local people. The government takes care of it. Often times, what is meant by rehabilitation is 'convincing'? At the worst, authority is used, official notices are served, orders are issued for arresting the community that resist for defusing.

Those who lived in Hosur for at least a decade would be able to say that the first circle of lands have been taken away for industrial purposes, the second circle was taken away by real estate brokers for constructing dwelling houses for sale; the third circle outside it are mostly going into the hands of NRIs who buy land, keep it fenced and call it 'farm house'. The people who originally belonged to this place are beyond this third circle—invisible and away from the place where 'development has been installed'. The local people have lost their identity, and piece of land they lived on, and ploughed to make a living. But, they have learnt to wipe their tears out with cash received as compensation.

The employment promise made to local is empty, in the sense, most of them who work here are Hindi speaking youth from the backward districts of northern India. Labourers are found to be costly here, and so they are brought from northern States. There are at least 100 units closed down in the past years showing several reasons, which resulted in job loss. There are companies with owners absconding where the bankers who lent them have appointed security guards at the gates of these companies with the hope that they would catch hold of the owner when they come to collect the left-over. There are also seven-eight years old companies that make book-adjustments to show loss, and shift to SEZ in Bangalore so as to enjoy the concessions afresh. The howls that the workers who lost employment make are viewed as a 'law and order problem'. The contract labour system prevails in most of the industries and factories now. This is the kind of employment that the government is talking about when they make statements that SEZs generate employment.

Another weird thing noticed is that the companies that buy several acres of land, use hardly one-fourth of the land for constructing industry, office or whatever. The remaining three-fourth of the land remains vacant appreciating in value. Once industries come up, the land value shoots up shortly. They earn an incredible value to the land. This is speculation and cheating the original owner of the land with the help of the government in the name of industrialization. The third SIPCOT works are on now. When so many acres purchased already remain unused, when so many industrial units remain closed down for long, the land acquisition has started again for the third SIPCOT. The SIPCOT website also reports about the amount of land acquired that remain unused and the amount of money locked up. This goes on. The land owners are getting bran biscuits in a golden-platter.

7. CAN'T THE COMPLEXITY SIMPLIFIED?

The concern expressed is of farm land being acquired, and of the false employment promises given to the local people. Minus a few cases such as the one in Oragadam, where people who protested against parting with land have been put in prison for a week or so, in all the other places the government uses the strategy of paying a higher amount in order not to let any hullabaloo take place, which could easily be politicised. Acquisition of farm land cannot be justified on any ground. Given the downward spiral currency value is getting, and the skyward flight land value is taking, unless the land owners want cash, compensation should be given as land in another location, coupled with justifiable basic infrastructure facilities. Just paying the present market value of the land is not enough—they must be compensated for the perpetual loss of income and given an alternative livelihood from Day One.

The issues besides the attraction shown with higher compensation (in some places like Oragadam) for cultivable land are many. It has happened in Cheyyar close to Kancheepuram, that a set of Village Panchayats have received letter from the district headquarters that they should send a resolution passed in the Gram Sabha stating that the community has no objection to common land in the use/custody of Panchayats being acquired for SEZ purpose—the bureaucracy directing an elected body. To get confirmed information on the number of acres to be acquired in Valasamudram Panchayat in Tuticorin district, the Panchayat President had to use RTI Act. In another instance, the

Sub-Registrar has prevented land being bought and sold because the area is notified for SEZ. After the local people protested against it, the Registrar has intervened and resolved the matter. In Oragadam, a cremation yard was relocated to another place by district administration, which then people found was run across by the NHAI Project. It is to be re-relocated again.

Set up business in a place where there is huge economic benefits like the SEZs which are duty free/tax free zones. Buy raw materials from where they are available at the cheapest price; bring labourers for employment from places where they are available for the lowest wages. Mobilize capital from cheapest sources. Sell in places where the products sell at highest profit. There should be 'no problem' of land, water, electricity, road, workers, capital, effluents discharge, environmental and labour laws. If required take agriculture land also. One needs to analyse what kind of CSR is this?

The swiftness the officials show in moving files relating to eviction of families from SEZ notified areas, and clearing up the land through bulldozers etc. is amazing. The pity is the interest shown, from the official side, on eviction of families and handing over the land to the private SEZ developer is not shown in Resettlement and Rehabilitation (R & R) Policy aspects. The number of people falling below poverty line could be considerably reduced, if provisions of R & R policy are implemented with the required sensitivity. This is the cause of tension in most places. Instead the victims are directed to go to court. Reference can be made of Mathur Panchayat near Cheyyar to interact with victims of forced displacement who half the time loiter around court premises in Cheyyar, and the other half around the pawn brokers shop at Mathur borrowing money.

Establishment of SEZs in areas that are really barren is welcome. The people would happily part with lands like it has happened in Perambalur SEZ (Tamil Nadu). Indeed, we are aware of the fact that it is moving from farming to other secondary and tertiary sectors that have made the rich countries rich. In such an event, preparations by the government should be underway to equip the youth with skills required for becoming employable in the SEZs, based on the industry requirements.

There are some Village Panchayat Presidents raised issues such as pressure on the civic facilities, especially the absence of sanitation facility for the construction workers employed in construction of buildings for SEZs. These workers who come from other States are made to live in make-shift tin houses, and cook outside on the open area. They defecate in the open and spoil the local water bodies for cleaning, washing etc. When the government makes pronouncements of clean villages the workers from far away States cause insanitation.

Let jobs in the SEZ be given to educated, technically sound youth from any part of the State. But, would agriculture also be provided the same amount of infrastructure, concessions, and support offered to SEZ? Millions have depended on agriculture for years. If agriculture were provided such all-out support, it would stand as well providing employment to millions. There is fond wish often expressed that they should also somehow hop in and find place in this development journey. The initiatives taken in this regard are insufficient. This is a concern.

It is time for the local bodies to be aware of, and be alert about announcements of SEZ areas, and be observant about the type of land acquired for SEZ and educate the local community on these aspects. We welcome industrialization, so long as it is set up on the barren land, does not play havoc to agriculture and rural livelihoods. We welcome industrialization so long as it does not cause environmental damage. Over use of environmental resource also amounts to violence. Ethics and self-discipline in resource use should be an overriding criterion of development.

Box 5.6: Local People get Employment where they are Pushy

The local youth (both boys and girls) over 1,000 of them have got employment in the SEZ units that have come up near Cheyyar. These youth belong to more than 20 villages including Mathur, which Mr. Thamiliniyan, Panchayat President, Mathur confirmed. He added that it was because of the struggle the local people waged against setting up of units without providing employment to local people. The recent development with regard to recruitment is encouraging. They consider local job applications also. *The Hindu* (2nd November, 2008) reports that as many as 1,112 persons belonging to villages in and around the Cheyyar Special Economic Zone (SEZ) in Thiruvannamalai district have been recruited by companies that have established their units there.

Source: *The Hindu*, 2nd November, 2008.

Identification, notification, and implementation of SEZ in the State of Tamil Nadu are taking place with mixed response from the population. The controversies surrounding the SEZ include forceful land acquisition using legislative provisions, for handing them over to private investors and property developers—and call it 'acquisition for public utility purpose'; booming real estate business and land brokerage encircling the SEZ area; agricultural lands being taken; deceptive employment promise offered to the local people, which in most cases have not taken place; shifting of unit to other SEZs on the termination of the concession period at the SEZ. These statements are all based on empirical studies carried out in almost all the SEZs in Tamil Nadu, corroborated by those who observe the development of SEZs from the inception. Thus, empirical verification carried out across SEZs within Tamil Nadu brings out several issues that are contradictory to the SEZ policy, anticipations of the government, and to the abhorrence of the society and environment.

Establishment of industries and service sector units can generate large scale employment. It also has high potentials to contribute towards national income. However, one widespread concern expressed by many, is that setting up of SEZ should not be at the expense of agriculture at a time when agriculture growth is decelerating. Truly, it is agriculture in India that essentially requires all sorts of encouragements, institutional support and infrastructure creation so that the deceleration is reversed. If at all, SEZ would do some good to the economy and to the educated youth, let it get established in real barren lands as reported by the people in a given region, and not as per the British-period records in possession of the government.

We should also take notice of the fact that there is hardly any country on this earth that has claimed that it prospered merely through agriculture or export of primary commodities only. Nor can one claim in the future that such a proposition would be successful in this globalised world. Equally so, no economist or political philosopher can argue that an economy can prosper completely dependent on other countries for food. At least India cannot do it, given the size of the population.

IV. MAJOR FINDINGS AND ACTION POINTS

The idea of SEZ is one of the elements of economic globalization which is principally based on free market capitalism. The rule of the market economy is that if somewhere has the richest human resources and the cheapest labour, the enterprises and business should naturally go there. Although SEZs bring opportunities for sharing best practices, innovative technologies and capital from allover, the basic drive is availability of trained manpower at cheap labour-cost, coupled with concessions and tax holidays here. Obviously, the basic intent should be earning profit, and not providing employment at ILO standards. This study conducted across districts in Tamil Nadu proves it beyond doubt that SEZ, as it intends to promote industrial corridors and technology parks, are coming up wiping out local livelihood resources and edging the poor landholders virtually to the margins. It has loosened their traditional stronghold.

The globalization policies of the government and the acquisition of farm land for SEZ affect agriculture or rural livelihoods—present or prospective, severe or slight could be made out from the inflation that wrecked household budgets and government finances in 2008. Many units closed down. Many units down-sized operations. Many units retrenched employees. But, unless you use RTI Act, the Project Officers of SIPCOT do not give you the data on number of units closed down in the last five years, or the number of workers who lost job because the units shuttered down. Vested interests countered rational concerns with misinformation of employment and economic growth. The apprehensions expressed by concerned Indians are brushed aside as emotive rhetoric.

In the new attention economy, if an idea can grab mind-space, that is half work done. There are reports that read that SEZs in China are successful. There are also reports giving evidences of thousands of SEZs in China closed down, or cancelled immediately after they were notified due to real estate boom, and uncontrollable grabbing of agricultural lands for industrial purpose. We should also take notice of the fact that there is hardly any country on this earth that has claimed that it prospered merely through agriculture or export of primary commodities only. Nor can one claim in the future that such a proposition would be successful in this globalized world. Equally so, no economist or political philosopher can argue that an economy can prosper completely dependent on other countries for food. At least India cannot do it, given the size of the population.

FOR WHOSE BENEFIT, AT WHOSE COST?

Many State governments in India are wooing the investors—both domestic as well as foreign—to commence business in their State creating a special *laissez faire* zone called Special Economic Zone (SEZ). So much so, when a firm that got approval to set up a unit within the SEZ of a State runs into problems due to local unrest or whatever, there is constant invitation from other State governments within India to shift the unit to their SEZ. Thus, each State is making allout efforts to provide all the facilities required to attract foreign direct investment or domestic investment. The Central Government has come out with a policy statement putting in a whole lot of tax exemptions and concessions. Many of the State Governments have also come out with

SEZ Policies with additional concessions and facilities. As on 11th August, 2008, India has got formal approvals for 513 SEZs, out of which 250 are formally notified. The government estimate is that these SEZs would take 1,781 sq.km, that is 1,78,632 hectares (or approximately 4,46,600 acres).

SEZs are duty-free territories for investors who are involved in manufacturing or in service provision; they are places for employment opportunities to the educated youth in a given State; for the State it is an indicator of FDI attracted; and regrettably in the opinion of the local residents they are special eviction zones. No one can deny of the pace SEZs have added to the growth of industries and services sector in the State. However, if one gets down doing a chain of interviews in the SEZ areas with a single question in mind: *For whose benefit, at whose cost?* One can get at the depth of the truth behind the statements why Union Rural Development Minister Raghuvansh Prasad Singh termed the promotion of SEZs as 'land scam' and why the local people call SEZs as 'special eviction zones'.

THE NATURE OF ISSUES

The main issues involved in land acquisition for SEZ are partly economic and partly social. Economic because of the involvement of compensation, and social because of the issues of resettlement and rehabilitation involved. If the developer tried to hit a hard bargain it becomes political. Once it becomes political then naturally the value of poor people's land escalates beyond imagination. But, the landholders and the SEZ developers have been playing the game of one trying to outsmart the other in the land deal. One short-cut that the SEZ developers usually take is standing behind the State government. They let the government machinery to deal with the landholders putting to use Land Acquisition Act. The landholders have been demanding that the private SEZ developers should approach them straight and the government machinery should not appear in the picture. The deal should be something like real estate business, where the government is nowhere in the scene.

The SEZ developers find using government machinery helps acquisition at reasonable costs 'by their own measures' and enables use of relevant laws for eviction where necessary. All that the company wants is land should be acquired for setting up the company, and financial compensation would be paid by the company to those who part with land at terms determined by the State. The question of rehabilitation or resettlement falls in the hands of the State Government to deal with, although the company might bear a portion of the expenditure.

DISCONTENTS

Investment Flow: The FDI and domestic investment expected by the government shall remain a distant dream, and what is confirmed is only the revenue loss that the government shall incur is a comment from a section of the globalization observers. The SEZ policy has also led to inter-ministry friction occurring in this regard, with the Finance Ministry bemoaning the prospect that the promotion of SEZs in the manner it is presently being conducted by the Commerce and Industries Ministry would cause a loss in revenue to the tune of over Rs. 1,60,000 crore by 2010 (as estimated US$36 billion). The Commerce Ministry tautly replied that the Finance Ministry's projections were merely based on 'paper calculations'. The Commerce Ministry actually expects an investment sum of Rs. 1,00,000 crore by the end of 2007 (roughly US$ 22.7 billion), which in turn, would result in a revenue gain of Rs. 44,000 crore (US$1 billion), besides creating hundreds of thousands of new jobs (Frontline, 2006). A recent report (SEZ, Fact Sheet) of the Government of India reports that the total investment that has flown into the SEZ areas as of June 2008 is Rs. 81093.495 crore; SEZs (both private and government) have generated employment for 3,49,203 persons (SEZ, Fact Sheet, GoI, 2008).

All said and done, the reports from other countries including China whose model India is said to have followed, is not encouraging. Empirical verification carried out across SEZs within India/Tamil Nadu brings out several issues that are contradictory to the SEZ policy, anticipations of the government, and to the abhorrence of the society and environment.

Agricultural Land Acquired: Although the Land Acquisition Act, 1897 states clearly, acquiring agricultural lands should be avoided, and if for some strong reason, it has to be acquired, should not exceed more than 10 per cent of the total land available for cultivation/to be acquired. But, in Oragadam and Chennankuppam areas, people's report confirm that out of the 2,200 acres acquired so far, only 1,500 acres could be classified as barren, in the remaining, about 400 acres were agriculture land that gave one time harvest a year, and 300 acres were two times harvested a year. The amount of cattle population has come down by less than half in the last three years for want of grazing land. Even the few cattle that are around they feed on the papers and foils thrown out of the companies, report the local community. This holds good for Bairamangalam near Hosur in Krishnagiri District also. But, at Bairamanagalam the farmers' vehement opposition to part with the cultivable lands (about 220 acres) has made the authorities and a private SEZ developer (company) to hang up land acquisition.

Involuntary Expulsion: The number of persons engaged in agriculture is declining year after year finding agriculture to be non-remunerative, there is this extra number from SEZ areas being 'involuntarily expelled from agriculture'. This is gearing up the pace of people getting out of agriculture in the State. Already studies are coming up that NREGS is dwindling agriculture due to shortage of labour for farm related works in villages. SEZ is accelerating this trend.

SEZ Concentration: SEZs are mostly concentrated in districts that are close to Chennai or Bangalore, e.g. Kancheepuram, Thiruvannamalai, Thiruvallur, and Krishnagiri. Those far away from Chennai, announced for the development of employment in poorer districts such as Thirunelveli, Madurai, Perambalur remain vastly unused. The investment that SIPCOT made in these areas remain locked up, or it is a kind of value appreciation viewed from the angle of developing real estate townships.

Real Estate Boom: SEZ, basically, is a plan for urban development (township) in rural areas. Once a SEZ develops it creates an artificial inflation in prices in that region, and especially the land price takes a skyward flight. That which was purchased for a few thousand rupees from the local farmers becomes saleable for several lakhs. Nanguneri Multi-product SEZ in Thirunelveli district (Tamil Nadu) was announced but hardly a few units have been set up there. But, the real estate business in the surrounding of about 30 km from Nanguneri to Munanjipatti is so busy, no local people can think of buying a piece of land there. The only people that thrive on the announcement is realtors, who are selling lands at exorbitant rates, reports *The Hindu* (dated 19th September, 2008)—India's National Newspaper. It holds good for Oragadam near Chennai also, where farmers have sold an acre of land for Rs. 14 lakh to the SEZ developer. In less than a year, the price of an acre of land has crossed Rs. 50 lakh.

Special Eviction Zone: At Chennanguppam near Oragadam, (Chennai) 100 Adhidrawida families, 87 of them got title deeds for house sites under the government free-house *patta* scheme, and 13 artisan families had got free land for dwelling from the *Bhoodan* land which was considered common land of the village. Those families have been asked to quit since the land is needed for Oragadam SEZ. They lose their dwelling houses, lands that they were cultivating, ponds that irrigated their lands, drinking water source, school, cremation ground, and so on. Although the SEZ developer and the District Collector have promised an alternative site for dwelling with facilities such as school, water supply etc. in the opinion of the local community, SEZ is a Special Eviction Zone. Of late, the SEZ developer through some unscrupulous elements is misinforming the public that the local school would be closed soon for want of children's strength, and so, they had better admit their children in some other school. The irate parents charge that it is a game plan of the SEZ developers to close down the school on the pretext of strength, so that they do not have to commit for construction of a new school in the location where resettlement is being planned.

Land Reforms and Land Ceiling: The efforts made through land reform measures, Land Ceiling Act, Bhoodan movement etc. obviously, were attempts to make sure that even a poor household should hold at least one or two acres of land for farming, which would be a source of livelihood and confidence. Ironically, SEZ is undoing the efforts made through Land Ceiling Act and Bhoodan movement. It is acquiring small pieces of land from the poor to be consolidated for the need of big industrialists. The farmer who knew nothing else than farming, is thrown out of his village snatching from him his only livelihood asset—the land at terms determined by the State. Thus, SEZ grabs land from the poor, and the voiceless and evicts them[2] to urban areas in search of wage employment, or further marginalise (and distance) them from accessing the benefits of growth. This study finds that Perambalur (near Trichy) is the only place in Tamil Nadu where lands that were completely barren have been acquired. The people who parted with the land are contented that they arrived at a fairly good deal as compensation.

Foreign Territory within a State: SEZ is supposed to be a foreign territory within a State. It is a separate self-contained township with all the facilities such as drinking water, sanitation, waste disposal arrangement and so on. A casual reading of the policy notes of the government would offer enough insights that this township (zone) would not seek the assistance of the local bodies such as Village Panchayats or town panchayats for any kind of service delivery. Therefore, once land has been handed over to the SEZ developer, the villages or Village Panchayats have no say over anything. Employees of some units in MEPZ (Madras Export Processing Zone) have gone to court citing that as per SEZ Policy of the government, building tax need not be paid, and the employees of SEZ units need not pay professional tax to the local bodies, which they have been paying until then.

Land Records: Agricultural Lands Records in India seems to be an interesting subject with a lot of confusions due to improper or dated records. The Nandigram and similar (not so vehement) oppositions of farmers from Tamil Nadu resisting to give agricultural lands have brought to light, that as per the government records the lands proposed for SEZ are barren, which actually is not. Perhaps, they were barren years ago. It has happened in Bairamanagalam near Hosur in Tamil Nadu. The same thing is reported about the lands in Singur, West Bengal—that the government used old land records of pre-*bargadar* period when the land was mono-crop. Over the past two decades, the land has become multi-crop.

The Employment Generation Myth: A chain of interview conducted at the SIPCOT in Hosur revealed that several industries have been closed down stating various reasons such as labour problem, the unit runs sick and so on. The reality as reasoned out by experts is that after enjoying the tax concessions of this duty-free zone for nearly eight or nine years, the private units make book adjustments for two, three years and close down unit in one SEZ and then shift to another SEZ start afresh with all the tax concessions again. There are industries shifted from Hosur SIPCOT to the newly developed SEZ in Bangalore. Once the industry closes the employees are deserted. Take the case of Jet Airways sacking nearly 1,000 employees stating economic efficiency of operations as the reason. Big business houses adopt the technique of offering VRS to employees (even Titan has done it at Hosur), and the smaller ones close down showing themselves as sick units. Big or small—many of these companies adopt the technique of having temporary labourers, and contract labourers only recruited through labour contractors or manpower agencies. The case presented of *Hundai,* Chennai puts across this point in Chapter 2.

In some places like Mathur Village Panchayat (near Cheyyar) for example, the assertive local Panchayat President has been able to influence the companies and has facilitated for almost 300 youth to get employment in the companies located in the SEZ—Thiruvannamalai. But, it requires constant struggle and capacity building of the local youth. If one did not dig the service conditions or the terms of employment, SEZs do generate employment. But, Mathur is only an exception because in many other places such as Oragadam and Sriperumbudur for example, employment of local people is avoided as far as possible. If at all they have taken, they have taken women workers from the locality, and not men.

Common Resources: It is not only lands or cultivable lands that are lost. Agricultural lands are lost, water bodies such as lakes and ponds are lost, water ways (drainage) are lost, trees are lost, cattle sheds, school buildings are lost, temples and places of worship are lost, and even dwelling houses are lost. This is about Oragadam, and Chennankuppam in Kancheepuram, and Mathur and Mankal in Thiruvannamalai. But, the compensation is paid only to private land holders and it is spoken in terms of 'cash only'. The compensation is also paid at terms determined by the State unless the local people scream to the extent that it gets sufficient media coverage or there is possibility for the issue to get political. There are no regrets about wiping out the common resources. The Panchayats are expected to understand that the State is giving it to private companies for industrial development, which is a 'common good'.

Local Panchayats Ignored: Special Economic Zone (SEZ) is one of the most controversial economic pursuits in India under the new dispensation of globalization. It is controversial not only because of the violation pointed out by local community that cultivated agricultural lands are acquired in several places, but also because it runs reverse to the spirit of the 73rd Constitutional Amendment Act. There are provisions in the Special Economic Zone Act 2005, and in the SEZ Policy, which completely unseat the Village Panchayat from the domain local bodies are expected to operate. The zones are announced with no consent of the Panchayats. Panchayats are instructed to send a 'No Objection' resolution passed in the Gram Sabha; the units set up at the SEZ premises need not go to the Panchayats applying for licence or for licence renewal; like in the case of industries in other areas, units in SEZs need not pay any building tax, or professional tax to the Panchyats and so on.

Village Level Democracy: One of the vital questions raised by the Village Panchayats in these areas is: 'What does Village Panchayat get as compensation for parting with the common lands in possession of the Panchayats?' The Village Panchayats get a directive from the district administration to send a Gram Sabha resolution passed unconditionally that the Panchayat does not have any objection to the acquisition of common lands/properties including water bodies, trees etc. by the State government for the purpose of setting up SEZ units. This explains the power of elected Panchayats in Tamil Nadu. Most Panchayats have meticulously carried out this directive from the District Administration so as to remain in the good books of the officials. However, eight Panchayats close to Cheyyar in Thiruvannamalai district passed resolution on October 2nd, 2008 objecting to the land acquisition and expressing their unwillingness to part with common lands, and resources like water bodies. However, later they could protect only a pond (4 acres of water spread area) from being acquired. Everything else is with a private footwear company (Lotus brand Shoes) now.

Resettlement and Rehabilitation: There is no legislation on Resettlement and Rehabilitation in India so far—either at the Cental level or at State level in Tamil Nadu. The Bill on R & R is still in nascent stage. The National Policy on Resettlement and Rehabilitation has got an acceptable shape and has come into force only in October 2007. The provisions of the erstwhile policies on R & R were applicable only when there were more than 400 households affected. The solace with the current policy—The National Policy on Rehabilitation and Resettlement, 2007 (R & R Policy) is applicable no matter how small the number of families affected. However, official unawareness of the provisions of the policy, and the tendency to wash hands off paying the cash compensation is resulting in social externalities, and diseconomies.

As Resettlement and Rehabilitation Act still remains in bill stage, it is possible that the officials involved in land acquisition put to use at least the R & R Policy, to provide a dignified resettlement and rehabilitation for those who part with their lands, houses, shops, work-sheds etc. for the sake of setting up of SEZs. Taking a short-sighted view of things with regard to land acquisition plays retrogressively. It ends up reversing all the poverty reduction efforts carried out pushing a considerable segment of farming families below poverty line taking away their only productive asset and the associated livelihood resources.

Compensation: The terms legislations prescribe for paying compensation to those who part with land is to pay the prevailing market rates. But, in practice it seems in many places the compensation paid to local people would be on par with market rates, or will it be less or more, is determined taking into consideration several other factors including the strength of collective voice of the people, and the political background of those who part with land. This includes social activists and the media pitching in providing strength to the landholders, and the political parties that plan to gain political mileage out of the crisis. Unless the local people demonstrated their collective bargaining power like it happened in Oragadam, or in Perambalur, or unless the issue is likely to become political the compensation settled is unfair.

Use of the Compensation Money: The way the compensation money has been put to use at places where reasonable compensation has been paid (Oragadam and Peramabalur for example) can be listed thus: New houses constructed, existing houses renovated and modified, purchased taxi for hiring out, purchased tipper lorry for hiring out, opened a petty shop in the main road, keep the money in the bank and look purchasing land in another place. In other places, where people have been paid poorly in terms of compensation (Mathur, Mangal for example), people have used up the money for settling down old debts, and others have used up the money in paying to the lawyers for fighting court cases to get reasonable compensation. Some families have used up all the gold jewellery in hand, and have also gone for borrowing to fight court cases. Land acquisition pushing the poor below poverty line could be literally noticed in Mathur and Managal. There are reasons to believe why Anti-SEZ Movement has emerged in Mathur village.

Sensibility in SEZ Development: If at all, SEZ should do some good to the local development: (i) let it get established in real barren lands based on actual surveys carried out in identified regions, and not as per the British period records in possession of the government; and (ii) the community unrest in SEZ can be avoided, if the National Policy on Rehabilitation and Resettlement, 2007 was taken as guidelines for resettlement and rehabilitation of people affected. The current tendency of making steadfast move towards eviction of people; levelling of houses; handing over the land to the SEZ developer, and paying 'cash compensation' to those who part with lands would only cause damage to agriculture, mock grassroots level democracy, and aggravate poverty. There is no meaning talking about Corporate Social Responsibility (CSR), having the company established stripping off the only permanent asset worth the name the poor farmer had.

ACTION POINTS

Land Records: The land records that the government keeps come from Mohal period, with slight modifications by the British Government in India. It is the British period records that are being used in many of the States in India including Tamil Nadu. It is this that is giving false information about various categories of land. The Department of Land Resources should accelerate the programme of updating the status and current use of various types of lands in Tamil Nadu. Land records and land administration should be computerised so as to identify barren and waste lands, and not to lay hand in cultivable lands based on old records.

Fundamental Right: One basic problem with the way SEZs are constituted is the lack of property rights for Indian citizens: if the State decides to take away a piece of land, there is nothing much the individual landholder can do. Nor can the compensation amount be argued beyond a fairly limited point—and the land is then resold to private parties at a vastly higher price. Given that this weapon is mostly deployed against peasants and other with no training or experience other than in traditional livelihoods, this needs reform. Fundamental right to raise objection needs to be demanded, and it should be respected.

Private Negotiation: The practice of SIPCOT acquiring land and selling it to the SEZ units need to be revised. The governments should insist the promoter-firm or firms do the negotiating with landowners without recourse to State fiat. Another issue is the preferential treatment for SEZs, on rules and facilities. These can be given to agriculture also instead of announcing loan waivers. SIPCOT may be involved only in acquiring the common lands with appropriate compensation to Village Panchayats. Purchase of private lands should be left to the companies (SEZ developer) or the units concerned to make private negotiations with landholders. The local R & R Committee along with Panchayat functionaries may oversee/facilitate this deal.

Land for Land Compensation: Instead of going for cash compensation, land for land compensation with assistance for land development and loan for cultivation could be a better deal. The government and the businesses fail to take note that land is not just land, but it has more to do with the livelihood, dignity, social esteem, culture and future of farmers and village and tribal communities. This requires to be taken care of, by providing land for land compensation.

Farm Land for Industry: Veterans of the Land and Land Reforms department say Singur and Nandigram happened not because farmers did not wish to part with their land but because they saw themselves being left out of the development process. "The farmer loses three things: land, livelihood and stability", says an official, requesting anonymity. Just paying the present market value of the land is not enough—they must be compensated for the perpetual loss of income and given an alternative livelihood from Day One. The approach should be respectable, and compensation should be fair, without pushing the landholders virtually to the margins with a bunch of currency in hand.

Involve Local Governments: The local community should be involved through the local governments in identifying areas for setting up of SEZs. There are certain provisions in the R & R Policy, 2007 such putting up in the notice board of the concerned Village Panchayats the extent of land to be acquired, the survey numbers, the common land to be acquired, the amount of compensation paid per acre, and how the common facilities are to be rebuilt, and what is the R & R arrangement being made etc. The Panchayats should also stand firmly where acquisition of certain kinds of land—be it private or government—would distress 'the common good' of the people, their employment/livelihood. Fully involve the Panchayats to enable grassroots level democracy to work.

Compensation: The R & R Policy, 2007 may be taken as guideline for providing compensation to the project affected families. The Village Panchayats wherever land acquisition for SEZ are to be commenced, the Panchayat functionaries should be sensitised on the provisions of the R & R Policy, and to include in the agreement the amount of time that would be taken for executing the R & R plan. The compensation should consider that a permanent asset is to be taken away once and for all. So, the amount or nature of compensation paid should be liberally fixed so as to allow the landholder to spend the rest of his life with dignity.

Compensation to Landless/Sharecroppers: The practice of providing compensation only to landholders, ignoring the landless labourers or sharecroppers who depended on that land for years should be done away with. Appropriate compensation should be paid to landless labourers and sharecroppers should also be designed. It may also be a plan of alternative employment. Land acquisition for SEZ has left the agricultural labourers at crossroads. The agricultural labourers are forced to migrate to Thiruppur, and Chennai in most of the places. It is time agriculture in Tamil Nadu gets all sorts of encouragements, institutional support and infrastructure creation so that the deceleration is reversed. The distress migration of agricultural labourers can be reduced. Setting up of SEZ should not be at the expense of agriculture at a time when agriculture growth is decelerating.

Project Level R & R Committee: Although the R & R Policy requires a local level committee to be formed with representatives from local Panchayats, local SHGs, local bank, NGO of that area etc. no project of the SIPCOT or private SEZ has this committee in place. They deal with individual farmers in isolation. The individual farmers fight their case individually, with very little role for the Panchayats or for collective bargaining.

Showcase Successful SEZs: Pressurise that the corporate firms or companies that establish units at SEZ should show case the successful R & R efforts made as a model to the world that ours is a socialistic democracy.

Cost and Benefit: The obvious question is why the State Government is keen on SEZs, and why cannot extend similar help to already existing industrial clusters. A related issue here is the lack of clearness on costs and proposed benefits in establishing an SEZ; almost nowhere do governments come out with clear statements on how the tax and other concessions will play out and the rationale for this. Doing so would help ensure rational public debate, of a sort that citizens could follow and decide on for themselves (IE, October 3, 2008).

Share in the Profit: Since land is converted into high-productive and profit making ventures, the owners of land are entitled to a share for their land—an important factor of production. Hence, displaced landowners are entitled to an appropriate share in the future profits from the new ventures taken designing compensation policies. A number of countries have designed policies in these lines (Ratna V. Reddy, Suresh B. Reddy, *EPW* August 4, 2007).

Return the Unused Lands: Where SIPCOT acquired land and remain unused for more than five years, it should be given to the Panchayats concerned or to the erstwhile landholders on payment of the amount that it was sold for. Further land acquisition in the name of Project—2, 3 etc. should be undertaken only if all the lands acquired in Project 1 got sold out and work commenced.

CONCLUSION

In deed,. we are aware of the fact that it is moving from farming to other secondary and tertiary sectors that have made the rich countries rich. In such an event, preparations by the government should be underway to equip the youth with skills required for becoming employable in the SEZs, based on the industry requirements. The government is holding talks for 'quota and reservations' in the private sector enterprises, while being otherwise busy doing the brokerage for the private companies to acquire farm lands in the areas they want.

Setting up of manufacturing units, and service provision through IT industries etc. are desirable for an economy to get on the fast track of development. The concern is that this should not create a smoke screen to make everything else obscure or trivial. This is a matter of serious concern when it comes to hit agriculture. Taking cognizance of the soil type and climatic conditions in Kelamangalam area (near Hosur) a District Collector who motivated a group of farmers to get down to cultivation of rose flowers setting up six green houses with the financial assistance of the NABARD, gets down in the next one year to grab lands for SEZ not being able to withstand the pressure from the instructions of the State Government. This has happened despite the fact that the local farmers have got a survey done by the State Agriculture Department and come out with a report that the land is 'purely agricultural land and that this village sends 4-5 loads of vegetables almost daily to places like Coimbatore, Erode, Bavani, Ernakulam and Chennai'. Higher level political lobbying by the local farmers, coupled with media coverage have put the idea of land acquisition on the back burner.

Agriculture cannot take back seat. It has to be given due place so as to avoid any possible food crisis in the future. Unmindful acquisition of agriculture land is also a threat to farmers who have trained themselves over the years in nothing else than farming. A country like India with the population crossing 110 crore, if it has to face a food crisis, it would take a magnificent proportion. Already the shift from agriculture to other sectors and the number of farmers who give up agriculture is alarming due to reasons such as agricultural commodities are the only products in this country for which the producer cannot determine price. Besides this if SEZ goes heedless in land acquisition, evicting farmers involuntarily from farming, it is a signal indicating a grave danger.

It is time for the local bodies to be aware of, and be alert about announcements of SEZ areas, and be observant about the type of land acquired for SEZ and educate the local community on these aspects. We welcome industrialization, so long as it is set up on the barren land, does not play havoc to agriculture and rural livelihoods. We welcome industrialization so long as it does not cause environmental damage. Overuse of environmental resource also amounts to violence. Ethics and self-discipline in resource use should be an overriding criterion of development.

NOTES

1. Nokia was established in Sri Perumbudur SEZ long before the Orgadam SEZ proposal came up.
2.. Expressions like 'the poor, and the voiceless' are deliberately used because lands that belong to big shots like VGP Realtors, MLAs and Ex-MLAs, and powerful Civil Servants are carefully by-passed. This could be directly observed during field visits.

REFERENCES

Aradhana Aggarwal (2006). Special Economic Zone: Revisiting the Policy Debate, *Economic and Political Weekly,* November 4, 2006.

Background note Special Economic Zones in India. [Online] Available: *http://sezindia.nic.in/* [accessed on 2nd September, 2008].

Balagopal K. (2007). Impact of Grant Industries, *Economic and Political Weekly*, September 29, 2007.

C.R. Bijoy (2007). Special Economic Zones: Profits at any Cost. [Online] Available: http: *www.countercurrents.org* [accessed on 2nd September 2008].

CII Notes on Special Economic Zone (SEZ), Confederation of Indian Industry, Core 4A, 4th Floor, India Habitat Centre, Lodi Road, New Delhi-110 003 [Online] Available: http: www. *http://cii.in/documents/wto/note%20on%20special%20economic%20zones1.pdf* [accessed on 2nd September 2008].

Erik, S. Reinert (2007). *How Rich Countries Got Rich and Why Poor Countries Stay Poor*, Carrol and Graf Publishers, New York.

Fact Sheet on Special Economic Zones [Online] Available: *http://meaindia.uic.in* [accessed on 2nd September, 2008].

GoTN, Department of Industries, SIPCOT—Citizen's Charter accessed from website: www.sipcot.com

Ignatius Chithelen (2008). Global Financial Crisis: A Long Way from Recovery, *Economic and Political Weekly*, September 2008.

Jet Staff Protest Retrenchment, *The Hindu,* dated October 16, 2008 (Madurai Edition) p. 1.

Lavanya Chandan (2008). Process of land Acquisition, [Online] Available: *www.legalserviceindia.com/article/print* [accessed on 2nd September 2008].

Mehra, R. and S. Gummage (1999). 'Trends, Countertrends and Gaps in Women's Empowerment, *Wold Development Report*, Vol. 27, No. 3, March 533-550.

Ratna Reddy, V., Suresh Reddy, B., (2007). Land Alienation and Local Communities: Case Studies in Hyderabad-Secunderabad, *Economic and Political Weekly* August 4, 2007.

Shankar Gopalakrishnan (2007). Negative Aspects of Special Economic Zones in China, *Economic and Political Weekly* April 28, 2007.

Shikha Ohri (2008). Special Economic Zones, [Online] Available: *www.legalserviceindia.com/article/print* [accessed on 2nd September, 2008].

Special Economic Zone Act of 2005 (2005). Government of India, *The Gazette of India*, Ministry of Law and Justice (Legislative Department), New Delhi.

Special Economic Zone Policy of Government of Tamil Nadu (2003). [Online] Available: *http://www.tn.gov.in/misc/sez2003.htm* [accessed on 2nd September 2008].

Special Economic Zone Rules of 2006. *The Gazette of India Extraordinary*, dated the 10th February, 2006.

Srikanth Srinivas (2008). Global Crisis, *Business World,* October 13, 2008, p. 34.

Standing, G. (1999). 'Global Feminisation through flexible Labour: A theme revisited', *World Development Report*, Vol. 27, No. 3, March, pp. 583-602.

CHAPTER SIX

National Rural Employment Guarantee: Experience from a Tamil Nadu Village

The National Rural Employment Guarantee Act (NREGA) is a flagship programme of the Government that directly touches lives of the poor and promotes inclusive growth. The Act aims at enhancing livelihood security of households in rural areas of the country by providing at least one hundred days of guaranteed wage employment in a financial year to every household whose adult members volunteer to do unskilled manual work. The Act came into force on February 2, 2006 and was implemented in a phased manner. In Phase I it was introduced in 200 of the most backward districts of the country. It was implemented in an additional 130 districts in Phase II (2007-08). As per the initial target, NREGA was to be expanded countrywide in five years. However, in order to bring the whole nation under its safety net and keeping in view the demand, the Scheme was extended to the remaining 285 rural districts of India from April 2008, in Phase III (UNDP, 2009).

NREGS IN TAMIL NADU

NREGS is being implemented in six districts of Tamil Nadu as a pilot in 2005-06 and extended to other districts in a phased manner year after year. This centrally sponsored scheme is implemented by the Department of Rural Development of the Government of Tamil Nadu. The Village Panchayats play the main role in the implementation of the scheme. However, the directions are from the BDOs, and the PO-DRDA. The scheme has been designed so well that it looks very much decentralised at the grassroots level and transparent to the beneficiaries. A rapid assessment was made in one of the NREGS villages in Dindigul district, viz. Kalikkampatty (Athoor Block). The idea was to record the views of the Panchayat functionaries and the beneficiaries about the benefits of the schemes to the rural poor, and constraints, if any confronted in the implementation.

Kalikkampatty Panchayat has seven hamlets with a population of 3,840, living in 1,038 families. The village has developed all infrastructures availing assistance under various schemes—both centrally sponsored and State sponsored. In recognition of the works carried under the total sanitation campaign, it received Nirmal Purashkar Award for the year 2007-08. Besides, other things like the successful SHG movement, the village is known for successful implementation of NREGS in Dindigul district. 1,000 individuals from 586 families have so far registered themselves with the Panchayat seeking work under NREGS. Implementation of the scheme started during the year 2006-07 onwards after the preparation of the perspective plan for a period of five years by the District Administration.

Box 6.1: Nature of Works Executed under NREGS

Year	*Nature of Work*	*Estimated Financial Outlay*	*Actual Expenditure (Rs.)*
2006-07	Supply channel renovation	10,00,000	9,64,380
	Desilting and deepening of pond (Kuttanikulam)	5,20,000	5,18,740
2007-08	Supply channel renovation (Gandhigram Oadai)	10,53,000	10,50,560
	Supply channel renovation (Nijamudhin Oadai)	3,70,000	3,67,840
	Supply channel renovation (Ariyanallur—neighbouring Panchayat)	10,53,000	9,49,295
2008-09	Shanmugam Pillai pond East Area improvement	10,00,000	Work under progress
	Murugan Thottam Supply Channel	5,00,000	Work under progress
	Karuppanan Pond renovation	5,00,000	To be commenced

In the last three years, the village has executed a total of eight works, seven in its own village, and one in the neighbouring village. Work in the neighbouring village was taken for want of work sites in Kalikkampatty and its hamlets during the second year of scheme implementation. On an average every year about Rs. 20 lakh is spent on various NREGS works.

Community and gender disaggregated analysis make two things clear: (i) majority of the women members (accounting for 72% in 2007-08 and 74 per cent in 2008-09) got employed under the scheme; (ii) 34 per cent of the households benefited are from the Scheduled Caste community. Thus, the scheme is found to have benefited women members in more numbers.

Box 6.2: Community Distribution of Employment Generated under NREGS

Community	*Gender*	*2007-08*	*%*	*2008-09 (Upto Dec. 2008)*	*%*
SC	Male	72	31	65	30
	Female	161	69	160	70
	Total	233	100	225	100
	Total Households	157	34	155	34
BC	Male	104	26	103	25
	Female	289	74	310	75
	Total	393	100	413	100
	Total Households	300	600	307	66
Total	Male	176	28	168	26
	Female	450	72	470	74
	Total	626	100	638	100
	Total Households	457	100	462	100

Box 6.3: Number of Days of Employment for Households

No of Employment Days	*Number of Households*			
	2007-08		2008-09	
0-20	34	7.4	73	15.8
21-40	43	9.4	148	32.0
41-60	63	13.8	162	35.1
61-80	91	20.0	42	9.1
81-99	129	28.2	18	3.9
100 days	97	21.2	19	4.1
TOTAL	**457**	**100**	**462**	**100**

For the completed year 2007-08, about 70 per cent of the families benefited with more than 60 days of guaranteed employment, of whom 21.2 per cent families availed 100 days of employment. During the current year, only half the estimated works are over and the remaining works are under progress and the person days of employment generated show that about 83 per cent of the families have about 50-80 days of work unused. Thus, the villagers are making proper use of the scheme.

The financial performance of the scheme in Kalikkampatty shows that the scheme in the last two years generated an additional wage income of Rs. 42.85 lakh to about 460 households in the Panchayat. The additional income generated per household works out to Rs. 9,315 in the last 20 months. It should be noted here that this scheme has enabled additional flow of money in the rural households, which in economic terms mean enhancement of human capabilities and functions. Key probes were into the households employed under the NREGS.

Box 6.4: Financial Performance of the Scheme

Particulars	*2007-08*	*2008-09*
Receipts: Opening Balance	595331	482752
Subsidy	2500000	1300000
Bank Interest	4621	4619
Total	**3099952**	**1787371**
EXPENSES: Wages	2607375	1678345
Bank Commission	9825	1597
Bank Balance	482752	107429
Total	**3099952**	**1787371**

Case 1: Ms Chikkammal: Chikkammal (62) lives in Kalikkampatty main village with her spinster daughter (Rajamani) who is about 40 years old. They belong to Backward Community. Chikkammal is unlettered, and Rajamani is a neo-literate. Chikkammal, although in her early sixties, still earns her living doing manual labour. Before the NREGS scheme, Chikkammal was an agricultural labourer. She used to get 3-4 days of employment in a week. The daughter goes for work in a handloom centre managed by Gandhigram Trust for over 25 years, and earns Rs. 40-50 daily. The introduction of NREGS serves as a great fall back for Chikkammal and her daughter during agriculturally lean seasons. Both of them (Chikkammal and her daughter) together have completed 100 days of employment under NREGS for two consecutive years now. Employment under NREGS has helped them earn almost Rs. 7,500 a year.

In their opinion income from NREGS is definitely an additional income, apart from the income Chikkammal earns through farm works, and her daughter earns through spinning. Like all the other NREGS beneficiaries do, Chikkammal also has a preference for NREGS work rather than the regular wage employment in the local farms. This is because the payment under NREGS is higher compared to wages that prevail for farm employment, especially for women (Rs. 50 a day) in this area. Both of them are members of local SHG as well.

It is interesting to note what they have done with the additional income. They have opened a Post Office Recurring Deposit (PORD), and a life insurance scheme for the daughter. They save Rs. 200 per month with the

PORD, and Rs. 101 with the Life Insurance Corporation of India. These two have become additional modes of saving now, apart from their regular savings with the SHG. Asked about their opinion on creating permanent assets, the daughter shared her plan to buy jewels once the PORD money accumulates.

Case 2: Viswanathan: Viswanathan (49), an agricultural labourer of Kalikkampatty village belongs to Scheduled Caste. He lives in this village with his wife, two sons and a daughter. Viswanathan is a neo-literate, and his wife is an illiterate. They live in a house provided to them under IAY of the government. For the construction of his own house under the IAY he has additionally contributed an equal amount of the money sanctioned under the scheme. He wants to see that all his wards get good educational standing, and get employed either in the service sector or in industries. The eldest of them is the daughter who is doing her Bachelors Degree in Education (B.Ed.) after Post-graduation. The boys are doing under graduation degree. He feels pride in repeating that he funded the educational expenses of all his children doing hard labour as an agricultural labourer working in other's farms. The family does not have own land or any other property. His children are his hope for the future. He underscores the family's dependence on PDS. He gets his entitlement of 35 kg rice from PDS, and borrows a Family Card from a neighbour for getting an additional 35 kg, which is sufficient for his family for one full month. He could manage rice for the family with a minimum expense of Rs. 70 per month under PDS.

Viswanathan and his wife have together completed 100 days of employment for three consecutive years. He has earned nearly Rs. 22,000 as additional income through NREGS, apart from the regular wage employment his family gets locally. NREGS has helped him stop borrowing money for educational expenses of his children. His preference is for local wage employment, as he thinks that his family has guaranteed employment of 100 days of work under the NREGS. Whenever there is no farm work around he would use 'employment guarantee' scheme. He thinks it is unwise and unnecessary to make the local land owner to wait for the sake of doing NREGS work, when the NREGS can actually wait, whereas the local landowner would want to use some other labourer in his place. Moreover, the farm wage rates for men too increased because of demand for labour caused by NREGS, which is another reason for him to feel happy about this scheme.

The local wages for agriculture and other manual works have increased from Rs. 70-80 to Rs. 140-150 for men, and for women from Rs. 30-40 to Rs. 90-100. That is opting for farm labour actually gives income more than what he could earn through NREGS. At the same time he can use his quota under the same. He plans his work. One of the purposes that NREGS contemplated seems to have come true in terms of increase in the local wages—both for men and women. However, the disparity in wages between men and women in farm employment remains.

He is also aware that the general wage level increase made agricultural operations unviable to the farm owners. Those who cultivate also shifted from food crops to commercial crops—from paddy to flower cultivation. We have options to choose from in terms of employment—is it local employment or NREGS. Earlier we borrowed for educating children, but now, we are able to manage without resorting to borrowing from money lenders. In the absence of this scheme we would not have been able to educate the children without debt burden.

Case 3: Veeraputhiran: Veeraputhiran (39) is an agricultural labourer in Kalikkampatty village. He lives along with his wife Rathi (34), two sons and a daughter. They own a house given to them under the IAY Scheme of the government, which they constructed contributing Rs. 60,000 additionally to the money sanctioned under the scheme. Both the sons are school dropouts. The elder son is learning two wheeler mechanism in a private mechanic-shed, and the younger son is assisting a local wiring contractor in household wiring. The daughter is studying in ninth standard in the local government school.

Veeraputhiran and his wife have together completed 100 days of employment under the NREGS for two consecutive years. Simply put, he says NREGS has eased life in the villages which was difficult earlier. It has given confidence in life that there is guaranteed employment and so life will go on hunger-free. He could not save any money in the past two years. But, he could avoid borrowing. He could spend around Rs. 1,500 in repairing his house, with the income he earned through NREGS works. His sons brought a DVD player for which he is paying on instalment-basis. He is happy that the local wages have almost doubled after the introduction of NREGS.

REGISTRATION

The scheme follows a systematic procedure in every respect to see that eligible persons get employment and thereby the minimum prescribed wage for the work. The first step in the whole process is the registration by the people who seek employment under the scheme. Everyone except the Village Panchayat President is eligible to have their names registered and get a job card. As such in this village 1,000 members have registered and got job cards in the last three years.

As the scheme is for providing wage employment to unskilled workers in the village almost everyone, even those who have never engaged in agricultural operations also get registered under NREGS and come to work. In the opinion of the Panchayat functionaries such people account for almost 50 per cent, which is a challenge in carrying out quality work. One inbuilt procedure with NREGS that offsets this weakness, to a considerable extent, is working in groups of 20s. Those who while away the time, evading work at the site, are chucked out by the members of the group the next day when such slothful people come to work-spot. This makes everyone to work.

It is also understood that everyone registers expecting that the government may in the future fix registration under NREGS as one of the essential criteria for getting benefits under other welfare schemes. In the last three years only about 63.8 per cent of the total registered beneficiaries attended works. The rest 36.2 per cent remained silent without making any request for work.

NATURE AND ADEQUACY OF WORKS FOR GUARANTEEING EMPLOYMENT

As the scheme encourages earthen works only, the village administration could identify only limited number of work opportunities within its jurisdiction. The village has very limited extent of *poromboke* lands, 2 rivulets (supply channels) and a pond. The estimated works in these common properties were not even sufficient for providing employment to all the registered workers in the first year of the programme itself. Therefore, the Panchayat had to approach the neighbouring Panchayat, which has more number of work sites. But, considering the future needs, the neighbouring Panchayat officials do not encourage letting their work sites for continuing work. That is, the Panchayat is forced to seek the help of other neighbouring Panchayats, which if materialised, costs at least 10 per cent more than the estimated cost in the form of transport/travelling expenses. Non-availability of work sites is the most serious problem the Panchayat confronts now.

STABILISATION OF WAGE AND IMPROVED QUALITY OF LIFE

One of the major intentions of the scheme is to assure minimum and equal wage to men and women in the rural areas. Guaranteeing employment means guaranteeing income to meet the basic minimum family requirements without difficulties. The interactions brought forth the fact that the local wage rates have increased for both men and women in the last 2-3 years; in the case of men it has increased from Rs. 70-80 to Rs. 140-150 and for women from Rs. 30-40 to Rs. 50-60. However, the wage disparity remains unsettled. Given the improvements in the prevailing wage rates, men folk prefer farm work to NREGS work with first priority, and women prefer NREGS to farm labour. As such, the women in the village worked more number of days. For example, during 2008-09, of the 638 person days of employment, men worked 168 person days and women worked 470 person days. The choice of NREGS and farm work now enable the people to choose the work to maximise their daily wage. This is one of the greatest benefits of NREGS.

The guaranteed employment coupled with the general wage rate improvements has brought a considerable improvement in the family income, which, in turn, started bringing changes in the quality of life. Those who struggled for making both ends meet now do it easily with the guaranteed (additional) income from the NREGS work; those who met the day-to-day family expenses are now able to save a portion of their income in SHGs, Post office and banks; some have life insurance policies; could spend some money for making improvement in the existing house, and constructing toilets. Apart from the economic benefits that the beneficiaries roll out, one social change that seem to be taking place in NREGS villages is that it enables people belonging to all religions and community to work together in groups and get along well. Kalikkampatty—a village—which was known for religious conflicts earlier, is now emerging as a village where people of different religions and community groups getting closer to each other unaware.

BETTER IMPLEMENTATION OF OTHER WELFARE SCHEMES

The village functionaries could convince the people in making use of other welfare schemes such as TSC, and becoming a member of SHG with individual bank account etc. NREGS has also geared up the operations of local SHGs. The beneficiaries of NREGS have been convinced to construct individual household toilets under TSC taking loan from local banks. The loan amount is being recovered in easy instalments from the wages under NREGS. The efforts taken in getting the NREGS beneficiaries constructing toilets under Total Sanitation Campaign (TSC) at their houses with financial tie-up with local banks by the Panchayat is worth emulating. In addition to the grants received under TSC, the Panchayat has helped the beneficiaries get loans from the local banks for the construction of toilets. That is convergence and networking are taking place consciously in this village.

CONCLUSION

As the scheme moves from pilot stage to wider implementation, it is time to map out, where the scheme has scored well and where it has been facing constraints. The scheme has provided a fall back employment guarantee for 100 days to the landless labourers, who otherwise depended only on seasonal employment in agricultural farms. Those who wisely mark these 100 days of employment making full use of the local farm employment (as primary) do really well. The availability of guaranteed employment, as contemplated by the scheme, has resulted in improvement in the local wage-rates for various kinds of labour works both on-farm and off-farm that the landless labourers are generally engaged in. That which was Rs. 80-100 for men has gone into a range of Rs. 120-150, and that which was Rs. 40-50 for women has gone into a range of Rs. 70-80. The total household income of landless labourers has increased, by the additional income they could earn under the NREGS.

Another very significant achievement of the scheme is that it has brought to light several encroachments of the common land supposed to be in possession of the Panchayats and the PWD. They include ponds, tanks, tank bunds, waterways, pathways etc. Although it has created internal grudges and feuds between the Panchayat functionaries and those who benefited by such encroachments so far, some of the Panchayat functionaries have shrewdly made use of this opportunity to expose such encroachments and have marked a clear line between private and common property. This has been possible, especially under the NREGS because the funds allocated every year is so huge that each Panchayat has to identify works year after year. This forces the Panchayats (or allows them to use the NREGS as a pretext) to look for each piece of common land, which otherwise had got covered under the assumption that land in possession of private people could be private property.

One of the Villages (*Kalikkampatty*) in Dindigul district has planned so well in integrating NREGS with the Total Sanitation Scheme (TSC) that the village has got Nirmal Purashkar Award which carry a cash prize of Rs. 5 lakh to the Panchayat. How was it done? Every individual who registered and got a job card under the NREGS was also made a member of the local SHG. The Panchayat administration has made an arrangement for a bank loan through the SHGs for constructing individual household latrines with a subsidy of Rs. 1,200 eligible under the TSC. The understanding is that the loan amount would be recovered from the beneficiaries when the weekly wage payment is made under NREGS. It became a big success. Every household owns a toilet now. The banker is getting the loan amount recovered; the village got Nirmal

Purashkar Award for achieving total sanitation; the Panchayat President got the District Collector's appreciation for implementing convergence of welfare schemes and programmes, which remains a wishful thinking in many of the policy notes—a success for constructive thinking and hard work.

All said and done, one of the grave dangers as expressed by landowners and landless labourers alike about the scheme is the deceleration it is causing to agriculture, and to allied sector. The official priority goes towards completion of works taken up under NREGS rather than the seasonality of agriculture, and availability of labour for farm works. This has caused severe shortage of labour to carry out farm related works. Coupled with considerable reduction in supply of labour for farm works and the hike in wage rates introduced by NREGS have created a situation where hiring labour for agricultural works is uneconomical. One widespread concern is agriculture is decelerating as a result of NREGS. This should not be left unattended to, and that a policy intervention is increasingly being felt.

REFERENCES

UNDP (2009). *The National Rural Employment Guarantee Act (NREGA) Design, Process and Impact,* Nreganet Series from UNDP, New Delhi.

CHAPTER SEVEN

Information Asymmetry: The State, Market and the Civil Society

INSTITUTIONS AND THEIR FUNCTIONALITIES

Individuals live and operate in a world of institutions (Jean Dreze and Amartya Sen, 2005). These institutions can be social institutions such as a family; a political institution such as a Gram Panchayat; or they can be an economic institution such as a bank or a market. We have state-led institutions. We have market-led institutions. Our opportunities and prospects depend crucially on what institutions exist and how they function. It is our policy with regard to the rules of the game and how these rules are put to practice that determines how extensive or intensive one can play. The region or the expanse of play in turn determines the range of human choices made available to an individual.

Democracy is an instrument of social equity and it operates through various institutions at various levels. The highest democratic body in India decided to globalize and move towards liberalization and privatization of economic activities about two decades ago. Since then, state-led institutions and market-led institutions operate on parallel lines. Several reforms have taken place in our democratic practice such as introduction of Electronic Voting Machines; citizens' Right to Information Act; social audit of National Rural Employment Guarantee Act and so on. Village Panchayats as the main democratic institution at the grassroots level institution have roles to manage the common property resources, besides ensuring the delivery of basic services such as drinking water supply, local school development and ensuring primary health care and disease control/prevention activities.

There is public provisioning of essential commodities, besides sale at open market. Public provisioning—be it essential commodities, drinking water, primary education or health care—operates parallel to the open market availability. Ensuring access to public provisioning, especially for the poor is within the control of the local bodies. However, markets operate through invisible hands and information asymmetry that nobody predicts precisely what it will be like the next day. This is partly a natural characteristic of the market itself; and partly because of the cartels that those who control the market are able to form. The services of public institutions naturally go as a matter of citizens' right to basic services. Markets operate on the basis of economic efficiency calculations taking into account profits and profitability. Liberal licensing, privatization, deregulation, decontrol, Single-window clearance—all these we come across in our daily lives these days—are also the concepts very much use in free-market economies.

There are instances where the economic efficiency calculations have provided wonderful results, for example, use of Electronic Voting Machines in India have spectacularly reduced the time taken for manual counting of papers in the secret ballot box. It has undone the need for diversion of battalions of staff in 'counting-duty' from various departments of the government, leaving their regular work high and dry. This is efficiency. Another best example is the cost per minute of call made in mobile phones, which is economic efficiency compared to the land-line phones we used to have about ten years ago. Similarly, introduction of technological innovations in water resource use through drip and sprinkle irrigation have reduced water use, and increased area coverage. This is efficiency of technology and reach of market.

At the same time, it also makes humans to think that instead of providing water to a habitation where the poor live, it can be packaged and sold for cash to the rich in the apartments. This deprives the poor of access to drinking water. Similarly, there are hills with inscriptions, stone carvings and cave temples that are considered as ancient archaeological treasures 'supposed to be' under the maintenance of Archaeological Survey of India or State Department of Archaeology, which are vandalised as sites for stone quarrying by the economic efficiency calculations of the private market forces. The rent-seeking behaviour of the politicians and the officials makes them turn a blind eye towards it. The Village Panchayat as a grassroots level democratic body looks on this defacement helplessly without being able to protect the hills which are actually Common Property Resources. The concerned department of the government sits away in the district or State capital, whereas the Panchayats because of the closeness have to witness the vandalism caused to such treasures. Thus, a democratic institution (the Panchayat) stands vulnerable to the forces of the market power. This is narrated with a case in this Chapter (The Case of Keelavalavu, Madurai).

The Markets and Panchayats, often cross swords especially because the former stands for economic efficiency and the later stands for social justice. There are instances where the economic efficiency calculations have provided wonderful results; and there are instances where they have thrown the poor out of their homes and farms.

The tentacles of market power and the vistas of its expansion are so overpowering to the extent of overshadowing the democratic ideals and democratic principles. They even go to the extent of micro-managing the local body functions putting to use the rent-seeking behaviour of officials and elected representatives. It starts in a humble way and ends up crushing the poor throwing them out of their homes and farms, as in the case of Special Economic Zones in Oragadam or Mathur (See Chapter 5: Special Economic Zones). At the same time there are places where the local bodies have been able to challenge the market, despite the fact that the State has been on the side of the market. An ordinary citizen has to face the activities of both the institutions almost on a day to day basis. He watches the interaction of democratic institutions with the market, and how markets deal with democracy, and also how the media—an important pillar of democracy—interprets it.

The reality of employment generation through letting the markets operate is very much true, notwithstanding the limitations and harassments that the workers/employees face. The fact that markets can also contribute to enhancement of individual incomes and thus can contribute to poverty reduction is not untrue. Interestingly one Hundai car manufacturing company in Sriperumbudur, Tamil Nadu can stand as testimony for employment generation as well as for constant employees' unrest. It has generated employment for more than 2,000 employees. But, at the same time, it is also known for ill-treatment of employees and workers unrest. This is especially because of poor democratic mechanisms in place to listen to employees' grievances and overruling the prevailing labour laws including Trade Union rights. There is no need for SEZ Units pay Professional Tax—neither by the employees nor by the unit—to the local bodies, as notified by the SEZ Act, 2005, and related Rules 2006.

The questions are: Is the unified voice of the employees heard? Do they have the right to organise democratically in order to sort out their problems with the Management? Do the public or the Panchayat body in the vicinity have the right to express and seek remedy to the negative-externality caused by the market forces? On the whole how democratic is grassroots level democracy? How democratic is organisation level democracy? How the grassroots level local bodies are challenging or overshadowed by the market power? What is the role of 'public' or civil society and the media in restoring the democratic ideals? Besides capital, what factors provide the market the power to command and overwhelm? How Village Panchayats can take on markets or deal with markets in such a way that it represents public choice? These are vital issues in the context of an emerging market economy such as India, for example.

Although state is an all-encompassing power, it depends on the state policy what ideals will a government follow. There are several ways of coordinating economic activity. It can be state-led. It can be market-led. It can be community-led and so on. It can be centralised or decentralised. The rules can be practised democratically with the principle of equity and fairness. It is possible the rules can be practised based on survival of the fittest or whoever proves mighty shall get the lion's share. Democracy is an engagement and strictly speaking democracy is only what you and I make as citizens. Markets tend to sabotage democratic practice is a widespread allegation by activists, NGOs and independent scholars. The cases narrated in this Chapter stand testimony to the fight the local bodies have to put up to be able to have access to information for local resource management. So, while it is true that democracy is only in what you make of it, most often, the practice of democratic ideals are governed by democratic institutions of the state. Markets subdue or overpower other forces, and at times the democratic institutions themselves—irrespective of their operating at micro level or macro level—have to pay heed to the power of the market forces when they stand as significant pillars of an economy.

INFORMATION ASYMMETRY

Market is a storehouse of capital, and capital is an instrument to have access to knowledge, information, technology 'and manoeuvring'. State is a storehouse of power and law making and so can exercise control over a vast pool of vital information including those of the markets' and the community's. The spread of computers and internet facilities has let open a vast pool of information and knowledge—some useful and many unusable. The general public or the Panchayats get access to information uploaded and published in the internet only. This information that is uploaded can be selective or lopsided, in the sense; one does not get all the information one requires to make a decision or to conclude pondering over certain things.

Case 7.1: Valasamudram, Tuticorin District, Tamil Nadu: The information available in the government websites or public portals are limited and introductory in most of the cases. The struggle local people of Valasamudram had to put up for obtaining information about a proposed Special Economic Zone (SEZ) cutting across that village could be cited as example. Valasamudram is one of the two hamlets (the other being Venkatachalapuram) that together make Valasamudram Village Panchayat in Oddapidaram Block of Tuticorin district (Tamil Nadu). On a sunny afternoon, cars and jeeps painted 'Government of Tamil Nadu' a little above the front windscreen came into the village. Those who got off the vehicle—seemingly government officers—walked talking among themselves towards the land where we had sown black gram and millets. Local people were only staring at them, not knowing the goings on. When a similar bunch of people visited the second and the third time, people came to know that they were government officials including the Project Officer SIPCOT, and others from the office of the District Collector, Tuticorin making a visit to acquire lands for setting up 'second SIPCOT'.

SIPCOT is a more familiar expression than SEZ in this area because there is already one SIPCOT in Veerapandiyapuram area near here. On hearing about the intention of the government regarding land acquisition, people got startled. That the people who handed over lands for setting up the 'first SIPCOT' in Veerapandiyapuram, Samynatham, and Gayaloorni areas have not got their compensation money fully settled yet. Many of the farmers have filed court cases that the government was delaying payment of compensation for the land they handed over several years ago. Hence, regarding the second phase the official communication was being delayed. Neither the Panchayat Office nor the individual land owners got any information. Meanwhile several private realtors started purchasing land giving prices higher than what used to be usually. This swelled the suspicion of the local people further. The public kept enquiring about it to the Village Panchayat President.

The Panchayat President wanted to confirm the truth behind the 'hearsay' and so enquired officials known to him at the District Collector's Office in Tuticorin. He could get only a hazy picture of the goings on that it is possible; they might take; and that there is a proposal being discussed; and how much land would be taken is not known yet and so on. But, the responsible persons that he thought would be in a position to give him the 'correct information' did not reveal anything significant. As a last resort he made a move on the 26th May, 2008 by putting to use the citizen's weapon: Right to Information

Act. He wanted to know the details of land being proposed for acquisition in the jurisdiction of Valasamudram Panchayat. He got a reply on the 5th June 2008 from the Public Information Officer that there is a proposal to acquire 928.30 acres of land in Valasamudram Panchayat.

This information remained mysterious until RTI was put to use. The people got confirmed information from the Panchayat President. It helped the Panchayat and the community to discuss and decide what can be done about it. It takes a Right to Information Act for a Village Panchayat President to get information about what is being proposed keeping his village at the centre-stage. This disguised nature of information the market and the State deal with; the information that remained mysterious to the local community and Panchayats was a real botheration until people were given this weapon called: Right to Information Act, 2005.

POWER WORKS AT THE GRASSROOTS

What does public power mean in the globalization era? Does it exist at all is a vital question. International Business concerns often prefer to work in orderly autocracies, rather than in activist democracies (George Soros). They can, of course, work in democracies when it (democracy) is emptied of its meaning. The emptying can be done through enforced local sacrifices and making the local people suffer or through silencing the public unrest using governmental power or police force—the instruments of the State to keep law and order. This can be set right during elections through populist announcements and give-aways.

International Business concerns do not prefer to work in activist democracies. Tamil Nadu is one of the most preferred destinations for International Business concerns to invest. What does George Soros infer here? Democracy in Tamil Nadu is willing to satisfy a whole range of tastes—not merely through the home made plain-vanilla to give you 'the taste of India', but through American Delight, Spanish Crunch, and French Cassata and so on. This is through bringing in FDI and setting up Special Economic Zones. If a democracy could declare catering to all the tastes, it implies that there are groups that are silently suffering or they are not able to make their noise into a unified voice. The money to buy the cassata slice (ice-creamy 'cash compensation') for the poor, obviously, comes from the market.

The irony is governments exist to act in the public interest. When can something be called 'public interest'? Only where the maximum benefit is gained by the largest number of people can we call it public interest. People in

Mathur and eight Panchayats in the neighbourhood question: How can acquiring land from hundreds of farmers for selling to one SEZ developer be called 'public purpose'?

Case 7.2: Mathur, Thiruvannamalai District, Tamil Nadu: The Mathur case is this. Lotus Footwear Company wanted to establish footwear manufacturing company near Mangal Kootu Road in Mathur Panchayat (Thiruvannamalai district of Tamil Nadu). The government has acquired 2,200 acres putting to use Land Acquisition Act. The farmers Kanniyappan (47), Dharman (61), Margabandu (46) and others who lost their lands, homes and homesteads are loitering in Cheyyar Court seeking justice. They are called 'PAP' in SEZ language. What is PAP? Project Affected People. The pity is all their jewels are said to be with the Pawn Brokers paying the lawyers' fees. Police force has been used to evict them from their homes and farms, and they have been behind bars in Vellore for 15 days. The charge was they prevented the officials from implementing the provisions of the Land Acquisition Act—the power of the state—noticeably. It is said the compensation money that these evictees declined to take has been deposited at the Court at Cheyyar. The earlier phase of land acquisition took place (in 1997) with the local people's expectation that many local youth would get employment. But, hardly any of the local people were employed in the units at Mathur. This has resulted in people feeling resentful or let down.

For a second phase in 2007, many people in Mathur and in the neighbourhood Panchayats received individual notices stating that their land falls in the area identified for SEZ extension, and so it would be acquired as per land Acquisition Act, and compensation would be paid. The Panchayats received notice requiring a Gram Sabha resolution with 'No Objection' for handing over the common lands for SEZ purpose. Mathur and eight other neighbourhood Panchayats passed a resolution in the Gram Sabha meeting to form an Anti-SEZ Movement, and that none of them would give: 'No Objection Certificate'. This flashed in the media. It, thus, appeared in *The New Indian Express*: *Will Cheyyar be Tamil Nadu's Nandigram? Government puts 10 villages on notice over land acquisition; eight of them oppose SEZ move.*

Meanwhile the Panchayat leaders got in touch with some activist groups, political parties, and institutions that could legally guide them providing the information on the procedures for land acquisition including the local committee to be formed for Resettlement and Rehabilitation, and the contents of R & R Policy, 2007 etc. This information symmetry and linkage provided by activists and institutions gave them additional mettle and moral fibre to stand firm against the land acquisition.

Two main demands of the people in Mathur and the neighbourhoods were: (a) employment should be provided to local youth in the units set up at SEZ in the area; and (b) the private land owners are paid compensation for the land they part with for SEZ, similarly, the Panchayats part with common lands. So, the SIPCOT or TIDCO should consider giving compensation to the Panchayat for the amount of common land acquired for SEZ purpose, which were in the maintenance of the Panchayats. The Panchayat shall use the amount for common development purposes with the approval of the Gram Sabha.

The Hindu (2nd November, 2008) reports that as many as 1,112 persons belonging to villages in and around the Cheyyar SEZ in Thiruvannamalai district have been recruited by companies that have established their units there. Upon empirical verification, this research team got this news confirmed locally. It is understood that because of the struggle the local people waged against setting up of units, local people have started getting employment. The recent development with regard to recruitment of local persons is encouraging. Some common properties like ponds have not been disturbed in the process, based on the demand of the Panchayats. Negotiations are going on about the issue of compensation to the Panchayats for the common lands parted with. It should be mentioned that the joint action of the Panchayats, and information provided by activist groups, and resource institutions helped them gain this status of sitting in a negotiation table, unlike taking Panchayats for granted in many of the places. The Bairamangalam case in Krishnagiri district, near Hosur in Tamil Nadu could be another clear example that demonstrated that grassroots level power works and makes the State and the market forces listen.

Case 7.3: Bairamangalam, Krishnagiri District, Tamil Nadu: The Government of Tamil Nadu through the TIDCO has made moves to acquire 3,600 acres of lands for setting up of SEZ at Bairamangalam, Kundumaranapalli, Anchettipalli, Sanamavu villages in Krishnagiri district near Hosur. Major portion of the areas mentioned are prime agricultural lands. But it has been mentioned in the notice served that it is all dry and barren lands. The farmers have given petition to the District Collector in the Grievance Day Meeting at the Collectorate. The District Collector has held a special meeting with 30 local representatives and Panchayat members from Bairamangalam area with a view to convince them. The classification of fertile lands as barren sent shock waves across the farming community and farmers took to streets. It got wide media coverage, which invited political attention.

The farmers of the area made the Assistant Director of Agriculture, Krishnagiri do an exclusive survey of the area and give a report about the nature of land, and the types of crops grown. The Assistant Director's report confirmed that the villages proposed for SEZ have large tracts of fertile agricultural lands, and variety of vegetables are cultivated and sent to several places in Tamil Nadu.

The Village Panchayat wrote to the Central Minister for Agriculture explaining the fertile nature of the area, annexing the survey report of the Assistant Director of Agriculture. Mr. Sharad Pawar, Minister for Agriculture seems to have written to the Mr. Kamal Nath, the Minister for Commerce, who in turn has sent a letter to the State Government, and the District Collector to drop land acquisition in Bairamangalam. This research team has the copy of the letter from the Ministry of Commerce. The Panchayats along with all the functionaries and community if they can talk in one voice and take appropriate measures, a Panchayat is able to make the Central Ministries to turn and look up. At Bairamanagalam the farmers' vehement opposition to part with the cultivable lands (about 220 acres) has made the State and the private SEZ developer (company) to hang up land acquisition.

Public power can be manifested through the Panchayat bodies, and democracy can be deepened through the provisions of the Panchayati Raj Act. Democracy is an engagement, and it is only in the making. The quality and vibrancy of a democracy depends on the citizenry. It has been proved in Bairamangalam.

Case 7.4: SEZ—Oragadam, Kancheepuram District, Tamil Nadu: Oragadam, at a distance of 45 km away from Chennai on Thambaram-Kancheepuram Road, is emerging as the new industrial belt. Oragadam Panchayat with 463 households has two hamlets viz. Oragadam and Chennanguppam, with a population of 1,150. Majority (about 80%) of the households belong to Scheduled Castes, and the rest of them belong to Backward Community, especially *Naidus* and *Vanniyars.* Agriculture, coupled with wage employment through agricultural operations, were the mainstay of the people.

When companies those were desirous of setting up units in the Oragadam area, they approached the State government to procure land on behalf of the companies. The SIPCOT along with the District Administration started acquiring land in Oragadam area putting to use the Tamil Nadu Acquisition of Land for Industrial Purposes (Amendment) Act, 2005 (Act 17 of 2005). That is the State attempted to acquire land from farmers and land owners on behalf of the private companies putting to use a legislature. This has happened in Mathur (Thiruvannamalai) and several other places in Tamil Nadu. The demand of the local people was: "let it be a free-market deal". It should not be something like the landowners compelled to part with land as per the Land Acquisition Act at rates determined by the State. Let the private companies that require land deal with the land owners directly. The process should not bring in government-machinery or the infamous Land Acquisition Act.

One big tool much to the advantage of market forces, that Government of India or Government of Tamil Nadu has given is implementation of the Central Land Acquisition Act of 1894 and the Tamil Nadu Acquisition of Land for Industrial Purposes (Amendment) Act, 2005, whereas the aspects relating to resettlement and rehabilitation is kept merely as Resettlement and Rehabilitation policy, and not as a legislation.

In the year 2007, contrary to the demands of the local community and Panchayat, the District Administration and the SIPCOT made site visits along with the representatives of the companies when the villagers remained silent onlookers. Subsequently, the government started sending notices and negotiations were to commence. They needed 1,642 acres of land from Oragadam and Chennankuppam areas. There were agricultural lands, and land meant for house-sites, and common lands. With a view to protecting the agricultural lands, the Panchayat took the lead to stage a protest against the proposed land acquisition. People assembled. It looked the protest would turn out to be road blockade. 37 members of Oragadam along with Panchayat President and Panchayat functionaries were arrested and jailed. They were in prison for one week.

Much soon the SEZ developers put money into mouths of individual land owners so that voice of resistance and opposition becomes feeble and unheard. Common lands having water bodies like lakes and ponds are lost, water (drainage) ways are lost, trees are lost, school buildings are lost, temples and places of worship are lost, and even dwelling houses and burial grounds are lost to SEZ in Oragadam and Chennankuppam. The Panchayat became weak not being able to protect the agricultural lands, and the commons. The Panchayat President says nothing works against the will of the government and the government machinery. He utters: '*Panchayats have a small limit within which they can swing so long as that space is not required by the State or the market*'.

RIGHT TO INFORMATION FOR CPR MANAGEMENT

Pragmatic approach to economic activity is that when the resources available are scarce, how to coordinate and allocate them in a 'socially equitable manner' is the concern of the State. It usually happens without losing sight of being politically correct; whereas how to put those resources into efficient use in a 'profitability sense' is the prime concern of the market. The interaction between State and market needs to be viewed from the perspective of political economy.

The state is an organisation for monopolizing legitimate coercive power. Using this coercive force, the state can coordinate and regulate activities of peoples and organisations (economic or otherwise) through laws, rules, and orders.

Basically the degree or scale of market operations is determined by state policies. But, then the problem is the state and markets are inseparably interdependent. Therefore, like the market wants to keep the state in good humour, the state wants to keep the market in good humour. When the hold of market (private forces) on the economy enhances, the state has to pay heed to be able to run the economy as well as polity smoothly. There is a kind of mutuality or reciprocity in the state market relationship. Often, in plain language the relationship is something like you scratch my back and I'll scratch yours. This, often enough, lets the people to stand away helplessly; and the civil society to shout slogans against especially the state and at times against the markets. When this marriage between state and market is overly blissful, the common man tends to get crushed, like happened in the case of Oragadam, Chennai above.

Government—an institution of the state—needs the common when it gets into its entity as a political party, and not when it is holding the power to rule or make law. Government cannot ignore the common man either because of the electoral politics and representative form of making the government. When the state tends to join hand with the market, there are also grassroots level democratic institutions such as Panchayats getting debased or demeaned, along with the common man. The rate of recurrence of Panchayats being put down (or disgraced) has become rapid after we adopt liberalisation and privatisation policies.

The best way the state can favour the market (or be unfair towards the Panchayats) is through de-control and deregulate when actually control and regulations are required; turning a blind eye to negative externalities that the market causes the common man; manipulate or suppress the information that the public might require about market. This is an observable fact quoted below for corroboration.

Case 7.5: Keelavalavu, Madurai, Tamil Nadu: Keelavalavu is a Village Panchayat at Melur Block in Madurai district—about 40 km from Madurai. It has eight habitations with a population of around 7,800. News appeared constantly in several Tamil dailies about the menace of illegal quarrying of granites. One of the recent pieces of news was that people in one of the habitations have been issued Family Ration Cards, with name of the habitation purposively changed. A key probe made on this issue, on the request of the

Village Panchayat President of Keelavalavu revealed that granite quarrying goes on unhindered within the prohibited limit of the historical site destroying the Tamil-Brahmi sites, which are supposed to be under the maintenance of Tamil Nadu Archaeology Department. Common property resources such as ponds and tanks around the quarry site, which are supposed to be under the maintenance of the Public Works Department (PWD), and the Panchayat Union are going traceless. The feeder channels to these ponds and tanks have been blocked with white stone blocks taken through quarrying. This has gradually resulted in local farmers making distress sale of land, which the quarry site agency grabs little by little.

In one of the habitations (Adaichankanmaipatty habitation) that is very close to the quarrying area none of the household has Family Ration Card printed the name of the habitation. The Ration Card shows that they belong to some other habitations in the neighbourhood such as: Colony Theru, Ammankoilpatty, Muslim Theru, Asari Val Theru, Pappakudi patty, and Chettipatty. In the opinion of the card holders, it has been done on purpose to do away the name of the habitation from the village map, so that in future, if required, the quarry agency would be able to have the records clear that no family ever lived in that habitation. The 56 families that live in this habitation (Adaichankanmaipatty) may have to find their way out and resettle themselves elsewhere, is the message.

People are not bothered very much for three obvious reasons: (i) the sentimental consideration towards granite agency because it usually gives donation during Temple festivals; (ii) change of name in the Family Ration Card has not prevented them from getting their essential commodities from the Ration Shops of the Civil Supplies Department; (iii) in the event of having to vacate and resettle elsewhere (which is very much likely) the people are positive that the granite agency would compensate them with money for the land they are stripped off.

Pieces of news appear continuously in the media that stone quarrying is under way within the regulated area, that is, within 300 metres of the protected limits of some monuments. The ASI and the State Archaeological Department can only watch helplessly. The Village Panchayat President has written petitions after petitions about the vandalism. He has received no reply from anywhere. Frantically not knowing how to save the common properties that are supposed to be under the control of the Panchayats, the Panchayat President is writing to the BDO, the District Collector, and even to Dr. A.P.J. Abdul Kalam.

RIGHT TO INFORMATION

The Panchayat President has started using Right to Information Act, 2005 as a weapon to fight against and to draw the attention of the officials who had thrown the petitions of concerned individuals and Panchayat functionaries, into deep freezer. There were a series of RTI applications filed to several officials concerned with mines, common property resource management and development activities in Keelavalavu village. They included:

1. Office of the Deputy Director of Geology & Mining, Madurai
2. Office of the Assistant Director of Agriculture, Melur
3. Public Works Department (Operation and Maintenance Division)
4. Block Development Officer, Melur
5. Revenue Department in Melur, Madurai

THE QUESTIONS RAISED

The samples of questions posed to various departments are presented below:

TO ASSISTANT DIRECTOR OF AGRICULTURE

- How many acres of 'cultivable lands' are there in Keelavalavu Panchayat area?
- What are the crops cultivated in Keelavalavu Panchayat ?
- Please give details of production of various crops (in quantitative terms) trends in Keelavalavu Panchayat in 1995, 2000, 2005 and 2008 ?
- As per your official records, what are the main 'surface irrigation sources' such as tanks, ponds, Oorani etc. for the farmers in Keelavalavu Panchayat ?
- What is the length of waterways (in metres or feet) that run within Keelavalavu Panchayat ?
- How many households in Keelavalavu Panchayat, as per your official records, are: (a) big farmers, (b) small farmers, (c) marginal farmers, and (d) agricultural labourers ?
- What is the status of agriculture in Keelavalavu Panchayat in 2009 ?
- What is the status of various surface irrigation sources, and waterways in Keelavalavu Panchayat in 2009 ?

TO REVENUE DEPARTMENT

- How many acres of common *porompoke* land are there in Keelavalavu Panchayat ?

- Please furnish classification-wise (each type of common land) acreage/ hectares ?
- Please furnish a map locating/indicating which are all the common lands marking their nature, and which are all private *Patta* lands ?
- Please give the list of factories, industries and mines, which are paying taxes, cess and charges to the Revenue Department, along with the amount they pay per year ?
- What is the procedure for eviction of unauthorised occupation of public places and private lands by unscrupulous people ?
- Which officer of the government (please give designation and address) can a Village Panchayat contact in this regard ?

TO PUBLIC WORKS DEPARTMENT (PWD)

- Please give list of PWD maintained surface irrigation tanks, ponds, *Ooranies* and other water bodies in Keelavalavu Panchayat in the table given below?

Sl. No.	Name of the water body	Type	Area (Water spread)	Do you have official boundary line marked?
1.				
2.				
3.				
4.				

- What is the length of waterways (feeder lines) to each of these tanks, ponds etc.?

TO BLOCK DEVELOPMENT OFFICE (BDO)

- Please give list of surface irrigation tanks, ponds, *Ooranies* and other water bodies in Keelavalavu Panchayat under the control of Panchayat Union (in the table given below)?

Sl. No.	Name of the water body	Type	Area (Water spread)	Do you have official boundary line marked?
1.				
2.				
3.				

- What is the length of waterways (feeder lines) to each of these tanks, ponds etc.

TO DEPUTY DIRECTOR OF GEOLOGY & MINING, MADURAI

- Kindly provide a copy of Quarrying Permit issued for excavation and removal in the quarries located in Keelavalavu Panchayat jurisdiction. The names of villages in Keelavalavu Panchayat jurisdiction are: (i) Vachanpatty, (ii) Adanjankammaipatty, (iii) Ammankoilpatty, (iv) Sakkaraipeerumalaipatty, (v) Kambarmalaipatty, (vi) Edachinankammaipatty, (vii) Kulichevalpatty, (viii) Keelavalavu.

- S.F. No. 296 is located in Keelavalavu Panchayat. Is there any quarry under lease officially approved in that survey number?
- What is the permit area given to the permit holder mining in Keelavalavu Panchayat area?
- How much quantity of granite blocks is taken everyday from the quarry referred to, and where are they taken to ?
- Kindly provide the amount of seigniorage fee and other fees the quarry permit holder/lessee has paid to the Panchayat?

These were the kinds of questions posed to various departments of the government. The main Department of the Government that is involved in this specific case that the Panchayat President is particular about is: Deputy Director of Geology and Mining, Madurai. This department (and a few other departments) had to be approached two or three times through various questions to be able to obtain relevant and sufficient information.

The idea of the Village Panchayat President was to find out and establish with facts if (i) indiscriminate quarrying was going on for several years even in areas beyond the permitted area for quarrying; (ii) irrigation water bodies and water ways have been blocked because of quarrying; (iii) agriculture has been hit severely and agricultural production has fallen drastically; (iv) no revenue to the Panchayat has gone from quarrying, which otherwise could have been used for local development works.

THE QUESTIONS RESPONSES RECEIVED

All the RTI applications filed brought response although the nature of response and adequacy of information received varied. There are several ways that officials deal with RTI petitions. One solace for the applicant (Panchayat President) at Keelavalavu in Madurai district (Tamil Nadu) who got down in this exercise is that never before he or any of the Panchayat functionaries have received a reply for their petitions in the past 3 to 4 years. But, they keep receiving some response or the other within 30 days for every RTI application they file. Putting aside the relevance, adequacy of information or triviality of the nature of response, one can say that people/local institutions do receive responses to the RTI applications filed. Some Public Information Officers write on the top of the RTI application: 'Most Urgent', and they instruct the relevant staff of the department to respond to the questions within 30 days. There are officers (e.g. Assistant Director of Agriculture, Melur) who have written a covering letter specifying that if the information sought by the applicant is not within our department, obtain it from relevant officers as per the Section 6 (3) of RTI Act, 2005 and send it to the applicant within time. Therefore, as a legislation RTI has made the citizenry to hold their head high, and the officials accountable, and responsive.

PROPER RESPONSE ON TIME

There are officials (such as Assistant Director of Agriculture, Melur, Madurai in this case) who sent information required by the Panchayat on time. The major crops cultivated in Keelavalavu village as per the records of Assistant Director of Agriculture are: paddy, sugarcane, and plantain. The data provided by the Assistant Director of Agriculture could help prove that agriculture has been falling year after year in Keelavalavu Panchayat. Paddy yield that was 2,929 tonnes in 1995 has come down to 1,542 tonnes in 2005, and 802 tonnes in 2008; Sugarcane that accounted for 3,384 tonnes has come down to 1,817 tonnes in 2008; Plantain that accounted for 166 tonnes has come down to 58 tonnes in 2008.

THE CONFUSION IN THE FEES PAYABLE

Some officials find out ways to return the RTI application to the applicant with a label on the top or with a covering letter stating: 'we do not accept postal order as fees payable for the information you seek, please send a Demand Draft'. There was no information such as in whose name the DD should be drawn, and payable at which bank etc. The Central RTI Act states that postal order or court fee stamp for Rs. 10 should be attached along with RTI applications. But, a Government Order of the Tamil Nadu states that court fee stamp or Demand Draft for Rs. 10 should be attached. The G.O. is silent about Postal Order. The Public Information Officers take it as an advantage for returning an RTI application without response to questions. There is also a State Bank of India account number given: 'Collection of fees under Tamil Nadu Right to Information (fees) Rules, 2005 (G.O. Ms. No. 989, Public (Estt.I & Leg. Dept. dated 7.10.2005) SBI Account DPC 0075 00 800 BK 0006. But the banker (Melur, Madurai) does not recognise this account number. Then the Panchayat had to go for court fee stamp only.

OFFICIALS WHO TAKE IT EASY

Some officials take it easy, and deal with the application with a sense of fun or amusement. This happens mostly in the case of Block Development Officer (BDO), who regularly deals with Panchayat functionaries, and for whom the face of the applicant is familiar. The response of the BDO Melur in Madurai district to an RTI application filed by the Keelavalavu Panchayat President (seeking the list of water bodies in Keelavalavu Panchayat under the maintenance of Panchayat Union Office) received after 30 days was: 'these informations should be available with the Panchayat Office'. The application has gone from the Panchayat Office. 'BDO-Panchayats' is a government officer who is in-charge for a cluster of Panchayats directly dealing with Panchayat related matters in place of the District Collector and the Project Officer, DRDA. When a Panchayat seeks information to get out of darkness about certain things about the Panchayat water bodies, the response was: 'these informations should be available in the Panchayat office'. The Panchayat President who assumed office for the first time was left perplexed regarding further step. The Panchayat President then sent an RTI application to the Village Administrative Officer (VAO), and obtained this information. The record showed 16 water bodies none of them maintained, and all of them under encroachment by the quarry agencies.

REPEATED KNOCKING REQUIRED

There are officials (such as Public Works Department, Madurai in this case) who provide information after you have very appropriately pitched your question, and when there is no evasion or dodging possible. For the first application to PWD, the response was that that was not the office meant to provide the information sought for by the applicant. Later, when questions were appropriately put across, 'that the list of ponds and tanks under the maintenance of PWD along water spread area, and if they have stones indicating the tank area limit have been put up', the response came. It was found from the information received (i) that most of the water spread area of the tanks are under encroachment by the quarry agency; and (ii) that nowhere tank boundary stone had been laid by the PWD; (iii) and that the length of water ways that bring precipitation or run off water to these tanks is 3,060 metres most of which are occupied by the granite quarry agency for their use.

Besides these, there are several vital information that the Village Panchayat could obtain which included: (i) quarrying was going on even after the expiry of the lease period; (ii) the area mentioned in the quarry lease permit is one, but the area where quarrying is done another (in the adjacent area); (iii) Lease period expired in 1993 but, quarrying operation carried out even in 2009 as per High Court directions W.P. No. 9988/2005. This is there in many of the cases.

THE CHALLENGE

The real challenge today is about finding the right balance between the market and the government, and determining the degree of operation. Both are needed. But, then when they become too close the civil society or the general public have to put up with things that are destructive to the common man, and the vulnerable. They can complement each other. This balance differs from place to place, and perhaps even time to time. It is clear that unfettered markets do not lead to social justice, like it has been presented in Keelavalavu case.

Information can be used as weapon in the fight of the civil society against bureaucratic-rigidity, irresponsible attitude of the scheme implementing officials towards the poor, and lack of transparency in development administration. Two vital things about Right to Information Act 2005 are: (i) somebody who seeks information need not express, why does she/he needs that information; and (ii) the reply from the officer should reach the addressee within 30 days of receiving the application. That she/he need not express why that information is needed; and how she/he will use that information puts the officer at swing. A right question properly worded and asked through an RTI application to the right department can change the way things are. There is no need for you to put the information received to use in order to set right things. Drawing the attention and making the relevant officer aware that we are alert automatically makes things fall in place. It sends across message to the erring officer and the private profiteering interests to measure their steps, and be watchful if they step beyond their limits affecting the general public or the poor. An alert civil society (including the local government) is required to manage the State and markets, when development ethics find the back seat in the temptation of the market to earn high profits, with hand in glow with rent-seeking officers of the government.

STATE SHRINKING

Another oft-repeated statement about State these days is, that the State is shrinking and the market is expanding. We need to bear in mind is that the

State never shrinks, only its nature changes depending upon situations. If you start comparing the largeness of its visible presence, it might look different. But, its endemic presence and competence to control do not go away. State is the instrument of the elite to control the system. The state cannot go away, because it is a repository of power. When we say it is shrinking we mean to say it is becoming smaller and smaller. But, it does not. Its intensity does not. Its power to control and the authority it commands do not shrink. It can stand up anytime, and grab you by neck—but the nature changes depending upon situations. The way it comes out might be different.

We are busy analysing what is being done, who is doing it, and how it is being done etc. But we do not ask: why is it being done? And whose interest is it serving? These are the questions we need to ask. So, on the face, it might look as if it is shrinking or expanding. You can take the US or Europe; anything that you do as an individual, institution or as a corporate is documented, with address, ID number, date and time. The dogs have a collar and you have an ID. And you are monitored. It is fast coming up in India also. The troika of our system remains: the market, the state and the elite.

SYSTEMIC INTERVENTION

It is true our problems are complex, something that cannot be resolved by one person or one institution, because the issues are systemic. To replace it you will have to have an alternative system. At least to draw the attention of the state you need a mechanism. Systemic thing can only be rectified systemically. Whatever the state does is systemic. Often, what an NGO tries to do is not systemic. Although sometimes, a Panchayat's intervention can create an impact when they properly use a tool like RTI, for a systemic intervention to take place many Panchayats, NGOs, research institutions, and the media should come together. When a Panchayat or NGO fights against illegal mining or everybody knows their fighting is meaningful. But, that is the end of it. It does not change anything. For the Panchayat it is a double difficult. On the one hand it has no autonomy and on the other notions such as local, small communities, reciprocal relationships, small independent markets in the face of globalization have become superfluous.

Panchayat is an important forum, which is within the access and reach of the common man. As an institution the Panchayat should remain in touch with the local civil society, and the media. Any and every response has to be structured. In bringing about balancing the Panchayat should make the civil society system resilient. For this to happen the Panchayats (which means local communities) should federate and talk in one voice, which require taking a stance. It must make the civil society really start talking. They should together project what their ideas are, what their expectations are and the way they look at grassroots level problems. Otherwise what will happen is that actual civil society discourse will never emerge. And Panchayat will start behaving exactly like what the State does at the broader level.

REFERENCE

Jean Dreze and Amartya (2005). *India: Development and Participation*, Oxford University Press, New Delhi. George Soros.

CHAPTER EIGHT

Dalits in the New Socio-Technological Milieu

I. INTRODUCTION

The total population of Tamil Nadu as per the 2001 Census is 62,405,679. *Dalits*[1] form almost one-fifths of the total population in Tamil Nadu. There are 107.12 lakh SCs, and 5.74 lakh STs in the State. It makes 19.18 per cent and 1.03 per cent of the total population respectively. Census of India 2001 reports that there are 76 Scheduled Castes in Tamil Nadu. Five out of the 76 community divisions within SCs constitute 93.5 per cent of the SCs. They are Adi Dravida (45.6%), Pallan (19.2%), Paraiyan (15.7%), Chakkiliyan (6.6%) and Arunthathiyar (6.5%). Interestingly, 35 community groups within SCs have reported population of less than one thousand. Among the districts Thiruvarur has the highest proportion of SC population to its total population, and the Nilgiris has the highest ST population in the State, followed by Salem and Nammakkal. *Dalits*, who account for a little over 25 per cent of the rural population in Tamil Nadu, live scattered allover the State, segregated from the rest of the people.

Society in Tamil Nadu is very broadly divided into three communities—Caste, Outcaste, and indigenous/*Adivasi* people (Sathianathan Clarke, 2007). First, by caste-community or caste-Hindus means those who are supposed to be upper caste people—the traditional land owners and those involved in respectable occupations. The outcaste means those 76 community divisions mentioned within SCs who were socially considered 'untouchables', and at the bottom of the Indian caste system (hereafter addressed as *dalits*). They were mainly engaged as dependents of the caste-Hindus, and were supposed to make a living by doing farm works, rearing animals, carrying death-messages across villages, burying dead animals, and making footwears for use by the caste-Hindus.

The social arrangement was such that one or a few of the *dalit* families depended on each one of the Caste-Hindus (traditional landowners) families. That is a family belonging to lower caste making a living by being dependent on the upper caste family, carrying out the works determined by the upper caste. They were historically considered the 'depressed class'. The birth of a child at the *dalit* family was taken that an additional hand was getting ready to rear the animals of the caste-Hindu, the family has been tied to. The Constitution of India affirmed that caste has been eliminated in India, and practising untouchability is considered a crime by law. In terms of social development the SCs have crossed several mile-stones, although problems of social discrimination overtly or covertly wake up sporadically.

The third community included the indigenous communities, which are not obligated to the Indian caste system yet, are marginalised. These have been grouped under the term *Adivasis*, and they are also referred to as Tribals or Scheduled Tribes (ST). India has 427 Scheduled Tribes—the Dravidian group dominate Tamil Nadu and southern part of India. They are variously addressed in different parts of the country. But, they want to be addressed as *Adivasis* (Gail Omvedt, 2000). One expression that covers both SC and ST is *dalits*, which this study also uses, although Government of India does not approve of this expression[2].

THE PROBLEM STATEMENT

The contention of many of the *Dalits'* organisation at the start of the globalization policies in mid-1990s was that globalization would hurt the poor, and the worst affected sector would be agriculture, and the worst affected section of the population would be *dalits* most of whom are dependent on wage employment in agriculture (Ramaiah, A., 2004; Haragopal, G.).

In reality, does globalization hurt the *dalits* or benefit them, is a vital question that required to be investigated. Even among the organisations that work for the welfare or rights of the *dalits*, there is strong difference of opinion when it comes to: *what does globalization offer to the dalits?* They stand divided in responding to a question like this (Gail Omvedit, 2000). Some strongly argue that globalization especially because of the increased mobility and connectedness has plenty to offer everyone, including the *dalits*. There are others who argue that globalization is a race against the unequals which results in survival of the fittest. It has a tendency to hurt the poorer countries and the poor (Anad Teltumbde). Hence, it surely affects the *dalits*.

Theoretically speaking, the market principles do not operate on preferential treatment or on positive discrimination for the historically deprived—be it in educational institutions or in terms of job reservation under quota system. Market goes by demand and supply forces and so it blind-folds itself to sentiments such as a section of the population in a given country has been historically marginalised and so they need to be given a helping hand, which a democratic governance system generally considers. A logical argument that follows this is, globalization is primarily knowledge-based social connectedness resulting in economic benefits for those with knowledge, information, technology or capital to invest. *Dalits* living on the margins of society get disconnected not being able to make way into any of these. These are only oft-repeated arguments by *dalit* organisations, the empirical validity of which requires to be tested.

Globalization has caused flourishing of manufacturing and service sectors such as computer services, banking services, insurance services, and manufacturing of secondary products and industrial goods. The argument is that *dalits* most of them being wage earners in agriculture stand close to nothing to gain from globalization. Is there or not any social and economic transformation taking place in the lives of the *dalits* as a fallout of globalization is a vital research question. That it cannot benefit them does not have to necessarily mean that it cannot affect them either. Similarly, that it has not been designed for the poor does not mean that even an enterprising poor cannot benefit by globalization processes. It can influence directly or indirectly; stealthily or explicitly. However, the real task hinges also in pinning down which is a fallout of globalization, which is not; and which is an upshot of general trend of development in Indian society. Hence, the study was carried out.

PROMINENT RESEARCH QUESTIONS

- What are the socio-cultural changes taking place in the lives of *dalits* as a corollary of globalization?
- What are the changes taking place in the livelihoods, and economic activities of *dalits*?
- Have the *dalits* been hurt or benefited by globalization, with substantiation for arriving at such a conclusion?
- What are the safety nets, if any provided by the state in order to protect the *dalits* from being hurt by globalization?

OBJECTIVES OF THIS STUDY

- To make an empirical examination of the in-roads that globalization processes have made in the lives and livelihoods especially of the poor *dalits*.

- To verify if the arguments put forth by the *dalit* organisations on the impact of globalization on *dalits,* if they are practically valid or are they only rhetoric, which are theoretical derivatives.
- To pinpoint whatever changes that have happened in the lives, livelihoods, tradition, and culture of *dalits* that could be attributed to globalization processes.
- To study the protective measures, which have been taken by Government of India and Government of Tamil Nadu in order to safeguard the *dalits* from the onslaught of globalization.
- To offer action points that could be paid attention so as to safeguard the interests of *dalits*, and *dalit* organisations, and to improve the quality of life of *dalits* in the changing socio-economic and political milieu.

METHODOLOGY OF THE STUDY

Methods and Tools Used: This is primarily a qualitative study conducted in nine districts of Tamil Nadu. Ideas have been drawn from several case studies of *dalit* villages in nine districts. The study has used tools in the qualitative research methods such as Focus Group Discussions, Chain of Interviews, Direct Observations, and On-the-Spot Analysis. Change in trends was analysed using techniques like Trend Change used by PRA practitioners. Matrix scoring was used to approximately quantify the number of people with various modern facilities, such as mobile phones, knowledge of computers, use of internet etc. The verbal data collected were cross-checked in other groups, and triangulated for validity. Diverse corpus of verbal data was collected from across districts from *dalits* living in different contexts.

The study was conducted over a period of two months in all the nine districts. Aggregation of data and similarities and dissimilarities were analysed, on the spot, and the background and reasons probed. Care was taken to see not only to collect data for the cases of interest, but also for cases that stand contrast or as oddity. It was not only *dalits* who were met and interviewed. Non-*dalits* living in *dalit* villages also were interviewed to get their views of the developments taking place in the lives of *dalits.* Existing literature on the subject was analysed to make sure the study comes in proper perspective. The commonalities that emerged in all the study villages have been captured as the main thread, there are also oddities reported appropriately specifying the contexts.

Data Sources: Primary data were collected directly from *dalit* hamlets and colonies using qualitative techniques like Focus Group Discussion, Chain of

Interviews, Direct Observations, and through On-the-Spot Analysis. The views of the caste-Hindus were also collected wherever required to record their views on the quality of life of *dalits*. The main sources of data are people in *dalit* colonies—men, women, youth and SHGs. Besides this, secondary data and policy notes have been collected from existing literature and websites of the Government of India and Government of Tamil Nadu. Relevant literature and concepts and secondary data were collected from published articles of referred journals, and Government of India sources like NSSO, and Government of Tamil Nadu websites like Adi Adrawida Welfare, Directorate of Employment and Training, TAHDCO, and Department of Rural Development and Panchayati Raj.

Data Analysis: The commonalities that emerged in all the districts were captured. Similarly, the oddities were sifted and documented as well. On-the-spot analysis and cross-checking of information through chain of interviews at the field level was done to recognise the validity of the data. Sufficient probing was done wherever required to get at the details.

Scope of this study: This is a single State study of Tamil Nadu. It covers specifically *dalits* meaning both SC and ST only, and not the poor from other communities. Reference is made to caste-Hindus only for the purpose of drawing similarity or contrast. The strength of this report is the intensive field-work carried out. The data and information presented are based on first hand information collected directly in the field rather than mere compilation of arguments based on existing literature and secondary data. The findings of the study emerge from a series of case studies conducted. From the number of cases visited, and the care taken in capturing and making on-the-spot analysis, the results can be generalised to the State of Tamil Nadu.

ARRANGEMENT OF THIS CHAPTER

The problem in reporting about changes in the lives of *dalits* in Tamil Nadu is that no single pattern emerges across districts. Each district in Tamil Nadu seems to offer more oddities than commonalities. This chapter is presented in five parts. *Introduction*—The Premise, Purpose and Design of the Study. This section provides an overall introduction to SC/ST population in Tamil Nadu, and has briefly sketched their historical background. It also provides the purpose and design of the study. *Basic Services and Quality of Life*—This section deals with the adequacy, and quality of reach of basic services to *dalit* hamlets. It also touches upon the improvement in quality of life of *dalits*, if any as a result of overall development of Indian economy. *Dalits, Livelihoods and Employment*—This section deals with the change in the livelihood pattern of *dalits*, and its social and economic consequences. *Social Exclusion and Inclusive Policies*—This section deals with the ways in which *dalit* community has been excluded by economic institutions and in the society. It also deals with policies that have served to safeguard the poor *dalits* from being hurt by the globalisation processes. *Findings, Conclusions and Action Points*—This last section summarises the major findings and action points.

II. BASIC SERVICES AND QUALITY OF LIFE

The notion of development should begin with delivery of basic public services to everyone of a country's citizen. It is particularly true of the *dalits* who cannot afford to approach the open market availing basic services such as education, drinking water or health care. The location of service institutions and the effectiveness of service delivery of these public institutions to *dalit* villages require to be analysed. Moreover, 'standard of living' and 'quality of life' are two different things. The later encompasses the former. While standard of living may pertain more to the income levels of individual families or communities, the quality of life is revealed in human dignity, social connectedness, civil and political participation and so on.

Viewed from this angle standard of living is only one of the elements of quality of life. The basic services that require to be analysed are: *dalits* ways to ensure food security, housing, electricity, drinking water, sanitation services, primary health care, basic and higher education arrangements, participation in local governance. Have the reform measures helped in providing access to these basic services required to be studied as well.

Food Security: There are two ways in which *dalit* community have their food secured. One is the Public Distribution System (PDS), and the other is getting foodgrains, cereals, pulses or oilseeds in return for the labour they offer to landowners in harvesting. The foodgrains collected during harvesting season is preserved for food security during rainy season. Other cereals, pulses or oilseeds are collected and sold for cash at the open market in the town and they bring home foodgrains for cooking. There are also share-croppers and cultivators among the *dalits*, who sell the harvested paddy, keeping aside the food stock they might need for rest of the year. This is the popular practice of ensuring food security at the local level by the *dalit* households. During seasonal shocks they also have the practice of selling their livestock and small stocks.

The other and more widespread practice of ensuring food security is the monthly supplies made by the PDS. The Civil Supplies Corporation through local Ration Shops supplies to all the BPL families rice, wheat flour, kerosene, sugar, and groceries at subsidised prices. As most of the *dalits* belong to BPL category they are entitled to get their quota of rice (35 kg a month for a family of five) and other essential commodities. Often the rice supplied by the PDS is found to be insufficient and so, they *dalits* have the practice of borrowing Family Ration Cards from well-to-do non-*dalits*, who do not buy rice at the Ration Shop. This supply is uninterrupted and the Government of Tamil Nadu has reduced the price of PDS rice from Rs. 2 kg to Re. 1 per kg. The *dalits* families have found this to be another good source of ensuring family's food security. However, PDS rice for many of the families is reported to be insufficient and so they buy the same quality rice in the open market where the price ranges from Rs. 8 to Rs. 13.

Housing: Dwelling house is an important indicator of quality of life. The house-site ownership and house ownership are mostly private to *dalits* in many of the study villages. Most of them have got official house-site *patta*. But, only a few have got assistance for the construction of house under schemes like IAY. The huts they have put up are vulnerable to fire and heavy wind. However, in each one of the study village at least 20 per cent of the families have been provided assistance for construction of house in different periods of time, under various schemes of the government like the IAY.

House crowding is reported to be a serious problem when sons get married, and start having a family of their own. The Government of Tamil Nadu reports that in the year 2005-06 alone, 42,195 new houses have been constructed for the SC/ST, and 21,449 *kutcha* houses have been upgraded to concrete roofed houses. However, compared to the need, the allocation each year seems to be too meagre. One common statement that comes about house allotment is that it is cornered by the moneyed, who can air big voice among the *dalits*, and to the real destitute who are voiceless.

Maintenance of the houses constructed on their own or the ones allotted by the government is very poor. The walls are weak and the thatched roof on the huts that they put up themselves might fly off a big wind. *Dalits* expect it to be repaired by the government.

Electricity: In each village visited it was found at least 15-20 per cent of the houses reported to be without even a single light facility. They reported that they were using the hurricane lantern or kerosene lamp for lighting purpose. Direct observation inside the hut revealed that in actuality only about 5-10 per cent of the houses remain with no electric light facility. Those who did not have power connection, they have taken unapproved connection on their own, and have put up bulbs. There are huts found with even multiple plug points for using fan, and audio players when as per records that was a hut with no power connection. In actuality most of the *dalit* huts are single light huts. They have either been officially provided by the government or illegally taken by *dalits* themselves from the electric line that cross their huts. Although this is common to SC and ST settlements, the menace of stealing electric power is more in SC villages than in ST villages. But none of the household ever approached to get power connection. The reason stated was affordability to get a power connection.

Cooking Gas: Households in 99 per cent of the ST villages, and in almost 90 per cent of the SC villages use only firewood for cooking. They use kerosene as the initial lighter. The supply of gas stove by the government of Tamil Nadu in some of the villages close to towns has set them to slowly change to the use of gas in place of fire. However, as most of the SC villages are remote, they do their usual practice of collecting firewood from the commons for cooking on their way home after work. The SC families think it would be additional expenditure buying gas cylinder every month, and so they feel reluctant to change to LP gas.

But, the STs are afraid primarily because of their fear about using gas. They think that they have heard gas might burst, and cost a woman's life, who was involved in cooking. The women have not even seen anybody using gas stove, and so are unaware. But, the men think that it might cause some fire accident for which they might be held responsible by the police. The Forest Department of the Government of Tamil Nadu in order to prevent the STs entering the forest on the pretext of collecting firewood have offered to help them supply free gas stoves, and arrange regular supply of gas. But, the STs in one of the study villages (Thirupur district) have declined the offer for fear of using gas.

Drinking Water: Inadequacy in the quantity of water supplied by the Village Panchayat is a common complaint in most of the study villages. It was observed that in nine out of ten villages *dalit* get water supply by common water collection points only. They have not got individual house service connections, like it has been given in the main village. *Dalits* in some of the study villages have demanded in the Gram Sabha meeting adequacy of water, and additional public fountains to reduce the rush in a few public fountains. It never materialised. They reported never to have approached the Village Panchayat to get a private house service connection as it involves paying a deposit, and installations charges which would work out to nearly Rs. 2,000. The *dalits* in study villages of most of the districts have only common water collection points, whereas the area where the elite people live get individual house service connections for water supply. However, they have not been pushed to the extent of buying water from private water suppliers.

Sanitation: Sanitation was nowhere in their list of priorities. None of the households own a toilet in any of the study villages. Even the one in group house, are not in use. However, it was found in one of the study villages in Cuddalore, toilets constructed completely free of cost by ADRA—an NGO after Tsunami, being used. Toilet was not there in the list of basic necessities at all. Asked about the toilet facility, their priority is about repairing the wall of their houses that might fall off and the roof that might fly off in strong wind. They defecate in open places only.

Box 8.1: Toilet—Not a Priority

Jeya (29) an SC woman at Semakottai Panchayat in Cuddalore district was curious to know why was this research team collecting information on aspects like delivery of basic services at *dalit* villages, and the use of various modern technological facilities in their lives. In an attempt to motivate the *dalits* to own toilets, a member of the research team put across how simple it was to construct a toilet making use of government subsidy under Total Sanitation Campaign. Later on, Jeya nailed it clearly that outsiders never understood priorities of the *dalits*. When our actual problem is getting rice at the PDS on time, and how to change the leaky roof of the hut we live in, we don't see defecating in the open or not owning a toilet as a big problem.

Health: Government health services are properly made use of by the *dalits*. The Health Sub Centres, and Primary Health Centres are properly being made use of by them. Hardly any family approaches private medical practitioners in the town for treatment, mainly due to affordability. Everyone of the delivery takes place at Government Hospital only—mostly at the District Headquarters Hospital. In some of the villages, they reported to have used the Emergency call number: 108 for making use of ambulance services. As far as health care services are concerned, *dalits* fully use the public health care services.

Basic Education: The Education for All Mission (SSA) has provided access to primary and upper primary level education to almost all the children in *dalit* hamlets as well. The SSA efforts with free education, free lunch, free uniforms, free books and stationery items, free bus-pass, and so on have largely helped SC/ST children to get enrolled in schools. No child that has reached the school-going age is left to hang around without being enrolled in *balwadi* (Child Care Centre) or at Union Primary Schools.

The current level of educational attainment found in *dalit* hamlets is that nine out of ten children reach upto completion of secondary level education. A little over seventy per cent of them reach up to higher secondary level education, and at least fifty per cent of them go to college level (or Polytechnic level) education. It is found *dalit* children proceed with average level educational performance as long as education is offered free—either in government-run schools or in government colleges. When it comes to paying for education, most of them tend to drop out due to problems of affordability. However, as most of them complete at least secondary or higher secondary level education, it could be stated that they can be well placed in educational attainment index. Of late, children from SC families are also admitted in private nursery and matriculation schools with a desire to enable them get English medium education. Nevertheless, this trend is found only in a very few villages with very few families who can manage to pay for private education. Nevertheless, technical courses offered by private institutions are found to be—financially—beyond their reach.

Even amongst *dalits,* SCs are better off with educational attainment compared to STs. The STs still have a long way to go even to complete upper primary level education. Again, with regard to STs near cent per cent enrolment has been achieved, but the habitual absenteeism is rampant, which is to a large extent better with SCs. As most of the ST settlements are located close to reserve forests, the children at school-going age develop taste in hunting rabbits and squirrels in the forest, or go for fishing in ponds, rather than go to school—their names are on roll though. Reform in Primary Education through SSA has helped increase enrolment of ST children in schools, but it does not help retention of them or prevent habitual absenteeism and eventual dropping out of the educational system.

Higher Education: Almost all the children from *dalit* settlements are in government-run schools, and as far as higher education is concerned many who pass out Higher Secondary Level education get enrolled in government arts colleges in the nearby town. A countable few pursue post-graduate studies as well. It is hard to find someone who pursues a technical skill oriented course. The exposure the *dalit* youth have on job prospects or employable skills is abysmally poor. They do not seem to acquire skills that would augment their employability. Give always like free lunch, free bus-pass, free-uniforms serve as the incentives to go to school at primary level; similarly, the hope about the quota based allocation of seats in institutions of higher learning make them pursue higher secondary education; and the vague understanding of 'reservations in jobs' make them complete a college degree too (Ashwini Despande *et al.*, 2007). But, they do not seem to realise that a college degree in arts with no job oriented skills or employable skills would help them very little in the job market. They register at the Government Employment Exchange and await call letter. They mark 'presence' at the service commission examinations, with the hope they would get government job. They have no idea of 'jobs and skill match' to be able to pinpoint what job would fit them in the private sector firms. They are not unaware that public sector employment is shrinking and only opportunities in private sector keep expanding as a result of liberalisation policies.

Educational Incentives: The Educational Loan Scheme has motivated a few youth from SC communities pursue post-graduate level education, and professional courses like B.Ed. and Polytechnic. Hardly anybody could be noticed from ST communities who have obtained an educational loan and pursue higher education. Amongst STs almost none could be seen in the study villages across nine districts in Tamil Nadu who pursue higher studies in colleges. Educational scholarships have helped many of the children from SC families complete upto collegiate level education. Yet, the parents do not even seem to have a rough idea of the amount of educational scholarships given in government colleges, and adequacy of it to complete courses their wards pursue. There is a widespread assumption in *dalit* hamlets that higher studies are costly, and that the educational scholarship would cover only a miniscule portion of the expenditure. This assumption prevents some of the parents from encouraging their wards to apply for collegiate education.

In the ultimate analysis it is found that SC children attain college level education and obtain certificates, degrees and diplomas. Some pursue even post-graduate level education. The educational expenses are mostly met out by the government, as almost all of them study in government schools and government colleges only. ST children are not prepared enough to complete even upper primary or secondary level education, due to absence of exposure neither to the basics nor to the comforts in life.

Employability: The problem with *dalit* youth with educational attainment is that they do not realise the need for cultivating employable skills to be saleable in the job market. Mere possession of academic qualifications, educational certificates and degrees, with no employable skills has only left the *dalit* youth disappointed and frustrated. With the shrinking public sector employment and increasing private sector employment they require guidance in cultivating employable vocational skills and entrepreneurial skills, which they are not exposed to. If at all they dream of government employment, they seem to have in mind only the class IV officers/clerical positions and peons. The scavengers in Municipalities are highly respected in *dalit* hamlets that they are monthly salaried class within *dalits*, and moreover they are employees of Municipality—a government entity.

Capability Poverty: It is dismal to find *dalit* youth having completed their graduation and post-graduation go for unskilled manual work in agriculture or for wage employment under NREGS, which are meant for unskilled labourers in villages. They lack exposure, and guidance. Still there are some inheriting an unfavourable combination of skills, or skills that are obsolete that cannot be cashed in or in the current socio-economic milieu. They lack employability. They lack vocational guidance and entrepreneurial skills. They are not trained in procedurally approaching banks to obtain a loan for setting up sort of self-employment or for obtaining some venture capital.

Box 8.2: A Wasted Offer

The Forest Department in Udumalaipet has floated to the STs in Indira Pudunagar an interesting proposal. That is the Government of Tamil Nadu has a scheme of supplying gas stoves to all the poor households in the State. But, it does not supply LP gas. The Forest Department has offered that it (the Forest Department) would supply gas to all the households month after month, on the condition that the STs shall not enter the forest to collect firewood. The STs have declined the offer. The reason stated by the STs is: '*Our women do not know how to light a gas stove. Suppose, she catches fire and burns with the gas, all men would be taken away in police custody that we set her on fire*'.

Thus, they do not have financial capital; they have no physical capital to hypothecate; they have very poor human capital in terms of capability. They suffer from 'capability poverty' as addressed by Amartya Sen. In many places they have no strong social capital worth the name. There are youth from *dalit* villages taken to cities like Chennai to work as labourers in construction industries and for digging pits for installing telephone cables in Mumbai, and to places like Thirupur and Erode to work in the garment industries. Their dream of getting government employment after graduation still hangs.

Civil and Political Participation: There are two things about civil and political participation. *Dalits* becoming leader of local governance system, making use of the provisions of the Panchayati Raj Act, and Constitutional 73rd Amendment Act is one. The other is *dalit* community airing their views in local decision making, and influencing development directions so that the decisions made in the Gram Sabha are not biased towards the rich or the caste-Hindus. They should be pro-poor, and pro-*dalit*. Unfortunately, the *dalits* in many of the villages studied do not participate in Gram Sabha meeting. The reasons stated for not participating are that (a) the presumption that they would not be heard, and (b) the reality that nothing that was passed as resolution in the Gram Sabha meetings held before have been materialised.

There are two types of villages found among the study villages. One is where *dalits* do not participate in Gram Sabha meeting at all. The other is where *dalits* participate, and flair up questions and cause hullabaloo so that no fruitful discussions take place. Most study villages belonged to the first category villages, except Keelkavarapattu in Cuddalore that belonged to the second category.

HOUSEHOLD ECONOMICS

A series of case studies of individual families was conducted in order to get hold of the household economics, meaning the expenditure pattern of a given *dalit* family, the income sources and how they manage especially the financial requirements of the family. Going by the definition of economics this is trying to understand how the hard earned scarce resources of the family are spent (allocated) on various items of expenditure. What is the savings or borrowings position of that family? How do they plan (if at all they do !) and manage these?

Items of Income	*Items of Expenditure*
Wage of the husband • The man gets anywhere between Rs. 100 and Rs. 200 daily during agricultural season. *Wage of the Wife* • The woman gets anywhere between Rs. 40 and Rs. 80 daily (seasonal) • NREGS income in some districts[3]. • Wage received in kind as paddy stock. • Paddy harvested from own land/share crop as foodstock, in case.	• Food expenses • Clothing (including uniform for children) • (Minimal on) education and health • Marriage and ceremony—family/relatives • Local Festivals • SHG loan repayment • Loan repayment to moneylender(s) • Pocket/snacks expenses of children • Purchase of home needs on instalment • (Contribution!) to TASMAC wine shop

It was found that the items of expenditure keeps extending, whereas the income sources are limited. Most of the families have no asset worth the name. In the order of magnitude the expenditure item that should actually find place next to food expenses is wine shop expenditure, and which should get third place is loan repayment to moneylenders. In *dalit* villages almost all the families owe money to private moneylenders. It drains away major portion of the earnings of the family, like the money thrown into the TASMAC wine shops. The amount of money borrowed for marriages and for giving compliments to marriages of relatives is considerably handsome, compared to the income levels of *dalits*. They join the SHGs mainly to get credit to be able to meet the consumption requirements of the family, and to repay the loan received from the moneylenders, and not with the intention of accumulating savings or taking up entrepreneurial ventures.

Box 8.3: Make Deposits at the TASMAC Shop

At Kovilpathu in Valivalam Panchayat of Nagapattinam when this team was interviewing there was a man (Subramani) constantly responding to our questions—no matter whether we asked him or asked the women around. The women constantly teased him as well. One of the women—Marie (who we came to know later as his wife) was rebuking: '*you talk like a Minister, but never bother to bring home the money you earn*'. Asked what he does with the money, all the women around say he cannot be seen in normal condition in the evenings. His—and many of the men in this village find a—bank in the TASMAC wine shop. Many of them deposit their income there. They all laughed. The wife (Marie) has to earn to feed the three children and the father-in-law who is aged. She is sending two children to the local Union Primary School, and the third one has not reached the school-going age. The husband didn't seem to bother. He laughed out listening to the wife narrating her story in a sickening voice. As we leave the place of discussion, the women talked behind our back that Marie will have her day that evening, after the husband returns from wine shop.

Money Flow: Money income is one important indicator of economic improvement of households. Various sources of money flow (income flow) into *dalit* families were analysed with a view to finding out if there has been any additional sources of income flow through multiple opportunities or enhanced choices created anew in the society. The sources of additional money flow into *dalit* families are through the following. Employment in NREGS, Self-Help Groups, Tamil Nadu Poverty Reduction and Empowerment Project assisted by the World Bank (TNVKP), the income that the youth make through employment in towns, cities and foreign countries as labourers or construction workers.

It was also found that NREGS either stopped or is not being implemented in full swing in all the districts. The main reason stated by Panchayat functionaries is: there is no place left uncovered in the previous year to take up for the current year. Self-Help Groups are in nascent stage in many of the *dalit* villages, if they are more than 3-4 years old, it remains dormant due to misunderstanding amongst members. The TNVKP is again in nascent stage in villages, which show a lot of hope to the people. The additional flow of money, at the moment, is from youth employed in the unorganised industry such as construction works in cities. But, it pertains only to about 15-20 per cent of the households in *dalit* villages.

DALITS, TRADITION AND POST-MODERNITY

Globalization has brought computer, internet, mobile and other technologies. These are meant to improve the 'quality of life' of individuals. The relevance and use of these technologies to *dalits* are discussed below.

There are clearly two different world-views of the *dalits*. One is of the aged generation, and the other is of the current generation. The notion of the aged generation comes from original tradition and culture that they got handed down. The world-view of the current generation comes from the influence of new technologies of the twenty first century, advertisement, and consumerism, which we address as post-modernity. Although the reach of various media to *dalit* villages is very limited, the influence of post-modernity among the youth is unrestrained. It puts in them unapparent desires, which have the potential to change their culture and tradition and determine the central social trends of the present. It profoundly affects everyday social life, for example, the social dimensions of information and communication technologies. The change in trend can be captured under spheres like education, employment, land ownership, expenditure pattern, marriage and ceremonies, food habits and clothing, facilities in life, and mobility.

Rathnavel (27), a *dalit* youth at Kodungal Village Panchayat in Villupuram district, had a mobile phone that he was often flicking on and flicking off during the course of an FGD with a band of youth by this research team. What is the price of that mobile phone? What is the use of it to him? And how much does he spend on it every month? He bought it for Rs. 1100 which is a basic model that he could find in the market, he said.

What is the use of it to him? Pat came the reply: *'I have two uses for this. One is I give 'missed calls' to my friends. If they have pre-paid balance in their mobiles, they call back to hear from me that I called 'just for fun'. And the other is, some labour contractors/logistics operators from the town call me to pass on information about requirements of labour in the construction industry in Chennai or Bangalore, and ask me to come with a team of youngsters to work.'*

How much does he spend on it? *None of us here recharge on monthly basis. This is a mobile phone with incoming calls free for life-time. Whenever, there is need to talk I buy a coupon for Rs. 10 and recharge. If I have excess money while at work in some place in the town, I recharge for Rs. 50. But most often, it remains with zero balance like how it is now. It rings with useful information when the labour contractor calls. We do not know who invented mobile phone, but sir, it is we who invented 'missed calls'*, he quips.

Mathivanan (32) of Veeracholapuram Village in Villupuram district was curious to know who we were and what we were looking for, when he found us in the local petty shop enquiring about the location of the Panchayat Office. The confidence in the language he spoke showed he was a local person, and the way he had dressed, and the mobile phone from China market made us wonder if he was really a native of that *dalit* village, and what was he doing. We found during conversation that he did belong to that village, but was settled in Chennai for more than ten years. He works for several labour contracting agencies in Chennai. He supplies labourers from his, and the neighbourhood villages for digging pits for installing telephone cables in Chennai, Bangalore, Mumbai etc. He earns his commission from the Contracting Agencies at Chennai, for every labourer he puts in touch with. By the time this conversation was going, he was surrounded by a team of youth (speaking in broken Hindi) who had come back home after completing a contract work.

The discussion with a group of women SHG members in Thinaikulam village in Thirupur district revealed that women find no use for mobile phones. One of the SHG women quipped: *I go for agricultural wage employment, and my husband is also a wage earner like me. Of what use do you think a mobile phone would be to us. Perhaps, you think, after completing my weeding work here, I can call my husband on the mobile to find out if he has completed bund construction work there.*

Besides the mobile phones, the One-Rupee Coin-operated phone is popular in villages. There is at least one Coin-operated phone in everyone of the village visited. The Emergency Call No. 108 for ambulance or fire service has been conspicuously displayed in almost all the villages visited. *Dalit* people in some of the villages reported to have used them beneficially, and in most villages they are either unaware or yet to use the 'call: 108 service'.

Pitchai (29), an ST youth in Indrapudunagar village in Thirupur district, was the only one having a mobile phone in the group of about 13 people (men and women) who were involved in an FGD with this team of researchers. Asked about the use of it and the money he spends on it, the reply was something unpredicted. He had got it as pledge for Rs. 200 he lent to one of his friends. The phone would be with him until his friend repays the money borrowed, he collects no interest for the money though.

Mahendran (20), Saravanakumar (22), Kalaiselvam (22), Vignesh (24) of Landai Village in Ramanathapuram district were listening to loud Tamil Cinema music inside a shed with a parapet wall. As we could see only a band of youth, we entered the shed with no hesitation saying: 'hallo'—as if we knew them before. They were all school dropouts, and who had completed class 10 or Higher Secondary level education, working in a Dubai based construction company. They were recruited by a recruitment agency run by a Muslim person, who has a recruitment agency in Paramakudi town in Ramanathapuram district. The construction company takes contract works from all over Dubai, and these boys are used as labourers on monthly payment. They stay together in a house allotted to them by the company. They cook their food. They earn INR. 10,000-12,000 every month. They get a vacation of three-months once in two years, when they get their flight tickets free. But no payment for the three months they are away from work.

At Landai Muslim colony in Ramanathapuram district all the people in that village are said to have converted to Islam. We could find a Mosque at the entrance of the village. Conversations with the villagers revealed that they got resettled in that village (Landai) and converted to Islam when there were constant caste-riots (between *dalits* and caste-Hindus) in the village they belonged to originally. Many youth from Landai Village Panchayat work as labourers in Dubai construction companies, recruited from Paramakudi *dalit* villages.

At Keelkavarapattu village, Annagram Block in Cuddalore district we could find a magnificent church at the middle of the village. It was said to be a *dalit* village, but most people have converted to Christianity, about two generations before, when the Arcot Lutheran Church of the Danish Mission was established there. The youth in the village remember that almost everyone of the *dalit* family has converted to Christianity when *dalits* were suffering from hunger. The Arcot Lutheran Church gave them food and health care services, education to children and taught them Bible too. Temple entry was a big problem in caste-Hindu villages, whereas Christianity invited the *dalits* into church.

The women buy modern home needs such as plastic chairs, stainless steel vessels etc. on instalment basis. They pay the dues on weekly basis to the supplier, who makes door delivery of furniture, vessels, and some electronic items like DVD players. Although moneylenders are widespread, operation of the sellers who give home needs on instalment are not many.

As far as training in computers is concerned, only a countable few have undergone training in the use of computers, but they are also not confident enough about working in computers. The elders have heard of computers, and a few have seen them in the Panchayat Office. But, none of them is aware of what an internet (*Inayathalam*) is. A few of the *dalit* youth who are aware of the use of an internet also, do not find any use for them in internet, nor do they have an e-mail ID of their own.

In the ultimate analysis of tradition and post-modernity, it could be said that unlike their parents, *dalit* youth are on the look out for employment elsewhere—either in the town or if possible go abroad as manual labourer. They are not ready to take charge of the land—neither as wage earner nor as owner. The mobile phone and Coin-operated phones come in handy to get in touch with labour contractors, and to step up their mobility as labourers. *Dalit* women and the aged generation do not find any use for mobile phones or computers. Even the educated youth who are on the look out for employment are looking for State services from the Employment Exchanges. They do not have any idea of using internet as a tool for putting them in touch with several employers in the market.

Finally, factors like conversion to Islam or Christianity could not be taken as an outcome of economic globalization of the current phase. It belonged to an earlier phase of globalization when religious missionaries from countries like France, Denmark, Germany etc. thronged India for essentially providing basic education, health care and religious services in Indian villages. The current tussle is: if they belonged to Backward Caste (BC) or Scheduled Caste (SC). This stems when some spiteful officers refuse to give them SC certificate reasoning out that their names sound like Christian's or Muslim's. They want to be addressed as *Dalit* Christians and *Dalit* Muslims respectively, whereas the contention of some of the officials is: Are you a *dalit*? Or Christian? Or Muslim? It stands there.

III. *DALITS,* LIVELIHOODS AND EMPLOYMENT

Poverty and *dalits* are almost synonymous. Historically, the *dalits* have undergone various forms of deprivation such as non-possession of land or any physical capital; deprivation of financial capital to take up entrepreneurial ventures; deprivation of human capability with only unskilled manual labour to eke out a living; and absence of strong social capital to participate in governance or to decide the development direction. The diversification in employment opportunities of everybody's life after globalization must have some impact in the traditional livelihoods of *dalits*. There are opportunities that globalization has brought for talents, and not for the talents of the non-*dalits* alone. They are not based on rural social hierarchy or traditional discrimination. Hence, an analysis into the change in trend, if any of the livelihoods of the *dalits* is inevitable in a study on *dalits* and globalization. We shall begin with the traditional livelihoods of *dalits* for the purpose of offering a background. Then, move on to the recent changes that are taking place in their livelihood patterns.

TRADITIONAL LIVELIHOODS OF *DALITS*

The activities and functions of *dalits* in traditional Indian society were very much limited and were directly pertaining to land, animal and rudimentary human services such as making footwears, hair cutting for the upper caste, carrying verbal circulars (messages) of death in the families of upper caste, burning dead humans, beating drums in death houses, burying dead animals, manual scavenging of night-soil and so on. The 'activities and functions' *dalit* community was involved in to eke out a living largely determined the social status of *dalits*. It is on these grounds that some social scientists argue that *dalits* have nothing to lose as a result of globalization. If at all they lose, it would be their misery; it would be their humiliation and social stigma (see Ramaiah, A., *Dalits* to Accept Globalization, TISS). Thus, the Scheduled Caste people were mainly farm labourers, attached to families of landlords. They were the working majority involved in the production of essential commodities for the entire community. There were no opportunities for multiple livelihoods. There were occupations one got trained by observation and practice, usually handed down from one generation to another. Similarly, the tribals, known as the STs were supposed to lead a life of hunters and gatherers.

Resistance movements by *dalit* organisations all-over India started gathering momentum against sub-human treatment of *dalits*. Partly, *dalits* had to put up with countless acts of humiliation before overcoming the resistance from vested interests to a significant level (Viswanathan, S., 2004). *Dalits* could register NGOs, and mobilise global funds to fight against caste based injustice and discrimination in India. The need for technology solution was recognised. Demand for technology was a felt need. As globalization started operating technologies started taking over several of the functions—be it passing on the message of death, shoe making or burning the dead bodies of humans. Passing on messages of death is instantly being done by one-rupee coin operated telephones in the villages, and mobile phones; shoe making has become a several million dollar industry; there are courses run by government polytechnics and private engineering colleges in footwear technology, which even upper caste people have started getting admission in; mechanisation is fast taking over manual scavenging, and Electric Crematoriums have come about for burning dead humans. Many problems that remained for years are being solved by technology and the knowledge that globalization has given access to.

DIVERSIFICATION OF LIVELIHOODS

The kind of livelihood diversification that has taken place after globalization was to be documented. So, the study attempted to list out the kind of livelihoods that the *dalits* were involved in, in recent times. Improved transport and telecommunication facilities have enabled mobility of younger generation of the *dalits*. The contacts that some of them could establish helps many in their village to take up diversified livelihood options. The mobility accelerates contacts. The facility to become mobile and be in touch through telecommunication facilities has enabled youth to move out of *dalit* villages, and work in varied fields. We shall give evidences of the empirical verification made.

Bands of youth from Tamil Nadu *dalit* villages work as construction workers, rod benders and manual labourers in laying telephone cables in cities like Mumbai, Chennai and Bangalore. At least 10-20 such youth could be identified in each of the study village in Cuddalore, and Villupuram. Similar statements could be recorded from other districts like Thiruvarur, and Nagapattinam that the *dalit* youth are employed in garment industries in Thirupur, Erode, and Coimbatore. There are *dalit* youth—reported by their parents in the study villages—employed in bus body building industries of Karur. There are *dalit* youth employed as casual labourers in the SIPCOT complex in Cuddalore. Panchayat Presidents from Thiruvannamalai have fought with the MNCs of SEZ in Cheyyar and have caused over 250 youth from *dalit* villages get employment at Cheyyar SEZ in Thiruvannamalai. There are youth including *dalits* from around Kancheepuram and Sriperumbudur working in companies like Nokia, Nixon, Lotus Shoes, and so on.

But, some of these companies reportedly prefer women employees, and *dalit* youth from far away places. It is also true that some of these companies avoid employing local youth, especially *dalit* youth as they find them to be quarrelsome, and absent from work when there are other works to complete at home. There are *dalit* youth being recruited as masons, rod benders, centring builders, and helpers from Paramakudi in Ramanathapuram district for construction works in Dubai. These can be listed as multiplicity of opportunities that *dalit* youth have found in the recent times, apart from the wage employment in agriculture—the only thing they were aware of.

THE OTHER SIDE OF LIVELIHOOD MULTIPLICITY

Close scrutiny of the nature of all these livelihood options that have opened up after globalization are 'unorganised kind of work' again. Despite the fact that they get higher pay, and it helps them enable money flow into the family, they are again into an unorganised and unsecured type of employment is the argument put forth by dissenters of globalization (Anand Teltumbde). It is true. But, those who fight saying that this is all unorganised and exploitative kind of work, often, have no solution to the problems of *dalits.* Momentarily, the diversified opportunity that globalization opened up has made way for *dalit* youth in considerable number find multiple livelihoods. Freedom to choose from multiple livelihood opportunities in itself is a kind of development, in the view of Amartya Sen. It is all the more necessary for *dalits* to become mobile, get exposed to multiple livelihood options that are opening up. They need to develop competence, get hold of new economic opportunities that come with globalization, which would eventually result in poverty reduction, and social well-being.

But this is only about the *dalit* youth (both the gender included). What is happening to the livelihoods of the middle aged; what is happening with *dalit* women who contributed considerably to the household income; and what is the role of NREGS, which is primarily said to be focused at *dalit* landless labourers? In the context of livelihood options of *dalit* youth, the discussion about the middle aged, and aged generation of the *dalits* is significant because it relates to intra-generational and inter-generational poverty. How does globalization help address the problem of intra- and inter-generational poverty?

THE NEO-LANDED CLASS

Globalization processes set manufacturing and service sectors on the fast track of development, at a time when traditional agricultural families (caste-Hindus) found agriculture after mechanisation non-remunerative. This led way for many caste-Hindus who until then found possession of land as an important indicator of social status to reconsider pursuits in agriculture and lay hand in sectors outside agriculture. Consequently, the current generation of the so called landed class have almost few to get down to doing agriculture. Nonetheless, their long-time inclination towards lands did not allow them to give up agriculture altogether. Not all of them give up; not all the land is sold out. Widely, they have started 'leasing out' lands to the *dalits* who used to work as labourers in their farms. Similarly, when the traditional land owners leave the village they leave it to some trustworthy *dalits* to plough their land on share cropping arrangement. The *dalit* who was hitherto a wage earner gets down to doing his own cultivation in the status of share-cropper.

For the erstwhile landed class, the fashion of knowledge-based employment, salaried job in the town, or a business in the town with other material possessions, plus cash in hand, and cash at bank started becoming the new indicators of social status. So, they found life outside agriculture brighter and so eventually they started selling off lands to *dalits,* who for quite a few years, had leased in lands from them. Some *dalit* organisations like LAFTI in Thiruvarur have worked towards assisting *dalits* to buy such lands with bank loan, through land purchase scheme of the TAHDCO or SHG loan. Only in Thiruvarur and Nagappattinam districts, over 20,000 acres have been transferred from caste-Hindus to *dalits.* This is witnessed in Thanjavur, Ramanathapuram and Salem as well. Thus a visible process of redistribution of land is taking place, where the *dalits* are becoming the new landed class, and the erstwhile land owners are moving to other sectors of the economy.

Dalits from being agricultural wage earners are becoming either as sharecroppers or as new land owners—size-wise with small holdings though. Other factors that work in favour of the shift is, the large pieces of land that were in the possession of erstwhile landed classes was non-remunerative putting machinery into agriculture, and hiring costly labour etc. Introduction of National Rural Employment Guarantee Scheme (NREGS) has intensified the demand for agriculture labourers and increase in the cost of labour in agriculture. After the introduction of NREGS, an important finding of several earlier studies on agriculture in Tamil Nadu is being disproved. *That is 'agriculture is overcrowded and underpaid'. It is no more overcrowded given the demand for labour for agricultural works. It is no more underpaid given the room labourers have for bargaining wages pointing finger at wags at NREGS, and the price primary commodities—be it cereals, pulses or oilseeds—that fetch in the market today.*

The demand for labour created by NREGS and the hike in minimum wages set by the NREGS has worked again in favour of *dalit* landless labourers to hint to their land owners to offer land on lease, if their land owners found difficulty carrying on with farming. Such lands from one landlord gets transferred either on lease or through sale into the possession of a few *dalit* families. Given the small size of holdings, *dalits* do not have to use machineries in agriculture. It has become farming by the entire household without involving machinery or hired labour. If at all additional labourers are required, it is met out through exchange of labour between two *dalit* families. Despite this shift taking place, wage employment in agriculture still dominates the *dalit* livelihood in villages.

Mechanisation is suitable only for large scale farming, or farming at a relatively bigger scale. Small holdings neither require machineries, nor is it feasible to use machines in small size land holdings in possession of the *dalits*. Moreover, the paddy straw gets damaged and become unusable while threshing, putting to use machineries. The straw cannot be used as animal fodder. Hence, the *dalits* still use family members in agriculture. The traditional land owners, who use machineries, find agriculture costly, and less remunerative. They are the ones leaving agriculture. They are the ones who lease out or sell off their lands to *dalits*.

Box 8.4: Forty acres declined to five acres

Dhakshnamoorthy (Reddiyar) of Pudupathoor Village—a caste-Hindu of the CPI(M) party in Thiruvarur (Vettaikaraniruppu) was owner of 40 acres of land that he used to cultivate paddy in. Not being able to get labour, and finding mechanisation in agriculture costly, he started selling off his lands piece by piece. The works of LAFTI—an NGO working to make the landless labourers as land owners in Thiruvarur district also influenced in his parting with land for the sake of *dalits*. Now, he owns only 5 acres of land. He wants to keep it for the social status he enjoyed as a landowner. But, he says that his son, who is working for the ONGC, is pressuring him to sell it off and go and settle with him in the town. He does not want to leave the village. He has no mind to leave agriculture. So, he is cultivating the five acres of land with him making use of a handful of labourers he hires whenever required.

Although small in number, this is a change taking place in favour of *dalits* in agricultural villages in Tamil Nadu. That is, the erstwhile landed class shifting to other sectors (outside agriculture) that globalization opens up, and the *dalits* fill up the vacuum created by the landed class, posing themselves as 'the neo-landed' class. Land as a 'physical capital' is doing away the 'landlessness' character of *dalits*; SHGs lending coupled with bank loan for agriculture provides them access to 'financial capital'. Their 'human capability' serves themselves instead of merely selling off their labour for wage. The value of their human capability has gone up with the new found physical asset and access to financial help through SHGs for agricultural expenses.

Much contrary to what was expected by the opponents of globalization, mechanisation in agriculture has resulted in many traditional landowners/ caste-Hindus giving up agriculture and *dalits* become tiny land owners. This shift in the erstwhile landless agricultural wage earners becoming the land owning class has introduced a new set of agro-social dynamics and agricultural production system in Tamil Nadu villages. That globalization would intensify widespread use of machineries in agriculture and so, the *dalits* who are mostly agricultural labourers would be thrown out of agriculture looks disproved in actuality. Those landlords who try to use machineries in agriculture due to shortage of labour for agriculture tend to quit agriculture and quit village itself. They settle down in towns with some business, or with their sons who are salaried. *Dalits* are emerging as the neo-landed class in agricultural villages.

Now, those traditional land owners who are still holding on to agriculture are suffering not being able to get labourers. *Dalits* who used to sell labour for wage are busy working in 'own lands', working for themselves—in the land that they leased in, or purchased. This further discourages the traditional land owners to continue agriculture, and it has a tendency to accelerate the process of land falling into the hands of *dalits* or in the hands of the realtors. The response of the traditional land owners who give up agriculture and are selling off their lands to *dalits* is: '*What befell on me today, awaits them (the dalits) tomorrow*', meaning the younger generation in *dalit* community are also looking for opportunities outside agriculture.

Thus, the fallout of mechanisation in agriculture has turned out to be in favour of the *dalits*. Introduction of machineries in agriculture and increased cost of agricultural labour coupled with new opportunities that opened up outside agriculture have resulted in landholdings to slip from the hands of the traditional landlords and fall into hands of the *dalits*.

TAKEN OVER BY MARKET AND TECHNOLOGY

Shoe-Making Industry: The *dalit* youth have become mobile. Not many of them are in agriculture anymore. The livelihoods that their parents pursued—be it footwear making or repairing the old shoes are closing down. The new knowledge economy found the potential of footwear market in India. Immediately, technology and capital took over footwear and shoe making. The MNCs have opened manufacturing centre for shoes, school shoes and footwear in several places of Tamil Nadu like there is one Lotus footwear manufacturing industry in Cheyyar SEZ at Thiruvannamalai. In another sense, they have incidentally gone into million dollar investment business, which youth do not find indignity in doing it. They pursue courses in getting trained in shoe making. The same thing holds good for beauty parlour, which has emerged from barbershop to beauty saloon to beauty parlour—several million dollar industry today.

Market Mechanism: From several parts of Tamil Nadu footwear showrooms place order with one or the other of the footwear manufacturer at Ambur or Vaniyambadi. Most of the industry owners are Muslims, and most of the shoe makers come from *dalit* community. Most often, the *dalits* are bonded financially like the *dalits* engaged in agricultural wage employment. But, the difference is more in the nature of tie-up. The tie-up at the shoe company stands because there is nothing social about it. It works on the market mechanism of paying the *dalits* on piece rate basis, and it is no social, arrangement for the *dalits* to try to get out of it. It is not payment made on the grounds of mercy or sympathy, which would be social, discrediting the value of labour involved for doing a job nobody else would choose to do.

Messages of Death: Messages of death are informed through one rupee coin-operated telephones or through mobile phones even in villages. *Dalits* are no more engaged in that.

Electric Crematoriums: As far as burning of dead persons are concerned there are many hospitals, NGOs, and charitable trusts that have started operating Electronic Crematoriums.

The drums-men: In Tamil Nadu villages *dalits* are still engaged in beating drums in death houses of caste-Hindus. The ones generally involved in beating drums are aged persons or middle aged men from *dalit* community. They own drums and they periodically beat them up and keep them as it should be. They are paid no fixed amount. The payment to the drums-men depends on the importance of the person who died, and how honourable the family is in the village. The youth are deviating from this and are forming 'Orchestra troops/band troop'. They have some additional instruments, and prefer to play as band troops outside marriage halls. The political parties give them opportunities to play to mark the invitation or in honour of political leaders visit to a town or locality. As this is not an occupation that would provide regular income, they take it up only occasionally upon invitation. However, the income from drum-beating or Orchestra troops never reach home. Reportedly, it goes down the bottle on the way to home.

Mechanisation of Scavenging: Manual scavenging has completely become a practice of the past in Tamil Nadu. It has been mechanised almost completely. Bands of *dalit* youth all-over Tamil Nadu (met for this study in Cuddalore, Villupuram, Thiruvarur, and Nagapattinam) with a modified auto-rickshaw fitted with a cistern and an electric pump offer septic tank cleaning service. They go round hawking if there is septic tank to be cleaned or block in the drainage to be removed. They print hand-bills with their mobile number and throw it inside compound walls of residential areas, and await phone calls to offer septic tank cleaning service. As this is not a job that many people would be willing to do, they charge from Rs. 1,000 to Rs. 2,000 per septic tank, and share the money. They found demand for septic tank cleaning service in the residential areas, and found a market to engage themselves in it. All of them are *dalit* youth belonging to families traditionally involved in sanitation and manual scavenging works *Swachchkar* community (*safai karamcharis*). They have improvised the method of cleaning using technology again. They do not physically land in the faecal matter. Instead, they have a motorised pump that sucks watery faecal matter from septic tank to the cistern that is attached to the auto-rickshaw.

Box 8.5: The pride of a newly wedded ST bride

This team of researchers happened to hold a discussion with an ST family (Arunthathiar—kamar) in Nagapattinam, where men are involved in sanitation works, and women are involved in rearing pigs and making baskets for a living. One of the women in the group—said to be newly married—mentioned she is not engaged in making baskets, and that she is just a house wife. She was not bothered that she did not earn making baskets. Asked why she doesn't do it: the reply was that her husband owns a septic tank cleaning vehicle and he earns not less than Rs. 250-Rs. 300 at least every alternate day. She doesn't have to put in a day long work to earn Rs. 40 making a basket. The pride that gleaned in her eyes in putting across to this team of researchers that her husband owns a septic tank cleaning vehicle, and so her family is well off compared to many others sitting around required to be documented.

If *dalits* have lost jobs because of the technologies brought about by globalization, there are jobs that were considered disgrace or shame to be engaged in such as carrying death messages, which one-rupee coin-operated phones do now; burning the dead bodies of persons, which Electric Crematoriums do now; mending the shoes of caste-Hindus, which industries have taken over; manual scavenging of night soil, which have been made mechanical now. The number of caste-Hindus that search for *dalits* to carry out such jobs of indignity is fast coming down. They go for technology solution, which has directly helped the *dalits* to wipe out qualities of 'untouchable nature' or indignity that they once had.

If all the scavengers involved in sanitation works at Municipalities, Corporations and government hospitals are *dalits* that is because they consider it a grace in being addressed as salaried class in *dalit* colonies. There is competition among them in getting employed as scavenger at Municipalities,

Corporations and in Government Hospitals. They do not consider it indignity. There is money in it, and so the element of indignity becomes too small to recognise. No matter whether they consider it grace or disgrace, that is also being mechanised fast.

Box 8.6: I am a Government Employee

Murugan—one of the participants in an FGD conducted at Kannaginagar near Panruti in Cuddalore district was loud mouthed and almost everyone with no trace of being dominated watched him talk to us. During the course of the discussion another person—a wage earner who introduced himself as Murugan's younger brother narrated that whenever he found difficulty in finding employment, him and his children used to eat at his elder brother's (Murugan's) house. The discussion turned towards marriage, when Murugan reported he spent nearly one and half lakh for his son's marriage. His son—a High School dropout, got married a year ago, is yet to determine how to run his own family. He got, besides other things, a Hero Honda motor cycle as dowry. The in-laws saw the family, and not the boy, said Murugan. Murugan looked a well-to-do person among the *dalits* who had assembled for the FGD with this research team. Out of curiosity and necessity we asked what was Murugan doing? And how did he manage to mobilise one and a half lakhs for his son's marriage?
He replied: *I am a government employee. Part of the money I got as loan from my office at Panruti, and the rest I borrowed from a moneylender.*
Which government office are you working in: *In Panruti Municipality Office.*
What are you there?: *I am a scavenger.*

INTER-GENERATIONAL LIVELIHOODS

The change taking place in the inter-generational livelihoods of *dalits* is considerable. The social stigma or social discrimination of *dalits* was mainly due to the type of activities and functions they were engaged in. The youth are no more getting into the shoes of their parents. Globalization and general trend in Indian society over the years has brought about several positive changes in the lives of *dalits*. The youth have become mobile. The youth get connected with the contractors in the town and are engaged. They are after multiple livelihoods and activities away from the traditional ones that attached social stigma in doing. The middle aged and aged *dalits* are in considerable number becoming land owners. The nature of agriculture they are engaged in is subsistence farming using family labour and so, they find agriculture remunerative. The landless labourers among *dalits* get seasonal employment in agriculture and under the NREGS during agriculturally off-season.

ROLE OF NREGS

The NREGS in the study villages have helped augment the income of the *dalits.* Those who wisely marked the 100 days of employment making full use of the local farm employment (as primary) have done really well. The availability of guaranteed employment, as contemplated by the scheme, has resulted in improvement in the local wage-rates for various kinds of manual works both on-farm and off-farm that the landless labourers are generally engaged in. That which was Rs. 80-100 for men has gone into a range of Rs. 120-150, and that which was Rs. 40-50 for women has gone into a range of Rs. 70-80. The total household income of landless labourers has increased, and the additional income they could earn under the NREGS. However, in some of the districts, Thirupur, Thiruvarur and Cuddalore, *dalits* complained that NREGS works were given hardly 15-20 days and then stopped. The Panchayats report difficulty to find place for providing employment in the consecutive years when NREGS is continuously implemented.

The hike in the local wage rates introduced by the NREGS has become a burden on the traditional landlords whose family members are not involved in cultivation. Therefore, the *dalits* are making use of the opportunity to demand higher wages, pointing finger at NREGS option. The traditional land owners finding it uneconomical to cultivate so they lease it out to the *dalits* on share cropping basis. The *dalits* put to use the entire family's labour in the land and reap good harvests.

ROLE OF SHGS

There are SHGs promoted by local NGOs. They are involved in saving and lending in a small scale in almost all the study villages. The vision of the women who have become members of SHGs is also very much short-sighted. They want to tide over the day-to-day consumption difficulties and to get a helping hand at times of a crisis. They have no vision or strong desire to come out of poverty permanently by making use of a social asset like SHG that NGOs and government offer all out support. But, SHGs have helped the *dalit* families tide over consumption difficulties and at times of crisis.

Besides SHGs, the Poverty Reduction and Empowerment Project implemented by the Government of Tamil Nadu with the financial support of the World Bank is in operation in some of the Project villages. This Project is intensively implemented in *dalit* villages. It addresses the issue of social exclusion by including socially and economically vulnerable people in *dalit* villages, that are especially multiple-problem households. The project is also involved in imparting various skill development and entrepreneurial training for *dalit* youths. This project is in nascent stage in many of the study villages. The prospects it shows for the improvement of the *dalits* are immense.

Box: 8.7: NREGS does well for this Family in District Dindigul

At Kalikkampatty in Dindigul district, Karupiah—a Scheduled Caste man proudly explains how he was able to manage his family expenditure without any private borrowings just as a wage earner. His is a family of four. He has an elder daughter studying in B.Ed after her Post-graduation in Tamil literature at Gandhigram University, and a son studying UG degree programme at Palani Andavar College in Palani. He is proud about financing his children's study despite his being a wage earner. His wife also goes to work whenever there is demand for female labourers during agricultural season in the locality. He says, his wife's membership in the local SHG, and the employment in NREGS could be attributed as two sources of money that give confidence to send his wards to college. He saves with the Self-Help Group, and earns at NREGS to pay to loan taken to finance the studies of his son and daughter. He is hopeful they would get employed and lead a life free of poverty.

Despite several positive changes in terms of livelihood and income, the quality of life does not improve with the *dalits.* This is mainly because they do not have the habit of saving. They do not hesitate to borrow (from moneylenders) for consumption expenditure, marriages, festivals and ceremonies. Most men in many of the study villages have the habit of hitting at the bottle all evenings, under the pretext of body pain. The operation of moneylenders has been liberalised in almost all the villages to the extent that *dalits* utter that without the operation of the moneylenders they cannot survive all the marriages, ceremonies and compliments that they have to give their relatives during marriages and local festivals.

The potential of SHGs has been used only to a very basic level. They look forward to borrow from group funds, and borrow from banks as well. They do not have the will to accumulate their savings, and see their money in their bank account, or buy some asset such as land, or jewel for the family. The main hurdle to this is, men in many of the houses drink and the woman has to feed the aged in-laws, and the own children. Globalization because of its intrinsic market nature has taken away many of the social stigmas that *dalits* used to carry around with them. But, the *dalits* have to find economic opportunities within the globalized context and get out of poverty.

IV. SOCIAL EXCLUSION AND INCLUSIVE POLICIES

EXCLUSIONARY PERSPECTIVE

It is true that there is an agrarian shift taking place in Tamil Nadu villages where *dalits,* although not in large numbers, are emerging as the neo-landed class. This holds good only for the wet regions or intensive agricultural districts of Tamil Nadu such as Thiruvarur, Thanjavur and parts of Trichy. At the same time another stark reality found mostly in dry regions or agriculturally not-so-busy districts of Tamil Nadu such as Kancheepuram, Thiruvannamalai, and Villupuram is, a major section of *dalit* population hold only their Family Ration Card as Asset No. 1 of the family. There is nothing else they have to list as asset worth the name. In districts like Ramanathapuram, the exposure they got through mingling with Muslim community has made them find manual employment in Arab countries.

Within *dalits* there are two classes that emerge. One is those who have managed to become small land owners or sharecroppers, and draw analogy with the caste-Hindus they acquired the land from; and the other is those who are still landless labourers and are completely dependent on Family Ration Card as the life-line asset of the family. The relative deprivation that the *dalits* undergo—no matter they have become landed class or still remain landless wage earners—is perceptible and definite. The Family Ration Card that ensures family food security plus the Registration Card at the NREGS that shows them the way to PDS shop are all the assets they seem to have. After a thorough interview with them, a direct observation of 'facilities inside the hut they live in' proves beyond doubt, what they stated was the bare fact and no exaggeration. It was analysed bearing in mind identifying any role of globalization in it.

Dalits are excluded from commanding livelihood opportunities, and choices. These are found in both material and non-material dimensions. The deprivations *dalits* experience are usually multi-dimensional. Therefore, the underdevelopment or backwardness of these groups can be understood now in perspective by using the concept of social exclusion. Exclusion of the poor from participation in and access to opportunities and activities is a major non-material dimension of poverty. The remedy appears to be in bringing the socially excluded close to society through a process of social inclusion. An attempt was made in the past in the southern States to bring these sections at par with the so-called upper castes by providing equality of opportunity in education and employment (Chalam, K.S., 2007).

The deprivation or exclusion that they go through in the study villages can be listed as follows. Absence of exposure and guidance exclude the *dalit* youth from catching up positions in the State services (Ashwini Deshpande, 2007); labour markets exclude them as 'misfits to the modern day skill-set requirements' (Carol Padhya, 2007; Thorat, S., 2004); the institutional credit markets exclude them as they do not write-up bankable/presentable proposals (Pallavi Chavan, 2007); the bureaucracy exclude them from having access to entitlements such as land *patta*, for example (Arvind Rajagopal, 2004; Thangaraj, 2006); the location of their settlement exclude them from having access to common basic facilities in the main village; the local elite group exclude them from participating in local governance (Mahamallik *et al.*, 2007). We shall offer illustrations below from the empirical verifications made.

Excluded from Institutional Credit Market: The institutional credit markets are prepared to lend the *dalits* against jewels or collateral securities, which not many *dalit* families possess. So, they are excluded from institutional sources of credit. Those *dalits* who own small pieces of land manage to get crop loan. But, majority of the *dalits* have nothing to pledge except the ration cards. Besides ration cards and stainless steel vessels, the recent addition to the things that the youngsters in *dalit* hamlets pledge include: mobile phones. The operation of the private moneylenders is rampant in all the villages in the districts under study. A chain of interview revealed that more than eighty per cent of the families are in the clutches of the moneylenders, and at least half of them under more than one moneylender. There are daily, weekly, and monthly repayment systems in vogue. There are families that have due to repayment in all the three systems. The opinion of the *dalits* is that they cannot survive unless these moneylenders operated.

There are SHGs functioning in some of the villages, but the SHG operations are basic and undeveloped. Almost all the borrowings—be it from the moneylenders or SHGs—are usually consumption-oriented, or festival and ceremonies oriented only. They are in a small income trap. So, nothing productive seems to be taking place as a result of savings and credit with SHGs. Intensive play of money lenders is one of the main factors that drain their incomes, besides the TASMAC shops. These two factors, viz. (a) borrowing from private moneylenders; and (b) men having the drinking habit, play devastating role in many *dalit* families. Besides this, there are also consumer goods such as plastic chairs, stainless steel vessels etc. that they (especially the women) buy on instalment payment. They need to find money for paying such instalments also.

Excluded from Participation in the Market Economy: Market economy works in favour of those who have capital, knowledge and information, or technology. It either bypasses the poor or affects the livelihood resources of the poor. A recent report of the National Commission for Enterprises in the Unorganised Sector of the Government of India, puts across that economic growth in India for the past 20 years has catered to only about 23 per cent of the population; and it has bypassed 77 per cent of the Indian population. They comprise the poorest of the country's people. Most of them are illiterate or having only primary level education, or suffer from malnutrition and ill-health. They belong to working poor or self-employed unorganised working class, including the *dalits*.

Excluded by Location of Dalit Settlements: Deprivation or social exclusion is relative, in the sense, in most villages, public institutions like ration shop, school, health care centre, play ground, drinking water supply, community hall are located in the main village. Usually, *dalit* settlements are away from the main village and so they are passively excluded from using these facilities. This is evident when in *dalit* villages (of most of the study districts) have only common water collection points, whereas the area where the elite people live get individual house service connections for water supply. Similarly, most of the poor who are in dire need of using PDS are in *dalit* settlement, whereas the Ration Shop is located in the main village, where caste-Hindus live.

Excluded from Land Entitlements: There are DC land *Adi Drawdiar* land and *Bhoodan* land given away to the poor *dalit* families by various governments in various periods. The SIPCOT in Kancheepuram and Thiruvannamalai districts are taking them for the purpose of establishing Special Economic Zone. These lands acquired from *dalits* at rates determined by the State. They are being sold to private investors and foreign companies for setting up manufacturing units. The *dalits* are loitering in Cheyyar, Vellore and Chennai courts filing cases against such acquisition. Thus, *dalits* are excluded from the traditional entitlement of land. This is a clear case of *dalits* put under active exclusion by the joint action of bureaucracy and the market power.

Excluded from Labour Market: The free education provided by the government since primary education until collegiate education motivates the *dalit* youth to pursue even college level education. But, to the blow of the *dalit* youth, they come to know about their capability deprivation only when they go to the labour market that in a market-oriented economy academic qualification count very little and only skill-sets (especially the technical and technology-oriented skills) that match the demands of the market fetch income. Acquiring such skill-sets require finance. Moreover, social and cultural capital (the complex and overlapping categories of caste, family background, network and contacts) play a huge role in urban, formal sector labour markets, where hiring practices are less transparent than appear at first sight (Ashwini Deshpande, Katherine Newman, 2007). Hence, having been excluded from the labour market they lurk in darkness.

These are some of the evidences on the denial of socio-economic opportunities found in the study villages. However, the blow on *dalits* has been, to a considerable extent, softened by reform measures coupled with social safety net arrangements of the State. These include inclusive policy on food subsidy, universal primary education, Health for all, National Rural Employment Guarantee Scheme, Self-help Group Promotion, Poverty Reduction project assisted by the World Bank and so on.

These measures have provided access to school education for *dalit* children, and food security of *dalit* families (including STs) in Tamil Nadu. The idea of using LP gas stove or owning a household toilet sounds funny to them. Their priorities are: *ration rice, fire wood from the commons, sufficient supply of drinking water on the common tap, and roof replacement of the house that keeps scaring them of falling off any time.* Making a qualitative analysis of the plausibility behind their priorities, and the exclusion (deprivation) processes in the economic, social and political sphere makes an interesting study. The *dalits* have largely been protected from the onslaught of the globalization through domestic reform measures and appropriate structural adjustments. In terms of addressing absolute poverty that globalization was feared to push the *dalits* into, adequate safeguards have been in place. In terms of relative deprivation, *dalits* have really lost. *Dalits* have also remained excluded from being enabled to profit from the opportunities and choices brought about by globalization.

It would be most unlikely for someone to exactly pin down that the reasons for *dalits* having been excluded in all the spheres mentioned above is a corollary of globalization. But, it could perhaps be uttered as absence of a favourable governance system in place. It could be due to the absence of or insufficiency of inclusive policies and affirmative action on the part of the government. It brings to light analysing the kind of inclusive policies in place, and their role in protecting the interest of the *dalits* as a kind of social safety net.

INCLUSIVE POLICY AND AFFIRMATIVE ACTION

Economically, *dalit* does not benefit anything through globalization—directly making use of the opportunity. Rather, the government had to protect the poor and the *dalits* from being sidelined or washed away by the market power. As a result of privatization and liberalization of economy many of the services like basic education, higher education, health care, transport, telecommunication, postal communication, banking, insurance, and employment gradually moved into the hands of the private firms and companies (Carol Upadhya, 2007). Moreover, the inflationary tendency and the price rise that got triggered as an upshot of globalization started showing on the poor. India is, perhaps, one of the very few countries that realised the immediacy in the requirement for introducing policies and affirmative action that insulate the poor from being severely hurt by this whirlpool.

The poor required to be protected from the market power. The government took responsibility to ensure that supply of essential commodities and basic services to the poor reach uninterrupted. It included food subsidy for the poor, universal primary education, quality health care through Rural Health Mission—health for all campaigns, National Rural Employment Guarantee Scheme (NREGS), Self-Help Groups promotion, introduction of Poverty Reduction and Empowerment Project in Tamil Nadu to indicate a few.

One of the theoretical underpinnings of the market-driven economy is that it would affect the poor initially when the reform measures are introduced. But, the poor would start finding place in the developed society, and enjoy the benefits of growth in the long run. The poor enjoying the benefits of growth is one, and the poor being insulated from being hurt by globalization is another. To enjoy the benefits of growth the requirements are: inclusive policies and ways to enhance the purchasing power. Getting protected from hurt is introduction of a series of subsidies to keep the poor silent.

Redistribution policies or inclusive policies have a direct bearing on the quality of life as well. The neo-liberal economic growth model and the associated reform measures in India have led to drastic changes in several sectors of the economy. Have these changes marked any positive impression in the 'quality of life of the *dalits*' who are most often—by location of their settlement—cut off from the main village? As standard of living forms only part of the quality of life, the consideration here is on the quality of life, which includes everything from look-and-feel of the *dalit* hamlets to digital connectivity, rather than standard of living *per se* by the conventional definition.

What kind of inclusive policies and affirmative action have been put in place in order to redistribute the benefits of growth and to insulate the *dalits* from being harmed? Improvement in real purchasing power is an indicator of development. But, what has happened is provisioning approach, where the government has supplied essentials and basic requirements in a highly subsidized arrangement.

Food subsidy could be stated as one of the measures of insulation from involuntary starvation. *Dalits* still depend on the food subsidy, or the paddy they collect in return for the wage employment they were engaged for by the traditional land owners. After 20 years of introduction of reform measures, the poor *dalits* still depend on PDS rice only, and they have no means to buy rice in the open market. When the 35 kg rice given is not sufficient, the *dalits* find some family in the village (most often a non-*dalit*) who would not eat rice supplied at the ration shop, and get that family's quota of rice to make good the shortage. Their dependence on food subsidy, fire wood in the commons, and the drinking water in the common tap is bound and almost predestined. Their wards work outside the village in non-farm related manual work, but the money flow into their families has not changed any remarkably.

As far as education is concerned *dalits* in Tamil Nadu have access to primary education. Education for all (SSA) has achieved cent-per-cent enrolment, and has remarkably reduced the dropout rates as well. The primary health care facilities have been improved to the satisfaction of majority in *dalit* villages through National Rural Health Mission. Tamil Nadu State has schools specially for Adi Dravida community. There are 1,053 Adi Dravida welfare schools, 282 Adi Dravida residential schools and 1178 Adi Dravida free hostels, 107 UG Institutional hostels, and 9 PG Institutional hostels, 17 AD Welfare ITI Hostels operating in Tamil Nadu for the welfare of *dalit* children. This is a process of developing an inclusive society, where *dalits* get opportunity for education, and higher studies. It is believed that the policy of caste-based reservation in educational institutions and employment will provide equality of opportunity to groups hitherto excluded from them.

Decentralization of democratic governance at the local level, after the introduction of the Tamil Nadu Panchayati Raj Act, 1994 and the Constitutional 73rd Amendment has offered to the *dalits* an opportunity to get Panchayat leadership on a rotation basis. In Tamil Nadu of the 12,619 Village Panchayat president's posts, 3,198 are reserved for women (general), 1,104 for Scheduled Caste women, 1,855 for the Scheduled Castes in general, 66 for the Scheduled Tribes in general and 27 for Scheduled Tribe women.

But for a few highly sensitive Panchayats in Tamil Nadu, where we were reported of expressive opposition of (some communities of) the Caste-Hindus not accepting *dalits* being addressed as Panchayat leaders and *dalits* ruling over them, in most of the places the transition has taken place without much commotion. However, the passive resistance to *dalit* leadership prevails sporadically.

The Government have emphasised the need for special treatment to these communities for improving their socio-economic status through implementation of welfare programmes under the Scheduled Caste Sub-Plan (SCSP) and the Tribal Sub-Plan (STSP). Steps are being taken in terms of reservation in educational institutions and employment, provision of scholarships, targeted economic incentives to encourage entrepreneurship as well as housing and infrastructure development schemes. In the Eleventh Five Year Plan, the outlay for 2008-09 is Rs. 835.82 crore. Of this, the outlay approved for SCSP and STSP are Rs. 442.06 crore and Rs. 1.12 crore respectively. In some of the study villages, the Poverty Reduction and Empowerment Project of the World Bank, is reported to be promising in the economic empowerment and skill development of *dalit* women and youth.

The youth have no hope in the job reservation policy as things are expanding more on the privatization front, and their fight to get reservation under the private sector looks more of fighting a losing battle, or it could only be a very distant dream (Carol Upadhya, 2007), At least forty per cent of the *dalit* youth have mobile phones, with a prepaid balance of Rs. 10 or Rs. 50 at the maximum. Although it is most often used for fun, and for giving 'missed calls' (*to state it in their own language*), it is also used for keeping in touch with construction and logistics contractors who would want to use the youth as manual labourers in the carrying out jobs in the town or in cities like Chennai, Bangalore and Mumbai. However, access to drinking water, housing and electricity is found to be wanting in many of the study villages. There are houses in *dalit* villages without electricity facility. But, it was found during direct observation inside the huts unapproved power lines have been taken by the *dalits* on their own. The toilet facility is almost zero and environmental sanitation is poor.

Despite positive discrimination, preferential treatment, and special component plan and presence of TAHDCO, *dalit* families suffer revolving within the same low-income trap. The factors that seriously hold them back are: the operation of money lenders who operate from the neighbourhood towns. They lend money for festivals, marriage expenditures and ceremonies and collect from daily wages, or on weekly basis with usurious rates of interest.

Whatever earnings that remains left over in the hands of the *dalit* man goes down the bottle at the TASMAC shops buying liquor. The earnings of women in *dalit* families and their SHG loan operations help them hold head above the water. In terms of managing the family expenditures, it seems to be in the hands of the women to a considerable extent.

Recognising the power of the market in marginalising the poor, the government keeps introducing inclusive policies and affirmative action with a view to insulating the poor, and providing positive discrimination and preferential treatment for the poor in general and *dalits* in particular. They include: food security through PDS, Education through SSA, Health care through NRHM, Employment in NREGS, Self-Help Groups, Tamil Nadu Poverty Reduction and Empowerment Project assisted by the World Bank, the income that the youth make through employment in towns, cities and foreign countries as labourers or construction workers. But, the operation of the local moneylenders and existence of TASMAC shops drain away all that the *dalits* earn.

SEZ and Dalits: There are some problems that *dalits* face, which can be straight away attributed to globalization, without a speck of doubt. One of them could be relating to land grabbing by the State for the needs of Special Economic Zone Development. For instance, at Chennankuppam near Oragadam (Chennai) out of 100 *dalit* families, 87 of them got title deeds for house sites under the government free-house *patta* scheme. Besides this, 13 artisans' families had got free land for dwelling from the *Bhoodan* land, which was considered common land. These families have received notice to quit the place, and they are to be resettled in another place—the reason stated is these lands are needed for setting up units under Oragadam SEZ. These *dalits* were cultivators and wage earners, and there were several other *dalits* involved as wage earners in these lands.

Caste-based Reservation: The policy of caste-based reservations provided equality of opportunity to groups hitherto excluded from education and State employment services. These policies have paid rich dividends in the form of increase in human development indicators. These attempts in the southern States provided opportunity for *dalits* in education and employment, enlarging the range of peoples' choices (Chalam, K.S., 2007). But, after globalization policies started operating the employment in public sector has come down drastically.

The annual growth rate of 'public employment' in the organised sector prior to 1991 was 1.52 per cent, which has come down in the negative to 0.03

per cent in the year 2000. The growth rate of 'private sector employment' in the organised sector during the same period has increased from 0.45 per cent to 1.87 per cent. The points of contention here is how many of the *dalits* could manage to get employed in private sector employment, which is hectically competitive; secondly, the terms and conditions of employment provided under the foreign companies that establish business here do not adhere to any of the labour legislations in vogue in India such as Industrial Dispute Act, Bonus Act, Trade Union Act etc. The SEZs are considered as foreign territories within India, and so they follow SEZ Act, 2005, and the related rules only, which rule out every local legislation including the payment of professional fees to Panchayats, which includes *dalits* panchayats as well.

Reservation in the Private Sector: Reservation for the historically deprived communities in public employment, institutions of political representation and higher education has been an important component of India's democratic politics. However, the privatization process concomitant with the withdrawal of the State from many spheres under the liberalization regime, have further narrowed and compressed the little space that the discriminated groups had gained till now (Thorat, S., 2004). Even among educated youth wage labour as a traditional occupation thus, continue to constitute a main occupation of SCs in the study villages.

Reservations are being debated once again in India in the context of privatization after globalization policies started operating in full swing. The moot question this time is a little different, viz. should the provisions of reservations for the deprived communities be extended to employment in the private sector against the background of a growing trend towards privatisation and liberalisation of the Indian economy? Under the new regime, the State has begun to withdraw from the economic sector and private enterprise is allowed to expand into areas of economic activity that were hitherto not open to it. As a consequence employment avenues in the State sector have been shrinking, making reservation in employment virtually meaningless (Surinder S. Jodhka, 2005).

This statement could be well corroborated with the empirical evidence that many of the educated youth in *dalit* villages are either awaiting a call letter from Employment Exchanges or they are involved in wage employment after graduate and post-graduate degrees. The youth seem to have no hope in Reservation Policies for two reasons: (a) reservations in jobs are cornered by slightly well-to-do among the *dalits* with the help of corrupt politicians and bureaucracy; and (b) the jobs that open up in private sector are mostly taken up by middle class and upper middle class youth who are ready with the qualifications and competence that these private companies look for. One ray of hope is the Corporate Social Responsibility that many private companies have started talking about seriously. In order to forestall criticism and the possible imposition of quotas, several companies have already taken steps to increase the diversity and inclusiveness of their workforce, for instance by floating internship schemes and training programmes for rural youth and Scheduled Caste engineers (Carol Upadhya. 2007)

Inclusive policies have helped protecting the *dalits* from being hurt, and to let them survive in the world that is becoming more and more competitive. It has not yet helped them take hold of opportunities and climb above poverty line.

V. FINDINGS, CONCLUSION AND ACTION POINTS

AGGREGATE ANALYSIS

Before getting down to drawing the important findings and conclusion, certain aggregate analysis require to be made. This should give an overall picture of whatever changes that have happened in the lives and livelihoods of *dalits* as a corollary of globalization. If the contention of some of the *dalit* organizations that globalization hurts *dalits* can be taken or is it only rhetoric without any empirical evidence; and if the *dalits* have gained or lost out of globalization. If they have gained or lost—what did they gain and what have they lost. This can be viewed from socio-cultural and economic points of view.

The first revelation that this empirical examination brought forth was that one cannot pin down exactly that most changes—for good or bad—that have happened among *dalits* can be attributed to globalization. The changes can be attributed more to the general trend of development in Indian society, and efforts of *dalit* organisations over the years. The direct-play of globalization is very little. However, it is true that some of the reform measures have played pivotal role in transforming their lives. Globalization has helped the *dalits* indirectly or inadvertently in some respect. The social safety nets and domestic reform measures carried out in various sectors have helped the *dalits* to remain protected (or unhurt) by the possible damage that the market forces could exert on the poor in general, and *dalits* in particular.

Causal Analysis of Deprivations: For many a social problem that the *dalits* were facing globalization has brought technology solutions. For many of the economic problems—broadly referred to as poverty or economic deprivation—*dalits* have not been able to make use of the opportunities brought about by globalization. A causal analysis mainly points out lack of exposure, basic capability deprivation and absence of physical assets or financial capital as the main reasons. But for the social safety net provided by the governments, *dalits* would have been severely hurt by the whirlpool of globalization resulting in further marginalisation.

Basic Services: There are two ways in which *dalit* community have their food secured. One is the Public Distribution System (PDS), and the other is getting foodgrains, cereals, pulses or oilseeds in return for the labour they offer to landowners in harvesting. The *dalits* families have found this to be another good source of ensuring family's food security. However, PDS rice for many of the families is reported to be insufficient and so they buy the same quality of rice in the open market where the price ranges from Rs. 8 to Rs. 13. Households in 99 per cent of the ST villages, and in almost 90 per cent of the SC villages use only firewood for cooking. Even if gas stove is given free by the Government of Tamil Nadu, the SC families think it would be additional expenditure buying gas cylinder every month, and so they feel reluctant to change to LP gas.

The house-site ownership and house ownership are mostly private to *dalits* in many of the study villages. Most of them have got official house-site *patta*. But, only a few have got assistance for the construction of house under schemes like IAY. In each village visited it was found at least 15-20 per cent of the houses reported to be without even a single light facility. They reported that they were using the hurricane lantern or kerosene lamp for lighting purpose.

Inadequacy in the quantity of water supplied by the Village Panchayat is a common complaint in most of the study villages. It was observed that in nine out of ten villages *dalits* get water supply by common water collection points only. They have not got individual house service connections, like it has been given in the main village. However, they have not been pushed to the extent of buying water from private water suppliers. None of the households own a toilet in any of the study villages. Even the ones in group house, are not in use. Government health services are properly made use of by the *dalits*. The Health Sub-Centres, and Primary Health Centres are properly being made use of by them. Hardly any family approaches private medical practitioners in the town for treatment, mainly due to affordability.

The current level of educational attainment found in *dalit* hamlets is that nine out of ten children reach upto completion of secondary level education. A little over seventy per cent of them reach upto higher secondary level education, and at least fifty per cent of them go to college level (or Polytechnic level) education. It is found *dalit* children proceed with average level educational performance as long as education is offered free—either in government-run schools or in government colleges. When it comes to paying for education, most of them tend to dropout due to problems of affordability. Reform in Primary Education through SSA has helped increase enrolment of ST children in schools, but it does not help retention of them or prevent habitual absenteeism and eventual dropping out of the educational system. The exposure the *dalit* youth have on job prospects or employable skills is abysmally poor. If at all they dream of government employment, they seem to have in mind only the Class IV officers/clerical positions and peons. The scavengers in Municipalities are highly respected in *dalit* hamlets that they are monthly salaried class within *dalits*, and moreover they are employees of Municipality—a government entity.

Safeguard Measures: The government has put in place insulation mechanism with a view to safeguarding the *dalits* from being hurt. The protective measures that have really worked in favour the *dalits* include food subsidy through PDS, Education for all, National Rural Health Mission—health for all, National Rural Employment Guarantee Scheme, One-rupee coin operated phones in the villages, Self-Help Group Promotion, Poverty Reduction and Empowerment Project of the World Bank in Tamil Nadu, to name a few. It must be noted that these protective measures are strictly against the principles of functioning of a market economy. But, the government in order to retain the socialist democratic character of the country or for fulfilling its responsibility of safeguarding the poor has taken these measures, stepping away from market principles. However, merely throwing money at people through direct cash transfers is not only indignity to the poor. It might work only as a political strategy, but it does work as a development strategy aimed at sustainable development. It does not translate outlays into outcomes. It looks only as a temporary solution for keeping the poor silent.

Technology Helps Wipe-out Social Stigma: As globalization started operating technologies started taking over several of the functions that otherwise served as the prime cause of social discrimination of *dalits*—be it passing on the message of death, shoe making or burning the dead bodies of humans. Passing on messages of death is instantly being done by one-rupee coin operated telephones in the villages, and mobile phones; shoe making has become a several million dollar industry; there are courses run by government polytechnic and private engineering colleges in footwear technology, which even upper caste people have started getting admission in; mechanisation is fast taking over manual scavenging, and Electric Crematoriums have come about for burning dead humans. Many problems that remained for years are being solved by the technology and knowledge that globalization has given access to. That it has come about in cities and in the towns of Tamil Nadu could be stated as evidence for it would extend to villages also in course of time.

Dalits necessarily had to lose their social identity in order to be recognised as equal citizens, and to come away from the sub-human treatment. Globalization has introduced several technology solutions for the social problems that the *dalits* were facing.

Livelihood Diversification: The kind of livelihood diversification that has taken place after globalization was to be documented. So, the study attempted to list out the kind of livelihoods that the *dalits* were involved, in recent times. Improved transport and telecommunication facilities have enabled mobility of younger generation of the *dalits*. The contacts that some of them could establish with outside the village helps many in their village to take up diversified livelihood options. Mobility accelerates contacts, and contact furthers social connectedness and economic opportunities. The facility to become mobile and be in touch through telecommunication facilities has enabled youth to move out of *dalit* villages, and work in varied fields. It is true that the jobs that open up are unorganised and insecure kind of work. But, the diversified opportunity that globalization opened up has made way for *dalit* youth in considerable number find multiple livelihoods. Freedom to choose from multiple livelihood opportunities instead of loitering in the age-old agricultural wage employment in the villages in itself is a kind of development.

Unlike their parents, *dalit* youth are on the look out for employment elsewhere—either in the town or if possible go abroad as manual labourer. They are not ready to take charge of the land—neither as wage earner nor as owner. The mobile phone and Coin-operated phones come in handy to get in touch with labour contractors, and to step up their mobility as labourers. *Dalit* women and the aged generation do not find any use for mobile phones or computers. Even the educated youth who are on the look out for employment are looking for State services from the Employment Exchanges. They do not have any idea of using internet as a tool for putting them in touch with several employers in the market.

Dalits as Neo-Landed Class: Another interesting finding of this study is that the traditional land owners (mostly caste-Hindus) or the landed class are shifting to other sectors of the economy (outside agriculture) that globalization open up. The *dalits* fill up the vacuum created by the landed class, posing themselves as 'the neo-landed' class. Thus, much contrary to what was expected by the opponents of globalization, mechanization in agriculture has resulted in many traditional landowners/caste-Hindus giving up agriculture and *dalits* become tiny land owners. This shift in the erstwhile landless agricultural wage earners becoming the land owning class has introduced a new set of agro-social dynamics and agricultural production system in Tamil Nadu villages.

That globalization would intensify widespread use of machineries in agriculture and so, the *dalits* who are mostly agricultural labourers would be thrown out of agriculture looks disproved in actuality. Those landlords who try to use machineries in agriculture due to shortage of labour for agriculture tend to quit agriculture and quit village itself. They settle down in towns with some business, or with their sons who are salaried. *Dalits* are emerging as the neo-landed class in agricultural villages.

Much contrary to what was expected by the opponents of globalization, and many of the *dalit* organisations, mechanisation in agriculture has resulted in the traditional landed class giving up agriculture and *dalits* to become tiny land owners. This shift in the erstwhile landless agricultural wage earners becoming the land owning class has introduced a new set of agro-social dynamics. This brings with it several interesting changes in the lives of *dalits* in Tamil Nadu. Besides this, the shift from sub-human existence as untouchables to land owning class, and the younger ones contributing very much positively to educational Status of the State could be two vital shifts, although quality of life index still shows poorly.

Two Classes within Dalits: One commonality that is very interesting is within *dalits* although there are several castes such as *Parayar, Pallar, Chakkiliar* and so on clearly, there are two classes that emerge within them. One is among those who have managed to become either as small land owners or at least share-croppers and draw analogy with the caste-Hindus they acquired the land from; and those who are still landless labourers and are completely dependent on Family Ration Card as the life-line asset of the family.

Additional Money Flow: Various sources of money flow (income flow) into *dalit* families were analysed. Money income is one important indicator of economic improvement of households. The sources of additional money flow into *dalit* families are through the following. Employment in NREGS, Self-Help Groups, Tamil Nadu Poverty Reduction and Empowerment Project assisted by the World Bank, the income that the youth make through employment in towns, cities and foreign countries as labourers or construction workers. But, as far as NREGS is concerned it looks like direct cash transfer taking place to temporarily pump in cash flow into rural households.

It was found that the items of expenditure keeps extending, whereas the income sources are limited. Most of the families have no asset worth the name. In the order of priority the expenditure item that should actually find place next to food expenses is wine shop expenditure, and that which should get third place is loan repayment to moneylenders. In *dalit* villages almost all the families owe money to private moneylenders. It drains away major portion of the earnings of the family, like the money thrown into the TASMAC wine shops. The amount of money borrowed for marriages and for giving compliments to marriages of relatives is considerably handsome, compared to the income levels of *dalits*. They join the SHGs mainly to get credit to be able to meet the consumption requirements of the family, and to repay the loan received from the moneylenders, and not with the intention of accumulating savings or taking up entrepreneurial ventures.

Has Globalization Directly Hurt Dalits? There are some problems that *dalits* face, which can be straightaway attributed to globalization, without a speck of doubt. One of them could be relating to land grabbing by the State for the needs of Special Economic Zone development. For instance, at Chennankuppam near Oragadam (Chennai) out of 100 *dalit* families, 87 of them got title deeds for house sites under the government free-house *patta* scheme. Besides this, 13 artisans' families had got free land for dwelling from the *Bhoodan* land, which was considered common land. These families have received notice to quit the place, and they are to be resettled in another place—the reason stated is these lands are needed for setting up units under Oragadam SEZ. These *dalits* were cultivators and wage earners, and there were several other *dalits* involved as wage earners in these lands.

Caste-based Reservation: The policy of caste-based reservations provided equality of opportunity to groups hitherto excluded from education and State employment services. These policies have paid rich dividends in the form of increase in human development indicators. These attempts in the southern States provided opportunity for *dalits* in education and employment, enlarging the range of peoples' choices. But, after globalization policies started operating the employment in public sector has come down drastically.

The annual growth rate of 'public employment' in the organised sector prior to 1991 was 1.52 per cent, which has come down in the negative to 0.03 per cent in the year 2000. The growth rate of 'private sector employment' in the organised sector during the same period has increased from 0.45 per cent to 1.87 per cent. The points of contention here is how many of the *dalits* could manage to get employed in private sector employment, which is hectically competitive; secondly, the terms and conditions of employment provided under the foreign companies that establish business here do not adhere to any of the labour legislations in vogue in India such as Industrial Dispute Act, Bonus Act, Trade Union Act etc. The SEZs are considered as foreign territories within India, and so they follow SEZ Act, 2005, and the related rules only, which rule out every local legislation including the payment of professional fees to Panchayats, which includes *dalit* panchayats as well. One ray of hope is that some companies have started taking seriously the factor of CSR. They have started eyeing on diversity in the employment they offer, and inclusiveness in providing employment to various caste groups so to manifest that they are following fair practices in recruitment.

Civil and Political Participation: There are two things about civil and political participation. *Dalits* becoming leader of local governance system, making use of the provisions of the Panchayati Raj Act, and Constitutional 73rd Amendment Act is one. The other is *dalit* community airing their views in local decision making, and influencing development directions so that the decisions made in the Gram Sabha are not biased towards the rich or the caste-Hindus. Unfortunately, the *dalits* in many of the villages studied do not participate in Gram Sabha meeting. The reasons stated for not participating are that (a) the presumption that they would not be heard, and (b) the reality that nothing that was passed as resolution in the Gram Sabha meetings held before have been materialised. Even at villages where *dalit* Panchayat Presidents are in power, their concern is about insufficiency of funds to be able to carry out development works. Minus certain rare exceptions, where moneyed caste-Hindu Vice-Presidents do not allow *dalit* presidents to present themselves as headman of the Panchayat, in all other places, the *dalit* Panchayat presidents reported finding funds to implement schemes to be a problem rather than the sabotage caused by dominant caste-Hindus.

CONCLUSION

Dalits are not what they were about 20 years ago. Years ago, it was near-slavery life attached to one landlord's family. Now, livelihood opportunities are diversified; there are academic degrees behind the name of *dalit* youth; mobile phones in their pockets; and they eye on State services for employment.

Most *dalits* depend on government services for making a living—be it food security, education of children, health care, drinking water supply, provision of housing, maintenance of houses, electricity, and wage employment. They remain insulated from the market forces. The need for them to approach the market has been put at barest minimum by the State services. The *dalits* are not prepared enough, or they have not been prepared sufficiently to face the market and live a life of their own, without depending upon the State services. The State cannot dismantle any of the services PDS, basic education, health and hand over to the private sector in an intention to reduce governmental involvement in these services. In tribal regions the Forest Rights Act is revolutionary but, it has remained only on paper. The STs do not have strong institutional mechanism or social capital to make it a reality.

These services have to necessarily remain with the government as long as ways are devised to improve the purchasing power of the poor and the *dalits* in Tamil Nadu. But as long as the poor remain insulated, they would not get an opportunity to participate in the market dynamics. If the widening rich poor disparity has been bridged, actions need to be initiated to improve the purchasing power of the *dalits* rather than providing the safety nets by the government.

ACTION POINTS

The action points for *dalits* in the context of globalization could point out ways in which *dalits* can be equipped to tide over the multiple deprivations that they are mire in. The causative factors of exclusion are: capability poverty, lack of exposure, absence of assets—financial and social. Underneath all these, two big stumbling blocks are: (i) drinking habit, and (ii) operation of the moneylenders.

The two big local or internal blocks have to be removed in the first place, to be able to see any impact in the rest of the efforts put in. The habit of spending their hard earned money on alcohol, and borrowing from the local moneylenders need to be addressed. This can be done best by training local women in fighting against alcohol, and by intensifying SHG activities. Even the existing SHG women can be trained in fighting against alcohol.

Strengthen SHGs and Intensify SHG Operations: The SHGs in *dalit* villages are in nascent stage. There is no indication that they would ever move beyond the stage of providing consumption credit. The SHG operations require to be intensified in order to gradually take them into the fold of SHG, and relieve them from local money lenders. The World Bank assisted Tamil Nadu Poverty Reduction Project can be very well used for this purpose. This shall facilitate increased flow of money into each household, and enhanced money circulation in rural areas.

Liberalise Education Loan to Dalits: Education can be one of the best means to tide over poverty. The assumption that higher education and education in technical universities is costly is the factor that keeps *dalits* students away from such institutions. Education loan for *dalit* students pursuing technical courses or short duration training programmes even with private institutions may be encouraged with adequate bank loan.

Vocational Training Centres: Getting academic degrees and certificates with no employable skills is a cause of concern. Equipping the entrepreneurial skills, skills to write bankable proposals, employable qualities and competence should be made compulsory in institutions of higher learning as recommended by the National Knowledge Commission. This can lead to participation in the market economy.

Private Sector Employment: In the context of rising political support for reservations in higher education and private sector employment, it would in fact be in the interest of private sector companies to formulate or support some kind of positive discrimination policy—statutory or voluntary—and to increase the diversity in their workforce (Carol Upadhya, 2007). But, this can be done with certain pragmatism, without getting down to support them taking into consideration only the historical deprivation this group has been suffering from. Instead, this can be done for the first generation employment seekers among the SC/ST families. As part of social responsibility companies can sponsor candidates from SC/ST families in educational institutions and recruit them later on, after they have been trained in the skill-sets that the company requires.

Liberal Agricultural Loan for Dalits: The traditional land owners in many districts are found to be disenchanted with agriculture, whereas *dalits* seem to be enthusiastic. When traditional land owners would like to lease out their land, the *dalits*, often find it difficult to accept for want of funds to take up cultivation operations. The money required for purchasing inputs such as seeds, fertilizers etc. is a hurdle in leasing in land. If this can be addressed through institutional sources of credit or SHG loans, *dalits* can become sharecroppers, and land owners in good number.

Employment Guarantee: The NREGS has played an important role in money flow into *dalit* households. NREGS also has augmented the bargaining power of *dalits*, when it came to agricultural wages. But, the Village Panchayats in many of the *dalit* villages find it difficult to locate where they can take up works under NREGS after a period of one or two years. All the possible public works within the Village Panchayats get over within one or two years of continuous work. Suitable modifications in NREGS or ways to ensure money flow into *dalit* households should be identified, when NREGS hits at the bottom rock. NREGS should not be a way of making direct cash transfer to the poor in the villages, mainly for keeping them silent, rather than contribute to any social rate of return or significant social outcome.

NOTES

1. For an etymological understanding of the word '*Dalit*' see Annexure 1 .
2. The terms 'Scheduled Caste and Scheduled Tribes' (SC/ST) are the official terms used in government documents to identify former untouchables and tribes. However, in 2008 the National Commission for Scheduled Castes, noticing that the word '*dalit*' was used interchangeably with the official term 'Scheduled Castes', asked the State Governments to end the use of the word '*dalit*' in official documents calling the terms 'unconstitutional' and to replace it with the term ' Scheduled Caste' instead. Adi Dravida, Adi Karnataka, and Adi Andhra' are words used in the States of Tamil Nadu, Karnataka, and Andhra Pradesh respectively to identify people of former untouchable castes in official documents. These words, particularly the prefix '*adi*' denote the aboriginal inhabitants of the land.
3. NREGS is not implemented in some of the study villages for want of places to work (projects). All the works have been completed in the first one or two years.

REFERENCES

Amartya Sen (2000). *Social Exclusion: Concept, Application and Scrutiny*. Office of Environment and Social Development, Asian Development Bank.

Anand Teltumbde. *Globalization and the Dalits, http://www.ambedkar.org/research/globalization and the dalits.pdf*.

Arjun Sengupta (2008). Planning for Inclusive Development, *The Hindu*, December 9, 2008.

Arvind Rajagopal (2004). Reforms with a Dalit Face? *Economic and Political Weekly*, December 4, 2004.

Ashwini Deshpande, Katherine Newman (2007). *Where the Path Leads: The Role of Caste in Post-University Employment Expectations*.

Carol Upadhya (2007). Employment, Exclusion and 'Merit' in the Indian IT Industry, *Economic and Political Weekly*, May 19, 2007.

Census of India (2001). *Data Highlights: The Scheduled Castes in Tamil Nadu*. Office of the Registrar General, India.

Chalam, K.S. (2007). *Caste-based Reservation and Human Development in India.* Sage Publications, New Delhi.

Francis Abraham M. (2006). *Contemporary Sociology: An Introduction to Concepts and Theories*, Oxford University Press, New Delhi.

Gail Omvedit. 'Call us *Adivasis* Please' (July 16, 2000). Special Issue with the *Sunday Magazine: Adivasi.*

Gail Omvedit. Capitalism and Globalization, Dalits and Adivasis, *Economic and Political Weekly*, Vol. 40, No. 47, Nov. 19-25, 2005.

Haragopal G. *Globalization and Dalits: Changing Role and Nature of the Indian State*, www.boell-india.org/download-en/haragopal.pdf.

Kameshwar Choudhary (ed.) (2007). *Globalization, Governance Reforms and Development in India*, Sage Publications, New Delhi.

Pallavi Chavan (2007). Access to Bank Credit: Implications for Dalit Rural Households, *Economic and Political Weekly*, August 4, 2007.

Ramaiah, A. (2004). *Dalits to Accept Globalization: Lessons from the Past and Present*, Tata Institute of Social Sciences, Unit for Social Policy and Social Welfare Administration, July 24, 2004, Mumbai.

Ruth Manorama. *Dalit Women: The Downtrodden of the Downtrodden*, National Federation of Dalit Women (NFDW), India. http://mrdagarna.se/upload/dalit%20%women%20%downtrodden

Sathianathan Clarke (2007). Dalits (Scheduled Caste, Scheduled Tribe Communities) of Tamil Nadu visited at: wwww.religion-online.org/showarticle—tamil e-library.

Stephen Cullenberg and Prasanta K. Pattanaik (ed.) (2004). *Globalization, Culture and the Limits of the Market: Essays in Economics and Philosophy*, Oxford University Press. New Delhi.

Sukhadeo Thorat & Narender Kumar (2008). *B.R. Ambedkar: Perspectives on Social Exclusion and Inclusive Policies*, Oxford University Press, New Delhi.

Sukhadeo Thorat (2007). *Human Poverty and Socially Disadvantaged Groups in India*, UNDP-HDRC, New Delhi.

Surinder, S. Jodhka (2005). Debates on Reservation, *Economic and Political Weekly*, October 29, 2005.

Thangaraj (2006). *Nilam, Saathiyam and Poutham*, Pavai Publications, Chennai.

Thimmaiah (2005). Implications of Reservations in Private Sector. *Economic and Political Weekly*, February 19, 2005.

Thomas, E. Weisskopf (2003). Globalization and Affirmative Action, *Economic and Political Weekly*, July 5, 2003.

Veena Das (2008). *Handbook of Indian Sociology*, OUP, New Delhi.

Viswanathan, S. (2004). *Dalits in Dravidian Land: Frontline Reports on Anti-Dalit Violence in Tamil Nadu* (1995-2004).

ANNEXURE 1

DALIT—AN ETYMOLOGICAL SEARCH

The word '*Dalit*' comes from the Marathi language. *Dalit* in Marathi language means 'suppressed', 'crushed' or 'broken to pieces'. It was first used by Jyotirao Phule in the nineteenth century in the context of the caste oppression faced by the erstwhile untouchable castes from the Hindu castes.

The word was also used by B.R. Ambedkar in his Marathi speeches in the 1920s and 1930s. The word gained widespread currency when the *Dalit* Panthers revived tne term in their 1973 manifesto. The *Dalit* Panther party was formed in April 1972, as a political and cultural resistance organisation. The *Dalit* Panthers sought to include the Scheduled Tribes, working people, landless and poor peasant women and all politically and economically exploited people's and people exploited in the name of religion. The *Dalit* Panthers movement and the concomitantly spawned *Dalit* school of literature in Maharashtra represented a new sense of pride, sharpened militancy and sophisticated creativity in *Dalit* people's search for identity and self-definition. The Marathi word *dalit* like the word black, was chosen by the group itself and is used proudly. None of the prevalent terms 'untouchable; scheduled caste; depressed classes; Gandhiji's 'Harijan' had the same connotation. 'Dalit' implies those who have been broken and grounded down by those above them in the social hierarchy in a deliberate and active way. There is in the word itself an inherently justified caste hierarchy.

Gandhiji's coinage cf the word 'Harijan', translated roughly as 'Children of God', to identify the former untouchables, though adopted for a few years, lost its support, particularly among the people it meant to designate. To many *dalits* the word is patronising, and is something of a pejorative epithet among *dalits* to refer to someone of their own who has internalised attitudes of inferiority and has an accepting view of his place in the Hindu world.

The terms 'Scheduled Castes and Scheduled Tribes' (SC/ST) are the official terms used in government documents to identify former untouchables and tribes. However, in 2008 the National Commission for Scheduled Castes, noticing that the word '*dalit*' was used interchangeably with the official term 'Scheduled Castes', asked the State Governments to end the use of the word '*Dalit*' in official documents calling the terms 'unconstitutional' and to replace it with the term ' Scheduled Caste' instead. 'Adi Dravida, Adi Karnataka, and Adi Andhra' are words used in the States of Tamil Nadu, Karnataka, and Andhra Pradesh respectively to identify people of former untouchable castes in official documents. These words, particularly the prefix '*adi*' denote the aboriginal inhabitants of the land.

In the context of traditional Hindu society, *dalit* status has often been historically associated with occupations regarded as ritually impure, such as any occupation involving butchering, removal of dead animals, removal of night-soil and leather work. It is reported that as much as one million *dalits* work as manual scavengers, cleaning latrines and sewers, and clearing away dead animals. Engaging in these activities was considered polluting to the individual who performed them, and this pollution was considered to be 'contagious'. As a result, *dalits* were commonly banned and segregated from full participation in Hindu social life (they could not enter the premises of a temple or a school and stayed outside the village), while elaborate precautions were sometimes observed to prevent incidental contact between *dalits* and other castes. Discrimination against *dalits* still exists in rural areas in the private sphere, in everyday matters such as access to eating places, schools, temples and water sources. Some *dalits* have successfully integrated into urban Indian society, where caste origins are less obvious and less important in public life.

While the Constitution of India has duly made special provisions for the social and economic uplift of the *dalits*, comprising the so-called Scheduled Castes and Tribes in order to enable them to achieve upward social mobility, these concessions are limited to only those *dalits* who remain Hindu.

Sources: Dalits. http://en.wikipedia.org/wiki/Dalit. accessed on 1st July 2009
Kameshwar Choudhary (ed). 2007. *Globalization, Governance Reforms & Development in India*, Sage Publications, New Delhi.

CHAPTER NINE

Managing Globalization from Below

INTRODUCTION

Globalization, as an international system, has now replaced several old systems. It has its own rules, logic and route that today directly or indirectly influence the economies, politics, environment, society, and thus lives of people of virtually every country in the world. Some consider that development brought about by globalization is environmentally disastrous and unsustainable. Some consider globalization will improve the chances for most people for great opportunity, democracy, and that the world after globalisation is getting flat with no disparities. Some want to get the economic right. Some want to get the political right. Some especially the Civil Society Organisations want to steer it to be people-centric. One considered view is that globalization needs to be managed well—through domestic policy interventions and appropriate institutional structures—so as to minimise the abhorrent effects on the poor and on their livelihoods.

This is based on the premise that economic and technological integration of economies, although have rendered a few positive results in terms of economic growth and access to technologies, the balance sheet analysis shows that it has created a few assets and a lot of liabilities, especially to the poor in India. The government is busy manoeuvring the economic growth rate, and pushing multilateral mega projects through. They have, perhaps, no time to address the equity question; they have no time to analyse if it benefits the rural poor. Eventually, the understanding is that economic integration benefits some, and hurts many. Especially, it has very little or almost nothing to offer to the poor in the villages. But, the plans rolled out one after another reveal sufficiently clearly that it grabs several things of the poor such as land, water, and other livelihood resources posing 'the economic efficiency of resource use' as the alleged reason.

THE EXTREMITIES

Decentralization or devolution of powers is found to be a good strategy for social development, whereas centralization, that is global integration, is advocated for business development. Tenet-wise these two concepts—globalization and decentralization—are at two extremities. The coincidence is that in India, these two concepts started taking position exactly at the same period of time. Interestingly, both the ideas were introduced by the Central Government of India—one for devolution of powers and the other for integration of Indian economy in the global free-market trend. This called for co-existence of both the concepts. But the fundamental clash in the basic tenets, often, makes the interactions inevitably incompatible or discordant. Decentralization believes in people's power and democracy. Globalization believes in population-size and market mechanisms. Decentralization asserts the rights of the locale in determining sustainable use of resources for livelihood needs, whereas globalization makes an 'economic efficiency calculation' in resource use. Decentralization revolves around democratic principles, and globalization revolves around the market principles.

There was a brain storming session held at Gandhigram Rural University in June 2009, where local body leaders, NGO heads, academics and researchers from the State of Tamil Nadu participated. The discussion revolved around identifying ways and means to manage globalization at the grassroots level so as to find ways to safeguard natural resources and rural livelihoods; and discover ways to make use of the opportunities instead of merely demanding to be in the protection of social safety net.

From the point of view of resource-use and the natural recouping ability of the environment globalization is unsustainable, was a common remark made all through the workshop. Secondly, the processes tend to take democratic institutions at the grassroots level easy. Thirdly, countries world over prove that while competition to put in the best of everyone's effort and sharing of technologies is good, unfettered free-market capitalism and reckless adoption of globalization policies result in economic volatility that even best of minds are unable to predict the tentacles and the fallout. When the speed, especially at the macro level, is reckless and overwhelmingly complex, the ability to visualise the likely repercussions become extremely difficult. This curtails our ability to pin down exactly the loose ends to prescribe solutions, before landing in a quicksand. Being a connected-economy limits the possibility for insulating. One solace is that the issues at the grassroots are considerably clear. That is, the micro level issues that affect ordinary citizens and rural livelihoods are sufficiently clear. The issues have been dealt with in detail in our earlier work [See Palanithurai, G. & Ramesh, R. (2008). *Globalization: Issues at the Grassroots*, Concept Publishing Company, New Delhi].

Another notable comment is that India has been cautiously slow or rather the government is not freely allowed by the leftist movements, local bodies and other civil society organisations to take the reform process too fast. Perhaps, this is one of the reasons how the country has been saved from the economic turmoil the world happened to face during the year 2009. Moreover, this turmoil does not bother the poor or the NGOs or the civil society that works for the ordinary citizens, because a downturn in stock market bothers only big investors and not the downtrodden people, unless it reflects in the prices of essential commodities. But, (Marxist and Gandhian) ideologists who, since the beginning of the introduction of the unfettered free-market capitalism, have been raising voice against it got a strong reason to increase the volume of their scream. It looked for India, for trying out globalization policies a coalition government at the Centre is good, so that the strings of control are multiple and the steering cannot be reckless.

The Central and State Governments of India cannot afford to ignore the rural poor, because they are the majority that determine who would hold positions of power in the subsequent elections. Therefore, while the government wants to accelerate the pace of globalization and privatization processes, there are also social safety nets introduced for the poor and those engaged in agriculture.

The general tendency observed about globalization during the discussions is that it benefits some who have (or have access to) capital, technology, knowledge and information, and political power centres. The support that globalization gets from the government is far too higher compared to what decentralization gets. The patronage of political players to the process of privatization and globalization is very much perceptible because in many a case they also turn out to be beneficiaries of globalization. The pity is that the many who are hurt are in the villages depending upon agriculture or traditional arts and crafts. There was also a prophecy expressed that globalization would fall on its own weight, mainly because its tenets do not take into account the nature's recouping ability. Man outrunning nature, rapidly depleting resources is hysterical and unsustainable. The drive towards economic growth rate fails to recognise that nature has only a limited amount of resources that it cannot sustain uncontrolled production and unrestrained consumerist culture. While making statement that globalization would fall soon, one concern concurrently expressed is that it is very much likely that globalization would cause damages to the natural environment beyond repair, before it collapses.

The factors of production commonly needed for any entrepreneurial venture (or for production function to take place) are land, labour, capital, knowledge and information assets. The rural poor generally have land and labour. But they usually do not own the other factors like capital, information and knowledge. The Special Economic Zones robbed them off their lands placing in their hands capital. In the SEZ bargain the land owners have been given a liquid asset (cash) in lieu of a permanent asset (land). Land value keeps appreciating day in and day out, whereas money value keeps descending. It is generally considered all-over India that the investment one makes in land is the wisest investment one has made. When this is the socio-economic reality, the government acquires land from the land owners in the villages to be given to private moneyed people to set up companies in Special Economic Zone. To the private investor, the money invested in the company may fail, but the money invested in land never fails.

Those who speak highly in favour of globalization tend to make reference to computers, broad band net connectivity, the mind-boggling amount of information available in the Worldwide Web, the drastic reduction in mobile phone charges, e-ticketing, e-banking, outsourcing that has become a trend all-over, and such other activities. Similarly, when they talk about technology they most often refer to high-speed computers, advancement in printing technology, mega capacity servers, and mobile phones. They hardly ever seem to think what percentage of villagers has access to broad band connections, and what percentage of villagers actually have any use to computer or e-ticketing or e-banking services or can afford to get telemedicine facility.

The condition of Information and Communication Technology (ICT) commenced in many of the villages is, they have either shuttered down, or are being used for playing computer games by school children for which they should put their signatures in a Users' Register to be shown to the sponsor. The number of Village Information Centres closed down in the past four to five years stand testimony to this fact. The original purpose of reaching the farmers with farm or price related-information did not materialise due to various reasons including non-availability of contents in the local language.

Given the rapidity of the dynamics, arriving at ways to manage globalization from below could only be timid, provisional and exploratory. The workshop came out with two sets of ideas. One is idea for managing globalization at the grassroots level; and secondly, the general preparations or full-scale action that any Village Panchayat should take up to be in a position to provide seamless administration at the lowest rung of a democracy like India. This would serve as agenda points for enhancing the efficiency of local bodies to face globalization at the grassroots level. That is in a way preparing the Panchayats and the community members. These preparatory steps are essential for any local self-governing system—be it within the globalized system or without it. Many of the points mentioned below are put across with the understanding that the Panchayats would take (academic and analytical) help from capacitated NGOs, and technical institutions and universities close by.

MANAGING GLOBALIZATION : GENERAL AGENDA FOR PANCHAYATS

- *Panchayat Level Data Bank :* One of the problems that slow down the development works in villages is non-availability of data on various aspects of life and resources at Panchayat level. The data on various classes of land may remain with the Village Administrative Officer (VAO), but it may not be available with the Panchayats. The Gram Sabha/Panchayat will not be in a position to plan tapping programmes in the absence of such data. The Panchayat should obtain such details from the VAO and keep them at Panchayat computer. Other vital data such as literacy, school going children at various levels, migration details, details of common assets and their status, details of common property resources, number of households with yard tap for drinking water, people with disability, old age people eligible to get government pension etc. should also be available.
- *General Identity :* The Panchayats should verify if all the households have Family Card, and each citizen has voter ID. The Panchayats shall help Persons with Disability to obtain relevant ID cards to avail the benefits of government schemes meant for them. Do children in schools use the free bus pass facility? The Official list of people below poverty line (BPL), and the one local Panchayats prepared should be available. These come in handy at times when relevant schemes are introduced by the State for safeguarding the poor. The poor, often, unable to establish/produce their identity have to remain away from benefiting from schemes that are meant to safeguard them.
- *Reaching the Real-Poor :* The poor have earned luxuriously over the years in terms of adjectives to describe them. They are 'the marginalised', 'the disadvantaged', 'the neglected', 'the downtrodden', 'the ultra-poor', 'the excluded' and so on. But, there are at the same time several schemes

of the Central and State governments meant for the upliftment of the poor. The real problem with such Scheme Implementing Officials is identifying the 'real-poor'. The Panchayat bodies, being close to the poor, should prepare a list of such people who deserve assistance through various schemes, and enable reach of schemes to the right people. For a Panchayat working systematically, reducing poverty in a time-bound manner is possible. The Panchayats need to be prepared for tracking the State of the real-poor, and lend a supportive hand. It should also ensure they cross the poverty line beyond the vulnerability point so that they would not fall back into the 'poverty-trap'.

- *Food Security:* The distribution of rice, *dal,* edible oil, and other essential commodities through Public Distribution System (PDS) is commonly taking place in Tamil Nadu. The Panchayats need to keep an eye on the distribution with a view to making sure that the articles distributed through PDS do not by-pass the real-poor. No family living within the jurisdiction of Panchayats should face food insecurity or unemployment. The Panchayats should make necessary arrangements through NREGA, and PDS to make every poor family survive.
- *Traditional Arts and Crafts:* The modernity has the tendency to sideline century-old traditional arts and crafts. This includes local carpenters, blacksmiths, goldsmiths, sculptors, brassware makers, potters, handloom weavers, silk weavers, artists, lock workers, and so on. For example, technology has taken over the lock industry, and it has handed over the lock market to branded locks. Although 'Dindigul lock' was a household name once, and it is still depicted as one of the traditional prides of India in the website of http://www.dico-lock.com the artisans involved in lock making at Dindigul are unable to afford three-time meal to their families. This is especially because the technology introduction in lock making by new entrants has rendered the traditional lock-making-tools uneconomical and their way of making lock outmoded. While newer technologies in the market have a tendency to wipe out the tradition, the Panchayats should guide the next generation youth to pursue skills close to their traditional occupation while at the same time putting to use modern technologies. This requires the Panchayats to establish linkage with technological universities, technical institutions, and concerned wing of the government such as District Industries Centre.

- *Make the Government Machinery Deliver :* People quietly go off approaching the private service delivery, when the service delivery with government schools, hospitals or postal service is poor. Another underlying reality, often, is people approach private service delivery not in appreciation; rather as the only alternative available in place of an inefficient or poor government system. This makes the private service thrive. This is one of the important reasons for government schools, and government health centres functioning in a sluggish manner. The educated villagers, Panchayat functionaries and other people considered important in the society never question or make a complaint. The best way to make the government machinery deliver is using the government service and constantly encourage when they deliver good service, and criticise or make a complaint to the ombudsman (or relevant authority) when they fail to deliver.
- *Water Conservation :* Research studies have shown that as much as 35 per cent of the fresh water is being wasted at the time of distribution in almost all the Panchayats in Tamil Nadu. Water is wasted during pumping, during distribution, during collection, and during household use. This is partly because of the negligence of the Panchayat level overhead Tank Operator, and partly because of the resident-community that do not attach any value for water. The Panchayats should take up water conservation measures including whole-hearted implementation of roof water and rain water harvesting arrangements. The hours of pumping and hours of water distribution to the households remain unregulated. It should also be regulated so as to reduce the power bill (pumping charges) and water wastage. This can considerably reduce the overall expenditure a Panchayat incurs annually.
- *Energy Conservation* : Besides regulating the pumping hours of water distribution, the Panchayats should put on street lights prudently. Use of sodium vapour street lights in Village Panchayats should be completely avoided. The Panchayat buildings, community halls, and SHG meeting halls can use the power-saver compact fluorescent lamps. Solar energy lamps need to be promoted liberally. The schemes available with the Ministry of Non-conventional Energy Sources can be made use of for this purpose. A Panchayat can attempt to get awards such as : Energy Efficient Panchayat. Use of cycles should be encouraged with slogans like: '*Cyclists save fossil fuel, save money for India, they don't pollute environment, and they are healthier citizens*'. Tree planting should

be taken up as a matter of pride during all important days such as 26th January, 1st May, 15th August, and 2nd October. This can contribute to the efforts against global warming, and climate change.

- *Solid Waste Disposal Arrangement :* All the Village Panchayats must have solid waste disposal arrangement. Each common drinking water collection point must have sensible waste water disposal arrangement. This must be a complete plan. The Panchayat functionaries should be made to understand that it does not stop at placing some dust bins, which is usually forgotten once and for all, allowing it to overflow. Collection should complete the full loop until safe disposal.
- *Education :* Education and Health are two prime indicators in the construction of Human Development Index. The Panchayat should maintain disaggregate village level data in various forms keeping in view a clear development perspective. It must have age, gender and community disaggregated data of educational status of the population. Status of children at various levels starting from pre-primary (*Anganwadi*) to primary, secondary, high, and higher secondary levels upto those who are away undergoing college and University level education should be available. It would require annual updating of data. It would give details of children who dropped out, and the number of youth who are unemployed with various qualifications. Local school should get the support of the Panchayat in enrolment of children, and the Panchayat should ensure quality education is provided in the government run schools.
- *Health :* The normal tendency even in villages is to avoid availing government health service for various reasons including insensitivity of the doctors, non-availability of medicines, corruption at second and third levels etc. This becomes a reason for private practice to thrive and flourish. This leads to unnecessary health expenditure to the citizenry. The National Rural Health Mission (NRHM) has augmented many of the facilities and systems in government health service. The Panchayat members should serve as a model in using government health services, and encourage the community members to use government services and be referred to government health service in the event of health complexities. Panchayats should play a vital role in making immunization programmes a success. Panchayats should ensure all the expectant mothers get due medical attention so that the village gets healthy babies. Panchayats should encourage institutional deliveries.

Panchayats in collaboration with government and NGOs may arrange for various general and specialised health camps.

- *Village Commons :* The village common property resources like ponds, tanks and *ooranies*, waterways, grazing land, common land, trees, and medicinal herbs should be protected by the Village Panchayats. In no circumstance, the Panchayats should allow such resources being wiped out in the name of real estates or establishment of industries. NREGA may be fully used to renovate and safeguard these commons. Setting up of small scale village industries or sheds for artisans may be encouraged in common lands, with the permission of the District Collector. Attempts for exploitation of these local resources by private profiteering interest should be carefully guarded against. These are resources that can generate local employment, and sustain local livelihoods.
- *Common Asset Building and Supporting Agriculture :* In order to undo the general comment 'that agriculture is being neglected by the government', the government has come out with new schemes and packages for supporting agriculture and horticulture. This includes schemes like IAMWARM for introduction of new irrigation technologies at highly subsidised rates, renovation of irrigation tanks by the PWD, and services like single window farm service called 'Agri-clinics', bank loan for precision farming, National Crop Insurance Scheme and so on. The Panchayat should serve as a connecting link between the scheme implementing offices of the government and the farmers so as to make use of such opportunities. The Panchayats should take up building of necessary common assets such as clearing of waterways, desilting of local ponds and other facilities. Panchayats should ensure these opportunities are properly made use of.
- *Banking Culture :* The Village Panchayat should encourage each household to open a bank account in local banks. It could be taken up like a campaign, with the assistance of NGOs that are involved in SHG formation. Formation of women SHGs by the NGOs could be encouraged so as to encourage banking culture and inculcate thrift and small savings at village level. The business of private money lenders should be completely done away with. Institutional transactions should be encouraged. Higher flow of money in the villages and in the hands of the poor can expand their choice and render greater freedom to their life.

- *Preparation of Youth :* Educated unemployed youth in the villages use up quite a few years before they discover that they should develop specialised skills so as to make a decent living. However, the desire to live a standard of living better than their parents live is found in almost everyone of the youth. This should be appropriately ignited in time by Panchayats by arranging for guidance and counselling sessions through capacitated NGOs, and educational institutions. The youth—educated or uneducated—should be encouraged to acquire technical or entrepreneurial skills that they can cash in on. Even those involved in agriculture may be orientated on modern methods of cultivation, water conserving technologies, pest management, and post-harvesting technologies. Youth with technical training skills should be helped to find employment in appropriate places. Entrepreneurship programmes of the government, NGOs and technical education institutions should be made use of, for which the Panchayats should facilitate, and have them connected.
- *Gender Equality :* Any asset creation—be it land or house—should be registered in the name of woman in the family. This would give them the power to decide and for the men in the family to recognise the lady of the family. The Panchayat functionaries should initiate such ideas, and encourage local men towards this. The women SHGs should be encouraged to own assets. The Panchayats may also entrust to the SHGs, the responsibility of keeping water collection points clean. The SHGs should also be guided to avail other government schemes meant for women and child development. The SHG may also pass a resolution that if men in any of the family take to alcohol, the woman cannot avail loan from the group.
- *Alliance Building :* Panchayats should not work in isolation. They should build alliance with other civil society organisations, media, NGOs, CBOs, community polytechnic, banks, agriculture extension offices, mission hospitals, technical educational institutions, and private companies that operate in the locality. This linkage would help get benefits of globalization for the Panchayats and the local people.

SWOT ANALYSIS

Before getting down to identifying strategies to manage globalization, it would be in order if the participants of the workshop were put to analyse and discuss the strength, weakness, opportunities, and threats found in globalization. The popular SWOT Analysis technique was put to use so as to get an overall idea. The following is the summary of the SWOT Analysis exercise. The points that emerged during the SWOT Analysis helped identify lead-points to discuss about ways to manage globalization.

STRENGTH

- India is blessed with a lot of natural resources and favourable climatic condition for production to take place uninhibitedly.
- India has a lot of human resources, and there is also educated and skilled human potential to take on, any competition from outside world.
- There is constant scheme-based effort made by the Central and the State governments to ensure minimum basic necessities to the people, assured rural employment and to provide them with communication, road and other basic infrastructure.
- The government makes 'domestic preparedness' efforts to enable India face globalization. This includes general infrastructure development such as road expansion, capacity building training programmes, entrepreneurial development programmes, computerization of banks, communication connectivity, etc. and new schemes in bringing about quality education, quality health care, rural poverty reduction programmes, urban poverty reduction programmes, and agriculture development programmes.
- Countries of the world view India as a favourable destination for investment, and human skills.

WEAKNESS

- The legislations and policies to make use of the natural resources are so weak from the point of view of regulating over exploitation of resources.
- There is still illiteracy, and plenty of unskilled labourers in rural areas. Going by head-count, India has the largest number of unlettered people in the world.
- Blanket-type (uniform) schemes introduced especially by the Central Government all-over India often results in locales getting mismatched. This holds good for NREGS as well.
- Despite the existence of constitutionally recognised local self-governance system, the bureaucracy has a tendency to take an upper hand in key decision-making of the local area development.

- The land holding pattern, by and large, is such that many of the agricultural engineering technologies could not be put to use. The non-remunerative nature of yield from agriculture does not offer the patience to the farmers to get to know of newer technologies relating to agriculture including post-harvesting technologies.
- There are plenty of small-scale and medium-sized enterprises (SMEs) including the ones managed by SHGs. They lack orientation on quality, package, branding and competition, which limit them at only local level; restrict competitiveness and scaling up, and eventually become commercially unviable, or existentially sick.
- The nuances associated with traditional crafts and arts are amazing. But, the weakness is that they are facing the danger of becoming extinct because of their dependence on government support, and lack of orientation towards market.
- There are certain traditionally respected products that have ethnic value such as *khadi*, natural dyed fabrics, home-made edible oils and hair oil etc. which are struggling to make an existence in the market. The concept of 'Be Indian Buy Indian' has become an old-fashioned statement. The concerns are: (a) these trades and those involved in such trades getting sidelined, and (b) the psychic-attraction towards foreign goods.
- There is great influence of 'cash economy' even among agriculturists. So, there is general tendency among the farmers to 'sell water' meant for irrigation, and sell even cultivable land for real estates, if it would fetch a good return in terms of cash.
- Despite governmental efforts on providing quality education, and quality health care, the patronage of people to government run schools and hospitals is insufficient.

OPPORTUNITIES

- The use of computers and internet is spreading cutting across disciplines and sectors.
- There is widespread introduction of technologies in all the fields from agriculture and fishery to designing fashion-jewellery and garments. Enabling reach and orienting farmers and artisans to use them are quite insufficient.
- The amount of information made available is plenty. But, enabling reach to villages is only limited. Moreover, the rural people are yet to

realise the power of information. This is an opportunity that people need to make use of.

- India has abundance of resources including medicinal herbs, indigenous medicines and local medicine manufacturing processes, which could be patented with proper geographical indications.
- The price of mobile-phones, and telephone charges have come down, giving opportunity to everyone to own a cell-phone. [Economic efficiency of such use (or villagers incurring such expenses) requires to be studied].

THREATS

- One of the greatest threats is over-exploitation of natural resources, which free-trade advocates as economic efficiency. The common property resources are cashed in or by private profiteering interest with the support of the government, or people with political connections.
- The fast reduction in the number of people in agriculture, and the perceptible migration of rural people to urban areas is a threat to urban civic facilities. At the same time, while the need for food production requires to be increased, there is a considerable chunk retiring from farming, handloom weaving etc. For example, handloom weavers retire by 2 per cent every year, but there is almost zero new entrants in that sector (Palanithurai, G., 2008).
- For Tamil Nadu to remain a food secure State is due to alternative income from livestock and small stocks. The reduction of grazing land because of lands being given for SEZ purposes, force rural people sell off their livestock (Palanithurai, G., 2008).
- The attraction people get in foreign goods results in indigenous products to remain on the shelf unsold. Those involved in traditional arts, and crafts such as carpenters, blacksmiths, goldsmiths, brassware workers, potters, sculptors are finding it difficult to find market in order to make a living. The arrival of branded items in the market, especially the ones imported, or manufactured by foreign companies located in India is a threat.
- The consumerist culture that is spreading fast even among rural people burns a hole in the pocket of even rural people, forcing them to live a life beyond their means. The consumerist culture has generally made the cost of living much higher even in villages. They have been forced to go in search of 'cash income' in order to maintain the facilities they have learnt to live with.

- Basic services particularly primary and secondary education, drinking water, and health services have become costly in the hands of private players in the market. Availing these services is beyond the reach of common man, when the governmental service is poor.
- The demand for alternative uses of (especially) land and water has brought into question 'the use-right of indigenous community' on these resources. There is constant unrest and struggle taking place to establish their use-right on these livelihood resources.

There is urgent need to reduce the 'weakness' and tide over the 'threats'. The strength and opportunities should be put to proper use in order to manage globalization. The strength should be efficiently used for seizing the opportunities, and the weakness identified should be gradually surmounted so as not to be gulped down by the threats. The points mentioned during the SWOT Analysis exercise greatly benefited while devising ways to manage globalization at the grassroots level and at the policy level. 'Domestic or local level Preparedness' to take on was felt essential, rather than allowing to be crushed in a stampede.

MANAGING GLOBALIZATION : PRINCIPLES AND APPROACHES

PRINCIPLES

There should be a set of commonly accepted principles to stand on, when we talk about development in the context of globalising nations. The workshop felt that it would be wise to make the principles revolve around three important tenets of development, viz. equity or inclusiveness, accountability and sustainability.

(1) *Equity :* Economic growth should result in equitable distribution of the wealth created. Globalization should not be a means for a few to accumulate wealth widening the economic inequalities.

(2) *Accountability :* There should be governmental accountability to the policies introduced with a view to backing globalization. Accountability of the local level institutions towards the local community should not be viewed easily.

(3) *Sustainability :* Ethics and self-discipline in resource use should be an overriding criterion of development. Overuse of environmental resource leads to unsustainable development. In environmental economics as well as in Gandhian economics, overuse amounts to violence. Development that cannot be sustained need not be supported.

Certain clarifications could be given as follows for the information of those who intensely oppose globalization. First, one should take notice that an economy cannot choose to remain a closed economy and stagnate. Several countries all-over the world has outsourced jobs in India especially in the IT, automobile, cell phones, and manufacturing sectors. This has generated considerable employment to the educated youth here. Tamil Nadu State alone reports creating almost 2.4 lakh jobs every year. The State Government of Tamil Nadu has the vision of creating additional 2 million jobs before 2011 (The Industrial Policy, 2007). India has, perhaps, the largest number of computer literate persons today. This makes one to think that there is need to open up. But, managing at the macro level is needed to determine which sector to open up, and to what extent to open up. The purpose of opening up should not be contended at showing economic growth rate on the paper, which makes no sense to the poor in the villages. Specific policy measures and schemes should be introduced to ensure equity in distribution of wealth.

Secondly, prosperity at the cost of depleting natural resources beyond nature's recouping ability cannot be encouraged. Thirdly, there is no country on this earth that has become developed merely through agriculture promotion or production of primary commodities alone. We cannot afford to brush aside things like industrial development, and digital connectivity in the name of *swadeshi*. However, national sovereignty and democratic character of the country or the local bodies need not be compromised for the sake of economic growth. Similarly, the decisions of the international bodies such as the World Bank, IMF cannot be imposed upon India to the extent that it could be addressed as imperialism by a section of the local population.

The workshop found three ways of facing or managing globalization. The approach we adopt for 'managing globalization' could depend on the sector in hand and the nature of issues each sector is likely to come out with. The nature of globalization processes is such that it cannot be let open completely, nor can it be blindly mentioned that it should be completely shunned. The cross-cutting nature of some of the issues is one of the reasons for this state of affairs.

The right approach for facing globalization could be adopting a cautiously selective acceptance approach; and showing resistive guarding wherever there is a need. The following are the approaches the workshop came out with. But, these approaches should be put to use in combination with another depending upon the changing circumstances or situation in hand. The approach devised as well as the nature of globalization processes is such that one cannot take hold of anyone of the approaches mentioned below, and stand on that firmly, once and for all. Two or even all the three of the approaches may have to be used in tandem. However, the actionable agenda points might be used independently of others, based on certain local priority.

APPROACH 1

Selective Espousal: This stems from the strength and opportunities that the workshop participants came out with. Selective espousal has a considerable amount of acceptance or optimism that globalization forces could be made use of, for the benefit of the poor as well. It may not be possible in all the sectors of development. But, selective manoeuvring could benefit. It should be mentioned without a pause here that 'local level preparedness' is a dire need. This goes to say that there are things that even villagers, especially the youth in the villages can benefit out of globalization. The need for constant capacity building and skill upgradation categorically goes with this approach. That is we need to take steps to offset the weakness and tide over them by constant capacity building exercises. This is getting prepared.

APPROACH 2

Resistive Guarding: This emanates from 'the threats' that the workshop identified. The threats are mainly to the land, water, soil, sand, trees and other natural resources. This requires resisting and guarding because these serve as livelihood resources of the poor. This (Resistive Guarding) is an approach to welcome globalization and industrialisation 'with certain non-negotiable ifs and buts'. That is it would be allowed without resistance at the local level provided it would not harm the natural environment by over exploiting resources; it would not emit smoke; it would not let out effluents into the fields or into our waterbodies; and it should allow the local bodies to exercise some of the powers like offering licence, renewal of licence, levying corrective tax and so on. If these conditions are fulfilled it would be considered for implementation, otherwise the community would resist. This is guarding. This is resistive guarding.

APPROACH 3

Expressive Disagreement : This is explicitly expressing disagreement through proper communication to the government, public opinion building campaigns, and media reports. If a move, in the name of globalization, undermines democratic character of the local bodies or goes violating the provisions of the Tamil Nadu Panchayati Raj Act, 1994, or other rules relating to river sand mining, or ground water extraction/privatization of water resources etc. there should be strong disagreement expressed about it. Panchayats as representative bodies of local community and managing trustee of local resources would take stand on certain announcements made, and the issues that originate due to the policies/actions of the government. The local community should record their dissent through media reports, telegrams to the government, and ministries concerned, and through fasting etc. This is blocking. This is expressive disagreement.

MANAGING GLOBALIZATION : SPECIFIC ACTIONABLE AGENDA

The approaches made out above could serve as a set of broad examiner for classifying policies and actions of the government relating to globalization. Subsequently, the workshop listed certain specific actions that Panchayats and peoples' movements can take to respond to the policies and actions of globalization. This is categorised as: (a) 'Grassroots Action'; and (b) 'Policy Advocacy'.

There are certain opportunities in the globalised world that even villagers can aim to get benefited. For instance, this can be of increase in the communication facilities that almost every villager gets access to. However, even the mobile phone facility cannot be uttered as benefiting the rural community if it was argued on economic efficiency or cost-benefit calculations. The drastic reduction in the telephone charges, knowledge enhancement with regard to sanitary practices and orientation towards quality standards in manufacturing practices and identifying multiple ways of reaching the consumers, SHGs and Panchayats getting access to computers and computer-aided accounting are some of the benefits.

This is based on the premise that even the poor in the villages can aim for seasonable gain if they put in efforts, and change or upgrade the way they work. Globalization requires people to remain relevant and deliver goods and services that the market demands. This is applicable to everyone including agriculturists, artisans, crafts-persons, business people, micro and tiny enterprises run by SHGs and those in services. The youth in the villages are fast getting oriented towards delivering to the demands of the market especially in Tamil Nadu, which is a good trend.

The grassroots action agenda listed out below are certain 'preparations needed at the Panchayat level' to face changes in the economy, society and the way political policies influence the lives, employment and existence of villagers. For many the agenda might look like 'essentials that any Panchayat must do'. But, we need to start from the bottom-most line, given the want of efficiency with which Panchayats function, barring a few exceptional ones.

GRASSROOTS ACTION

(1) *Information Dissemination :* The information about the knowledge economy reaches the villages very poorly. That is despite the reach of print and television media to the rural villages, the exposure and amount of information an urban elite gets, is much higher compared to what reaches a commoner in the villages. Awareness about the changes taking place in technology, knowledge, and business processes should be made available to villages, so that there is possibility for traditional ways of doing things to get updated. Educational and technical institutions should take steps to spread information, conduct capacity building training programmes and arrange for exposure visits. Thus, enabling information-access to villages is essential part of managing globalization from below.

(2) *Setting up Globalization Observatory :* The Panchayats that are constantly in touch with technical institutions and departments of the government are, to a considerable extent, familiar with the issues that could be addressed as fallout of globalization policies. The functionaries of Panchayats should keep an observant eye on the interactions that this Panchayat is making with outside world, and the influence of outside world on this Panchayat. If something is found to have a tinge of neo-liberal economic agenda, it should be taken for public hearing in the Gram Sabha. This requires setting up of a Globalization Observatory at the Panchayat level.

(3) *Public Opinion Building :* The Globalization Observatory should have local analysts, who would work like a local research team. They should be in a position to understand the repercussions of certain initiatives of the government, or private companies nearby and build relevant public opinion. This would help build informed-citizens. This would strengthen the ability and power of Gram Sabha to take appropriate decisions. The local analysts team need to be in touch with institutions that are constantly watching globalization so that they get access to sufficient information, knowledge and development that take place. Building informed-public is a vital task in the globalization context.

This is essential in democratization of globalization at the grassroots level.

(4) *Forming and Expanding Networks :* The participants felt that absence of 'ethics' in business as one of the concerns of free-market economy. It is more companies-centred and not people-centred. One proposal could be organising and expanding the networks or forming forums that raise majority voice or common concerns in a collective manner. It should help add an ethical dimension to globalization. Aspects such as ethics, society, equity, and sustainability of resources should be the focus of this network. Such a collective expression is required to build opinion, and make the poor people's voice heard.

(5) *Forming Occupation-based Group :* Most rural entrepreneurs including farmers are working in isolated compartments—without one knowing what the other person in the same or similar trade is doing. In a connected world, being isolated is weakness—weakness in mobilising the funds required to carry out uninterrupted production, and weakness in the marketplace as well. Moreover, this does not allow collective production and collective decision-making as to what to produce, in what quantity, to what kind of consumers, where to sell and at what price etc. Forming artisans, entrepreneurs, and small and medium-sized rural producers into occupation-based groups would enable them have easy access to bank credit. This would enable them to have access to capital, which can buy technology, knowledge and labour and so on. This shall help patenting as well.

(6) *State and the Basic Services :* The State while promoting liberalization, privatisation and globalization policies should not make way for weaning away from providing basic services. The basic services include primary and secondary education, drinking water, public health and referral service to territory level hospitals. Leaving education, health etc. to private corporations as part of Corporate Social Responsibility (CSR) programmes or on economic efficiency calculations might work out sporadically. But, it cannot be a pretext for the government to withdraw itself from delivering such basic services to the citizenry. Matters such as provision of rice, *dal* and other essential commodities at fair price, housing for the poor, irrigation infrastructure and such other things cannot wait either. The private schools and hospitals should be accredited for quality and for the efficiency of service delivery. But, price-wise it is often unaffordable to the poor. The Panchayats should

urge towards this. The Panchayats should develop proper vision and have say on all these 'State and market related matters'.

(7) *Conservation of Environment and Ecology :* The 'economic efficiency mind-set' created by globalization is such that it converts almost anything into financial terms including human kidney. The natural resources like land, water, sand etc. are sold in an unregulated manner by private profiteering interests, often with hand in glove with corrupt officials. The voice raised by the Civil Society on these issues is either sporadic or episodic. Relevant Panchayats with the support of NGOs, Print and Television media should take up issues on natural resource depletion. Wider public opinion needs to be created on resource depletion. Panchayats should exert pressure for implementation of The Tamil Nadu Ground Water (Development and Management) Act, 2003, and The Tamil Nadu Panchayats (Second Amendment) Ordinance—2003 regarding rain water/roof water harvesting. Rain water harvesting and tree planting should be taken up at Panchayat level with all seriousness. Similarly, Panchayats should be made aware of the Tamil Nadu Minor Minerals Concession Rules, 1959 along with the newly inserted Rule 38-A, G.O. Ms. No. 95 dt. 1-10-2003 of Industries Department along with the recommendations of the panel on river sand mining. This would empower the Panchayats with knowledge on these issues such as ground water extraction, rain water harvesting, river sand mining and the ways to tackle these issues legally.

(8) *Capacity Building at the Local Level :* The youth requires to be guided to take up skill training based on the demands of the market. Skills such as two wheeler mechanism, automobile mechanism, catering and hospitality skills, skills required for front office management, computer-aided designing and so on. One of the changes brought about by the knowledge economy is the shelf-life of knowledge and skills have become too brief. That means even the educated and skilled youth needs to update their knowledge constantly to remain relevant in the job market. Training oneself in occupations that are entirely new is one, and modernising the existing ways of doing agriculture, horticulture, art, and crafts is another. Youth—young boys and girls—from poor families should be assisted (if required even financially) to undergo short-term entrepreneurial courses in technical institutions, recognized computer centres, industrial training institutions, and polytechnic colleges. They should be assisted to get financial assistance through government

schemes for self-employment, or job placement based on competence. This can enable the rural youth grab opportunities and reduce rural poverty levels. This can also serve as (a) action for inclusiveness, and (b) action for reducing excessive crowd in agriculture that the Eleventh Five Year Plan document emphasises about (PC-GoI, 2007).

(9) *Development Negotiation :* The Special Economic Zones (SEZs), notified by the government in many a place, is found to have been indiscriminate in acquiring land for setting up of SEZ units. One of the lessons regarding land acquisition is that wherever people's mobilization has been strong, indiscriminate land acquisition has been stopped. The Panchayats should take a strong stand on this aspect and negotiate that: (1) only barren land would be sold out for setting up of SEZ; (2) each land owner who gives land should be entitled to get a house-plot; (3) each family that parts with land would be entitled to employment for one person from that family, and if required the SEZ unit would arrange for training and absorption. Panchayats need to assess—with the help of technical institutions, if required—the opportunities and benefits of globalization, i.e. if the benefits are likely to outweigh the risks/cost. The Panchayat should take it as a matter of right to authoritatively decide if they should permit a given industry to find location in their Panchayat jurisdiction or not. It would assess the land, water and other resources the industry would gulp down, the number of employment it would generate and the adequacy of the effluent treatment plant to the installed production capacity and so on. The help of technical institutions can be sought, and Right to Information Act, 2005 can be put to use wherever required.

(10) *Demanding Clean and Transparent Administration :* One of the lessons that the field visits made for the purpose of this series of studies was that wherever the Village Panchayat President or Panchayat functionaries have been assertive, they are able to get things done for the common good of the Panchayat. Where Panchayat President has been evasive or the people are not demanding, things do not fall in place. Legal instruments like the Right to Information Act (RTI Act), and roping in the service of the Vigilance, and Anti-corruption wings, using the service of the Public Information Officer at Collector's offices have paid results. Taking matters to the attention of the media including television media have paid results. The Panchayats should not hesitate to use these democratic and legislative instruments for the purpose of

cutting the corrupt officials down to size. For instance, the government machinery cannot turn a blind eye towards poor pollution control norms adopted by industries. Local people cannot be kept in darkness merely by concealing information.

(11) *Training to Farmers on Full-loop Agriculture :* There is no dearth of schemes for agriculture and farm related activities. Department of Agriculture should revitalise and breathe life into its agri-extension services, and conduct training programmes to farmers on the complete loop of making agriculture economically viable and commercially profitable. It should begin from soil testing to selection of seeds, to post harvesting technologies, and to agri-commodity marketing arrangements. The agri-extension services require renewing and perking up with greater intensity. The agri-clinics are expected to take on in a full scale. The Krishi Vigyan Kendras (KVK—Farm Science Centres) that are inactive could also be put into action to prepare materials (booklets and leaflets) that can explain the schemes available for agriculture development starting from soil and seed quality testing to post-harvest technologies. Panchayats can organise 'farmers' forums', which can demand various services, education and information from the Office of the Assistant Director of Agriculture in the concerned districts.

(12) *Make use of Geographical Indication System :* There are produces that small producers sell as 'commodities' in large quantities in gunny bags. They can grade and sell them as 'products' for direct sale to the consumers. There are products (and commodities) that are region specific like Nilgiri Tea, Manaparai *murrukku*, *pathamadai* mat, Tirunelveli *Halwa*, Kancheepuram silks, Marthandam honey, *Mannachanallur ponni* rice etc. In other parts of the country also there is no dearth of specialisation such as Assam tea, Coorg coffee, Darjeeling tea, Bengal cotton, Gandhigram khadi etc. These need to be branded indicating especially the geographical origin and the indigenous nature of the product. These products can be value-added and patented as well. Local NGOs and technical institutions can assist.

(13) *Sanitary Measures :* One of the non-tariff barriers effectively used by importing countries after global trade started picking up is sanitary measures. This is adhered to more in food and beverage items. That is ensuring cleanliness of production processes, the packaging, and the presentation in the market. This is, perhaps, based on the learning some of the importing countries have of : (i) the personal hygiene practices

adopted in some of the developing countries, and (ii) of the technology and poor facilities available in production operations and in the packaging area. The staff working in food and beverages industries should be imparted training in cleanliness and personal hygiene behaviour; and the technology and facilities available in production process and in the packaging section require improvement. This is about sea-foods processing, for example. Conforming to these sanitary practices is good even from the point of view of health care. The small producer firms should be prepared towards this, no matter if the products are exported, or sold in the domestic market.

(14) *Demand for Social Safety Net :* Globalization leaves behind those who are weak, and vulnerable to competition and international standards. Similarly, globalization has almost nothing to offer to those in villages; instead it has a character of exploiting the livelihood resources of the poor. Globalization also has the tendency to widen the gap between the rich and the poor, and the knowledgeable and the illiterate, technologists and the traditionalists and so on. The government should be pressurised to bring in appropriate policy interventions to safeguard the interest of the poor, illiterate, and the traditionalists and others that research studies indicate as being affected. NGOs and research institutions should identify such class of people and take it to the notice of the policy makers.

(15) *Corporate Social Responsibility (CSR) :* There are big companies and firms with known names like Tata, The Ford, TVS, Ajim Premji Foundation, Kingfisher, Bill & Melinda Gates Foundation involved in supporting social development projects in the area they work. They have their vision of community development and poverty alleviation. Moreover, many of the CSR funds are cornered by Cricket Clubs, or for sponsoring Tennis and Cricket players. But, scores of other smaller firms that has several million turnover each year do not involve themselves in social development causes. Perhaps, it could be because of their non-orientation towards social causes. There are also industries that sit on farm land, employ child labour and then have CSR programme which is meaningless. Civil Society Organisations, educational and research institutions and media should sensitise them on these issues to take up Corporate Social Responsibility activities for poverty alleviation.

(16) *Make Your Voice Heard :* When there is a negative impact of globalization on the poor or in the villages, or a deterrent to the grassroots level democracy, it should be brought to the notice of the media. The affected

Panchayats should be in a position to hold a press meet and explain the retrogression.

POLICY LEVEL

(1) *Resource as a Ruling-Constraint :* Indiscriminate use or exploiting environmental resources more than the recouping capacity of nature is one of the main reasons why resource use is to be watched. No explanation, including the 'economic efficiency of use', cannot be taken as a reason for over-exploitation of resources such as ground water. Be it acquisition of land for setting up of Special Economic Zone (SEZ) or water for dyeing industry, water should be made as a ruling constraint. The price the firm pays for procuring water should be excessively inflated so that there is rational use of water; so that the industry finds ways to recycle used water; so that technologies for recycling waste water is installed.

(2) *Demand Proper Measure of Growth :* There is a strong feeling among environmentalists that growth is reported in India with wrong calculations. That is growth is reported without taking into account the entire cost incurred (including social and environmental) in bringing about economic growth. The natural resources used up or degradation caused to the environment so as to achieve economic growth is never taken into account, nor reported. Therefore, growth should be reported after subtracting for environmental degradation. That is downside adjustment for environmental damage should be done in order to correctly measure growth. Civil Society Organisations should demand proper measure of economic growth. Otherwise, it would amount to erroneous calculations and reporting or even deceiving.

(3) *Equitable Infrastructure Development :* Infrastructure development in the spheres of road development, sea-port and air-port development, infrastructure for Special Economic Zone (SEZ) and IT industries draw considerable attention of the State, whereas infrastructure development in some of the primary sectors such as agriculture, horticulture, irrigation, fisheries and fish landing centres, milk processing, seed processing and storage, post-harvest storage etc. do get very scanty attention. Adequate lobbying needs to be done in order to ensure equitability in infrastructure development.

(4) *Anti-Dumping Duties :* The Government of India, it is reported, has taken

more than 60 anti-dumping measures in order to protect the small producers (WTO, 2009). It has taken measures like imposing anti-dumping duties to control reckless import of certain goods that might, otherwise, affect the small producers in India. Reports from research institutions should go to appropriate policy making bodies to enable the government take proper steps to protect small producers. University Departments and Research Institutions should take up constant research on trade dynamics and what is happening to domestic industries as a result of imports, FDI and FII.

(5) *Right to Levy Corrective Tax :* The industries that pollute land, water, sea etc. usually go scot-free. They might have an effluent treatment plant of abysmally low levels of tonnage capacity. That would satisfy the reporting requirements of the pollution control norms prevailing in the country. But, in actuality, it might be causing damage to the environment, land, water, air etc. of that area. The Village Panchayats and Civil Society Organisations functioning in that area should demand levying of corrective tax from such polluting industries. The Panchayats may also be permitted to levy this tax, and use the money for reclaiming the affected land or cleansing of water. This can considerably reduce the negative externality. The corrective tax levied should be ruthlessly high so that the firm reduces, in the first place, letting out effluents.

CONCLUSION

Policy initiatives that promote large-scale privatization of natural resources especially land and water are real challenges. This remains a real threat to the rural livelihoods. However, given the geographical area of India, and the size of population, the government argues that it is only miniscule. No matter whether it is miniscule or large-scale, if a policy initiative floated in the interest of privatization would displace the poor, make the land owners landless, and distance the poor from accessing livelihood resources, such policy would be addressed as retrogressive only. No matter whatever be the contribution it makes to the economic growth of the country, the poor does not have to understand what it is all about. No policy should, even inadvertently, attempt to marginalise the farming community, or further marginalise the poor.

Similarly, any policy that does not guarantee a fair price to the primary producers—when it can assure huge profit to the agents and secondary producers—would be addressed as retrogressive only. When setting up of industrial units in the SEZs can enjoy duty-free existence, and avail tax concessions in almost all the transactions for almost fifteen years, while at the same time if any policy initiative was made to cut down subsidies for agriculture, it would be addressed as retrogressive. Opening up to the introduction of technologies in various sectors without making sufficient domestic preparation, or capacity building, would be addressed as retrogressive only.

The issues are, by and large, clear. The force of globalization pushes subsistence agriculture to commercial agriculture. Moving from protectionism to competition is the trend. Moving from primary producer to value-addition is what the market demands. The state is not as big as it used to be. In the globalized economy, the market has outgrown in size that it can decide the direction an economy takes. This is true for India as well. The solid example is when the country faces an economic turmoil, the Prime Minister calls for the meeting of the private-player-giants in India not to aggravate the situation by taking knee-jerk steps.

The concern is if the rural people, rural small scale producers and agriculturists are aware of the developments, and the fix they are in. Some communities that feel the pinch raise voice through Panchayat forums, NGOs and Civil Society Organisations. But, is there anyone who has the time to study the direction the economy is taking, and to spell out in clear terms what the future holds for the rural people. Owing to sporadic voice raised by the Civil Society Organisations, the physical and material supports are forth coming from the government in the form of schemes and social safety nets. But, the psychic drive or cultural influence of globalization is going deeper than anything else even in villages that they are after 'cash income' and want to make carbon copies of city life at their levels stretching to the extent of selling off their lands to realtors in order to settle down in the town. It has become a thing of the past that the extent of cultivable land that one owned determined one's social status. The current trend is the number of saleable housing plots one has that determines one's wealth. This is fast converting several cultivable lands into housing plots. The basket of suggestions given in this chapter to manage globalization is an outcome of a two-day workshop (held at Gandhigram, Tamil Nadu). This would be of use to Panchayats and NGOs who would draw suggestions from here, improvise if necessary, and implement them to save the poor and the local resources that they depend on.

REFERENCES

Government of Tamil Nadu (2007). *The Industrial Policy, 2007.*

Jeffery Sachs (2005). *The End of Poverty*, Penguin Books, London.

Palanithurai, G. and Ramesh, R. (2008). *Globalization: Issues at the Grassroots*, Concept Publishing Company, New Delhi.

Planning Commission, GoI 2007-2012, *XI Five Year Plan.*

Robert Gilpin (2001). *Global Political Economy*, Orient Longman, Hyderabad.

Stephen Cullenberg, Prasanta K. Pattanaik (2004) *Globalization, Culture and the Limits of the Market: Essays in Economics and Philosophy*, Oxford University Press, New Delhi.

Thomas L. Friedman (2000). *The Lexus and the Olive Tree*, Anchor Books, New York.

Thomas L. Friedman (2008). *Hot, Flat and Crowded*, Allen Lane, England.

WTO (2009). *http://www.wto.org/english/res_e/statis_e/statis_e.htm* accessed on 26th December 2009. *http://www.dico-lock.com/product2.htm* Accessed on 26th December, 2009.

Index